ST(RIPPED)

A Story of Shedding, Shifting, Shining, and Finding Strength

NICCOLE HENDRICKSON

LANDON HAIL PRESS

Copyright© 2025 Niccole Hendrickson
All Rights Reserved

This book or any portion thereof may not be reproduced or used in any manner without the express written permission of the publisher, except for the use of brief quotations in a book review.

Paperback ISBN: 978-1-959955-66-5
Hardback ISBN: 978-1-959955-67-2

Cover photography by Talia Kite Photography
Cover design by Rich Johnson, Spectacle Photo
Published by Landon Hail Press

Although the author and publisher have made every effort to ensure the accuracy and completeness of information contained in this book, we assume no responsibility for errors, inaccuracies, omissions, or any inconsistency herein. Any slights on people, places, or organizations are unintentional. The material in this book is provided for educational purposes only. No responsibility for loss occasioned to any person or corporate body acting or refraining to act as a result of reading material in this book can be accepted by the author or publisher.

This book is dedicated to the young girls and goal-getting women who know their magic lies within. To those who are in relentless pursuit of excellence, who believe in their impact and internal power.
This is for the women ready to turn inward, embrace their true selves, and take full responsibility for their mind, body, and soul.
It's for those who are prepared to navigate the transformative journey of resilience—through the challenges and the s(tripping) away of who you thought you were and what you thought your power was—only to fully own the strength revealed in your authentic self.
May this inspire you to lead a life united in purpose and passion.

CONTENTS

AUTHOR'S NOTE 1

DEAR READER 4

INTRODUCTION 7

PART I: WHO ARE YOU, ANYWAY? 13

CHAPTER 1: Your Formation, Like It or Not 15

CHAPTER 2: Why Your Circle Matters 42

CHAPTER 3: Values + Guiding Principles 68

CHAPTER 4: Becoming is Letting Go 82

CHAPTER 5: Passion, Goals + Goal-Getting 127

PART II: EXPECT THE UNEXPECTED | ST(RIPPED) 145

CHAPTER 6: The "St" in St(ripped) 147

CHAPTER 7: Grit, Perseverance, Determination 164

CHAPTER 8: Falling Back into your Vision + Foundation 189

CHAPTER 9: Becoming Happens in the Darkness. Leverage It. 216

PART III: UNITING PURPOSE X PASSION 251

CHAPTER 10: The "Ripped" in St(ripped) 253

CHAPTER 11: What No One Can Take Away.................. 278

CHAPTER 12: Passion Evolves, Purpose Stays 301
CHAPTER 13: Fearless in your *WHY* 329
CLOSING LOVE NOTE 340
ACKNOWLEDGEMENTS 343
ABOUT THE AUTHOR 345

AUTHOR'S NOTE

Life has a way of breaking us open. Exposing what is deep inside, revealing the foundation on which we were built, and testing our capacity. Sometimes, it's slow and subtle; other times, it's a full-blown reckoning. For me, it was both.

The trials I faced—the ones that brought me to my knees—were not just painful interruptions; they were the tools that shaped me into who I am. In the moments when I felt the most torn down, undone, out of control, and uncertain, something sacred and beautiful was flourishing within me, deep underneath the shattering. What looked and felt like absolute destruction was actually construction—of a stronger, more aligned, and more honest version of me.

This is a story of that becoming. And not just mine, but maybe yours, too.

ST(RIPPED) is more than a memoir. It's a map. A field guide forged in the fire of personal loss, raw truths, unexpected turns, and undeniable growth. It's a tribute to the people who stood beside me, held up the mirror, and helped me face parts of myself that I hadn't been courageous enough to encounter alone. It's about the ones who believed in me when I forgot how to, who saw my magic and deep impact when I struggled to see it, and those who challenged me to become my more. It's about confronting what's uncomfortable, meeting myself in the silence and the darkness, and discovering that my deepest drive came not from proving something to the world, but from returning home to myself.

Every scar, every setback, every lesson has left behind key points of instruction. Not always in words, but in wisdom. That wisdom, which I discovered in the process, became the framework for how I rebuilt. How I reimagined. How I dug deep and created the life I knew, deep down, was possible. A life that was not defined by what I had lost or compromised, but by what I was finally willing to claim.

This book is structured into three parts:

Part One is about my roots and discovery, my foundation, and the people who helped build it.

Part Two dives into the shadow—the growth that came through heartbreak, confusion, and surrender.

Part Three is the rise—the alignment of passion meeting purpose, and what it looks like to live from that place.

Each chapter ends with interactive reflections, opportunities for your own personal exploration and empowerment. These pages are filled with stories lived by me and experiences that challenged my character. They are intentionally nonlinear, just like life itself. You may find pieces of yourself in them. I hope you do.

As you read, you will come to understand the concept behind ST(RIPPED), my powerful story of shedding, shifting, shining, and finding unshakable strength.

To protect the privacy of friends, family, and other individuals referred to in this book, some names have been changed and details excluded.

ST(RIPPED)

The building back up comes after the breakdown. But remember: do not fear walking in the dark. The rise of light radiates most brightly after the darkest of nights.

Enjoy the journey!

xx
Niccole Hendrickson

NICCOLE HENDRICKSON

DEAR READER

First, thank you. Thank you for picking up this book, for trusting me to speak into your life, and for allowing me the honor of walking alongside you on this journey. Whether you're here to be inspired, challenged, encouraged—or maybe all three—I'm so grateful you're here.

Before you dive into the prompts and reflections ahead, I invite you to pause. Grab a journal, your favorite pen, and a cozy cup of coffee or tea. Settle in. This space is for *you*.

As you move through these pages, don't overthink it. These prompts and interactions aren't meant to be perfected—they're meant to *open you up*. Let them soften your heart, clear your mind, and stir your spirit. Allow yourself to be seen, felt, and maybe even st(ripped)—layer by layer, letting go of what doesn't serve and making room for what's real.

If, along the way, you find yourself curious about the work I do and how I might support you more personally, I'd love to connect. You can apply to work with me through my website, or, at the very least, let's be friends on Instagram. I'd love to cheer you on, right where you are.

Now, take a deep breath—and begin.

With love and leadership,

Niccole

ST(RIPPED)

P.S. I'd be honored to share your acts of courage and commitment to your evolution. If a moment from your journaling through the *St(ripped)* post-chapter reflections speaks to you, capture it—tag @niccolehendrickson and use hashtags [#st(ripped), #warriorst(ripped)].

You are the warrior we're all inspired by, and your journey has the power to spark something in others, too.

IG: @niccolehendrickson
Website: www.niccolehendrickson.com
Email: niccole@niccolehendrickson.com

Instructions for Post-chapter Reflections

Before You Begin

This is your moment to pause. To turn inward. To get honest.

Grab your journal and a pen that feels good in your hand—something that invites flow, not perfection. Set a timer for five minutes per prompt. This isn't about getting it "right." It's about getting real.

Before you press start, place both feet on the floor. Close your eyes. Take a few slow, grounding breaths. Let the noise settle. Feel your body. Come home to yourself.

And then… begin. Let the words rise without judgment. Be curious. Be honest. Be open.

And most of all—**enjoy** what unfolds.

xx
Niccole

NICCOLE HENDRICKSON

INTRODUCTION

"The privilege of a lifetime is to become
who you truly are."
—Carl Jung

St(ripped) is the revealing of the character and grit harnessed when we are without our believed comforts, it is the discovery of strength that is built and earned.

We were all splashing around, playing, laughing, and enjoying the fruits of our grandparents' labor and their devotion to providing us the most beautiful lived-out legacy: being together as a family, and making memories *all* together. We were in Las Vegas, twenty-one of us in total: twelve adults and nine kids. I still can see the lounge chairs lined up all around the pool, the bronzed bodies and colorful swimsuits, brightly colored painted toenails, fabulous hair, sunnies on, and smiles in full-on mode.

I giggle when I remember all the details of our fashion and accessories, only to realize, thirty-plus years later, how all of these items have made a full-fledged comeback, and we are rockin' the very same fashions, while desperately trying to achieve the ease of those times.

Our parents were close by, set up in a way that at least a few of the aunts or uncles had their eyes on us at all times, however there was a shared comfort among all of us kids that became a known safety net: one another. As children, we played and thrived, looking for no one else but the others' company. We were everything to one another, and no one else mattered beyond our unit. My cousins were the only friends I needed or wanted in my early formation.

To this day, I can remember being five-year-old Niccole on this family vacation and suddenly being consumed by a burden; this burden of bad words flooded my mind. Where did they come from? How did I learn them? I couldn't get them out of my head. They started dominating my thoughts, consuming me and my ability to have fun and be free. It was as if the depths of my observations became my own thoughts and I couldn't escape the thought reel of these negative words, possible meanings, and how I was to process them.

In the blink of a moment the freedom that comes with being five was robbed by this burden of unstoppable thoughts that I couldn't eliminate and fix on my own. The burden was tied to both the disruption from the bad word reel in my head as well as an annoyance that I couldn't overcome it on my own and dive back into the play time with my cousins. To me, the bad words were a metaphor for the irrelevant things that would later occupy way too much of my headspace and thought processing.

I ran to my parents and started to cry. "I can't make them stop, the bad words, the interruptive thoughts. They are on repeat in my head."

My mom and dad looked at me with a level of curiosity and concern at how overwhelmed and consumed I seemed to be. Then, both of them kindly talked me through the

release of this burden, this overanalysis of a thought, and gave me the permission to let go...
Let go.
To just be.
Be free and in the moment of my youth.
I returned to the splash area, still heavy with thoughts, and I curated a tune to switch my thought patterning into one of release and peace...

This memory is pinned in my mind forever and always. It reminds me of how intricate my mind was and is to this day. This memory serves as proof for how powerful the energy and focus can be to a specific thought and how we can manifest something so much bigger and consuming, without fully intending to do so, when we breathe energy into the thought.

I believe this marked the beginning of how hard I can be on myself, for whatever reason. I just took on this expectation of perfection, deep judgement of myself, my thoughts, and my ability to navigate them. I was never given this burden, I took it on. While the situation is laughable to me today, it is nevertheless still powerful. It sparked my conscious connection to just how influential my mindset was and the boundless power it held.

At such a young age, it would have been terrifying to acknowledge this level of connection, but I think it would have been so damn useful and wise, had I been able to navigate what it meant and how I would utilize it. This marked my first time feeling and experiencing my depth and complexity. Clearly, my parents were very wise, compassionate, and tuned in to me, as a child. Instead of gaffing me off, they embraced what I brought to them and then helped to facilitate a solution. This experience was the first time I felt "different" for being so deep at such a young age.

All throughout my childhood, I watched and studied everything around me, always taking mental notes and allowing my curiosity to flourish. But I kept my observations to myself, storing them in my mind to use or learn from later. But sometimes, I discovered, that mental space or archive needs to be cleaned, cleared, or filtered.

As I grew up, I began to think of this headspace like a backpack that can get too stuffed or crowded or heavy. And I learned that when our mind is "heavy" with too many thoughts and too many stored up details and feelings, it eventually impacts our physical wellbeing. In the same way, overloading or overtaxing our bodies impacts our productivity and the mindset's ability to balance, rest, or expand into new areas.

It took me some time to learn how to let go of some of the weight on my mind. Ha! Let's be honest! This would remain a lifetime focus of mine.

Throughout my childhood, I also took very seriously the idea upholding of my family name and a commitment to my integrity and my word. I thought about how my actions or lack of actions would impact not only my future, my goals, and my relationships, but also how they would impact the family, who worked diligently, generously, lovingly, and bravely to provide the life I was living.

For me, this never felt like a burden, though. It was empowering to decide how my path would not only be a branch of legacies I was proud to be a part of, but also powerful fuel to determine the path I wanted to travel with confidence, in order to fulfill my own legacy. I was far from perfect in my choices.

Oftentimes, I did disappoint the family name, my bigger aspirations, and the road forward. But I was no stranger to the life I had to live, in addition to the "rules" and "parameters" I also needed. After all, rules, parameters, and expectations are simply guardrails. I was and am living here to decide when a guardrail needs bending.

I believe we need structure, we need parameters, we need guidelines, morals, and consequences. At the same time, equally, we need to push boundaries in order to see what we are made of in the end and, more important, in the process. Sometimes, I think I wanted a big structure, so I could push the infrastructure it was built upon, to test the confidence and the threads it was woven with and seek out whom I would become in the end.

St(ripped).

St(ripped) of the need to hold it all, do it all, become it all on my own.

NICCOLE HENDRICKSON

PART I

WHO ARE YOU, ANYWAY?

You are responsible for your own happiness.
You are responsible for the energy you bring and how you show up.
You are responsible for waking up every day and doing the work to make progress on what matters.
You are responsible for defining what matters to you.
You are responsible for telling the truth even when it is really hard.
You are responsible for paying for your life.
Nobody owes you anything, but you owe yourself everything.

—Mel Robbins

NICCOLE HENDRICKSON

CHAPTER 1

Your Formation, Like It or Not

You cannot change who you were born to, the circumstances in which you were born, or the conditions you were raised in. While this can be incredibly frustrating, depleting, challenging, and unfair, for some there is power in knowing you can dictate your future, your vision for your life, and the choices you make, in order to navigate your future. We all have a choice in how we respond, how we utilize our conditions, and how we formulate our future and then show up in it.

Defining Examples of the Family Who Set the Tone for Curating Your Life

My grandfather, Papa was quiet, stoic, mentally strong, focused, determined, sharp, thoughtful, and tirelessly committed to doing life differently than he had lived it. He wouldn't force his children or grandchildren to learn from his experiences and suffering. He set out to fully live a life that would prove to the world that you do not have to keep being the cold-hearted, unapproachable hardass the times crafted you to be.

NICCOLE HENDRICKSON

Born in Lane, South Dakota, in 1922, Papa was raised by a stern, no-nonsense German mother. Papa was the third born of five sons. He spent most of his youth during the Depression. Like in most other struggling farm areas, living in South Dakota presented life challenges no little boy deserved. There was more famine, darkness, and solitude than any hints of love and compassion.

Papa quit school at the beginning of eighth grade. He spoke poor English, and his grammar was lacking, but the final straw for him was being teased for his poorly repaired overalls. The shoulder straps were uneven, and each was connected to a different-colored buckle.

All the children attending his single-room school were poor, but Papa was below the norm of his classmates. He received little pushback from his parents about leaving school. Most likely, they needed all the free help they could get on their impoverished farm, which had few animals and limited crops.

When Papa was twelve years old, his father died of asthma. The local coroner came to the farmhouse, but once he had completed his business, before he departed, he handed Papa two large buckets and told him to bury them away from the house. He gave strict orders not to look in the buckets and to bury them simply.

Like any curious twelve-year-old, he couldn't resist taking a peek. Inside the buckets, he was horrified to find his father's blood, which had been removed through the embalming process.

Later that year, he was sent to Montana to live with an uncle. He packed his belongings, albeit very spartan, and he arrived with one chapter book, the clothes on his back, and the shoes on his feet. His uncle gave him a single-shot .22-

ST(RIPPED)

caliber rifle with a damaged front sight post and let him live in a small camper trailer. Papa was left alone for months at a time. He subsisted on canned meat, vegetables, and peaches, while he performed his duties, overseeing his uncle's sheep. His uncle visited him routinely, to resupply his water and food.

By the time he was seventeen years old, the young Papa had exercised more independence and responsibility than most adults during their lifetime. After spending his adolescent years watching over sheep and working the land, he became physically strong, mentally undisturbed, and anxious to experience life outside the ranch.

In 1939, at age seventeen, he informed his uncle of his desire to join the army. Because he was not yet eighteen, he needed his uncle to sign the papers enabling him to enlist. At this point in his young life, any opportunity to explore, evolve, and make money was an adventure worth taking. He was ready to leave the fences and "safe haven" of the ranch.

This would be the first time Papa bet on himself. There would be more serious wagers soon to come.

When I was a young girl, I forged an incredible bond with my Papa, a man who I believe embodies the ultimate power of choice. At the age of seventeen, he boarded a train in Montana and reported to boot camp at Fort Bliss, Texas. Following completion of boot camp, he received orders to Schofield Barracks, Hawaii. There, Papa was trained as a crew member on an anti-aircraft battery.

His crew and entire unit were moved to Pearl Harbor to serve as security forces for the airfield and harbor. During this period, WWII was raging Europe. Germany had invaded neighboring countries and forged an alliance with

Imperial Japan. Meanwhile, America was determined to stay neutral and out of the war.

Life on the island was unlike anything Papa had ever experienced. He earned fifty dollars a month and sent money home to his mother. He spent much of his free time fishing the local waters and enjoying fish-fries with his fellow soldiers. Then, early on the blue-sky morning of December 7, 1941, Pearl Harbor was attacked by Japan.

A few months later, the Army advertised the formation of a new unit, the 101st Airborne. Interested soldiers were encouraged to apply. Those who made the final selection would receive an additional $50 in "jump pay." Papa signed up and was sent to Fort Bragg, North Carolina, where the airborne unit began their training. Later, they moved to Fort Benning, Georgia, for jump school and further training. Finally, his unit returned to Fort Bragg and continued training in North Carolina and neighboring states. It was like he had won the lottery.

My Papa was born into very challenging times, but he decided to make something of his life. Little did he know he was signing his life over to fight for every ounce of this freedom. To me, he was a living example of courage and a devotion to curating the life he believed he was not only worthy of, but deeply committed to, for his children. He paved a clear path for me, as a young girl, and how he brought to life the "even if" mentality.

He modeled for me a relentless mindset and commitment to better himself. He demonstrated great humility and how, no matter what your start to life looked like or which interferences arise, you have the power to decide!

ST(RIPPED)

The bond I forged with my grandfather, Papa, taught me self-worth, outdoor knowledge, independence, trust, respect, patience, and boundaries. He also taught me that being disappointed with someone you loved was okay. He demonstrated that some thoughts are reserved for your mind and heart only. He showed me how powerful the small details of knowing someone were.

I'll never forget how proud he was to show me the sunflower garden he'd grown for me one summer. As we drove slowly down Rocky Lane and onto their property, the sunflower stalks were over five feet tall. He stood waiting for me in his Wrangler jeans, pearl-snap long-sleeve shirt, cowboy boots, and a snapback hat that sat perfectly on his crisp white hair.

Proudly, he stood before this magnificent garden with a huge smile, awaiting me and my excitement as I exited the car. I ran to him and followed him through the sunflower fields. This was love and attention to detail. A life lesson on what it felt like to honor something small in someone you loved. What it felt like for the person giving and the one receiving, who'd been granted a gift that would last a lifetime.

His intentional act of kindness had an effect on my soul; This experience impacted me for my lifetime. I was seen, loved, and met with the greatest that love could deliver. In turn, the fruits of his labor, intention, and love were met with my acceptance and gratitude.

Some of the most defining moments of my childhood were fearlessly navigating the outdoors, learning how to shoot a shotgun, shuffling cards, swinging on the porch swing while taking in the moment, rides to the ice cream shop, and embracing the simplicity of life when fishing, while also keeping in mind how the person who caught the first fish, the most fish, and the biggest fish would be paid out, once we returned from the adventure on the lake. Always a win! Then, grilling on the coal-fired BBQ.

My grandfather's willingness to explain the same thing over and over again, like the damn birds. I asked the same question, summer after summer, about the birds. I swear my desire to learn about them was rooted in the experience he provided by demonstrating so much patience, love, and passion, whenever I asked him about the birds. Either way, I loved every second of the explanation. I loved how happy he became when speaking about their details. I also loved the moments we shared when the various birds popped up on their perch right before our eyes, while we sat, swinging on the porch.

Summer after summer, my brother and I stayed for two weeks at my grandparents' house in northern Arizona. These became some of the most sacred memories of my lifetime. My memories are full of lessons in the power of listening, observing, trying new things, making mistakes, and learning from them. They are about how to live in fullness with minimal comforts, about why being an observer will teach you more than speaking, internal peace, creativity, the power in being bored, and the dangers of being wrapped in fear.

They remind me there is no separation between generations, only an unwillingness to stay curious about one another's relativity. Last, just because the flower is gorgeous doesn't mean you should pluck it from its happy soil. Some things are meant to stay and remain beautiful right where they are rooted. Not all things are meant for us to covet.

ST(RIPPED)

Boy, did I learn this lesson the hard way one summer! We were zipping around on our four-wheeler, hair blowing in the wind, full of laughter and freedom. As my brother was driving us around the orchard, we circled a little patch of flowers. I asked him to slow down as I leaned to the side to snag a beauty.

The fun quickly ended when hundreds of tiny, translucent thorns pierced in my hand. The agitation and pain grew quickly; my palm was on fire and pulsing with a stark reminder: you don't get everything you want without a cost.

My brother promptly drove us to the porch, where I sprinted up the four stairs, through the screen door, and into the kitchen, where my grandma was preparing lunch. I immediately told her what had happened, as tears filled my eyes. As my grandma hustled to greet me with loving, open arms, my papa quickly retrieved some duct tape. I spent the remainder of my afternoon vigorously applying and then ripping the duct tape off my palm, hoping to extract all 100+ translucent thorns from my hand.

Not everything you want should be yours to hold and have; some things in life are meant to be acknowledged, adored, and passed by.

A catfish! Can you believe it? There are fish that have whiskers! To this day, I still get a kick out of those plump fish with whiskers and start to giggle. My Papa loved to fish. He loved the preparation that went into a day on the lake: the gathering of the mealworms, a simple sack lunch, water in a canteen, a foldable backless military-grade stool to sit on, a couple of fishing poles, and, most important, your patience.

I have vivid memories of setting up our stuff beside the lake. The tall grass lightly dancing in the breeze, the fishing supplies so simple in their repurposed containers, the faint but genuine smile that glimmered on Papa's face as we staggered out to the water, leaving us plenty of room to cast our lines and wait. We waited, hoping to catch the first fish. Then waited for the next, hoping for the thrill. You waited patiently because that was what we were there to do: *just be.*

As the day rolled on and boredom tried to creep in, as a kid, I started to do silly things, like modify to my imagination's content and wildly casting my line, hoping my dad or papa wasn't paying attention. I could blame the snag on the grass in the lake or on my sibling, who was also messing around. But it was me, my loss of control for *just being*. The days on the lake were the threaded memories of experiencing internal peace, the power of presence and simplicity.

These moments were lifelong teachers, imprinted on my internal matrix. These moments later proved part of my valued foundation for connection and mental peace that I leaned into. These moments, these forged relationships were my gravity.

The multi-faceted woman: *she wears many hats that all embody impact, creativity, influence, and passion. She knows no limits and never settles for a single responsibility. Her life is full of vision, love, and purpose.*

My Grandma Ruby was just that, the multi-faceted woman. There wasn't a space she didn't beautifully curate, a meal

ST(RIPPED)

she didn't fill with love, or a conversation where she missed a detail. She was astounding.

I learned there was no such thing as a measuring cup in Grandma Ruby's kitchen. You had to learn to *trust your senses and create.*

Brunch was on full display. The stove was already heated to perfection, and all the items needed to create a spectacular meal were lined up on the island, ready to contribute to her notable creation.

"Niccole, my apple, peaches, pumpkin pie, can you please gather the egg order?" she requested with her warm smile.

I stayed close to her side in the kitchen, studying her every move and securing easy access to a hug and kiss whenever either of us desired them. Before I headed out to gather the egg order, she kissed my head and grinned ear to ear. She never missed a detail. I wore my denim, lace-trimmed, heart-pocket apron, the pocket perfectly sized for my notepad and pen.

I wore it over a lavender shirt, cream headband, and "cat who ate the canary" grin on my face as I made my way to the living room to collect the egg order, including how many eggs and how each family member wanted them cooked.

"Grandma, we will need four fried eggs for Dad, two scrambled for Mom, two for my brother, 2 for me, and three for Papa."

Out came the prized bacon grease. Minutes later, we had all the eggs cooked to everyone's specifications. The fluffy biscuits came out of the oven, simply perfect every time! Golden brown, just over the size of a silver dollar, soft inside but firm in structure and delightful. These beauties filled anyone's soul to capacity.

After the eggs came the breakfast meat: venison, bacon, and Jimmy Dean sausage patties, piled high on a platter. Next, Grandma's famous gravy. I was mesmerized by her ease in the kitchen. She'd reach into the flour container with her bare hand and sprinkle flour into the saucepan, first by the handful, then easing up to a drizzle. She carefully mixed it in with the wooden spoon to create the perfect consistency.

And last of all, my favorite, her fried apples. Good God, I couldn't get enough of these. They had a smell that consumed me. The cinnamon, sugar, and apples were brought to the perfect heat, making a near liquifying delight for the tummy. They were nothing short of *marvelous*!

No one ever left Grandma Ruby's table hungry. We never left without a heart full of gratitude. Never left without priceless wisdom. The oval-shaped table at Grandma and Papa's was full of love, empowerment, observation, and listening. This is where trust and growth occurred. Everyone's voice was heard and our presence validated.

This table served as the foundation for my inner strength. Just as the table grew in length, one leaf at a time, as more guests joined the festivities, so did my developing voice and courage. Each year, my capacity grew, along with my knowledge and my understanding of generational history that provided me an edge. It fueled a curiosity far too expansive for my age. Still, I tucked those golden nuggets of information away in my observation compartment, which I kept in the back of my mind, a place I could access whenever my strength or my certainty

ST(RIPPED)

faltered. This was my empowerment place, where I gained courage from witnessing resilience and honor before my eyes.

My seat at this table became my platform for life. The age range spanned from seven to sixty-five, but I never felt the age gap.

Every time I paid a visit, my grandmother fulfilled a project in its entirety. Her creativity knew no end. She was the most resourceful person I knew, making magic and impact out of very little. She was transformational in every conversation, no matter the subject. She was rooted in truth, grace, and faith.

Many kids can remember their first opportunities at independent phone conversions with friends. Me, I clearly remember my sacred phone dates with my Grandma Ruby. No topic or conversation was off the table. She always lent me wisdom and patience, giving me a safe place to land emotions, questions, and my own life's uncertainties.

She helped me to better understand my dad, my parents' choices, and why it didn't matter when other kids were mean and unrelatable. She reenforced how my firm commitments to developing my character, honor, presence, and emotional intelligence were what mattered. She helped me understand the power of "coming back to my foundation," no matter what. She often told me I cannot control how others show up, but I can commit to dignity and respect; I can impact the trajectory of my life by staying focused on myself.

The compounding effects of her wisdom and love became my most outstanding teacher in becoming a young lady. Our bond was an integral part of my most challenging teenage years and as I became a young woman. I had her presence, mentorship, and unconditional love; I always had a balance of free will and accountability.

In later years, when the holiday season came around, I would walk through my grandparents' mudroom, up the steps, and into their entryway to find every square inch of the house bursting with Christmas spirit. Not one surface was left untouched; and the magic increased as I moved through the house and approached the kitchen. The aromas of cinnamon, sugar, and crackling fire overcame my senses. I was engulfed by the cozy, welcoming magic of the season.

Every step into the house welcomed me with a feeling of relaxation, safety, and love. There was so much but not enough, at the same time. The more I saw, the more I wanted to discover. My Grandma Ruby's artistic touch and intention to ignite the season's spirit kindled in my soul, whether I liked it or not. This home opened anyone's soul to joy and connection. It freed every visitor of doubt about whether magic and love existed.

As I moved through the kitchen and into the dining room, I came upon small shelves carefully curated with Christmas decor and intricately embellished with homemade treats, ranging from fudge to sugar cookies, peanut brittle, chocolates, hard candy, and thumbprints. These unique sweets were the result of my grandmother's culinary prowess and her sensory decorating. She didn't miss a detail.

Her smile was full of contagious pride and joy. This woman lived to make a home for her people and provide an experience that captured all of your senses, leaving you feeling nothing short of love and care. Her validation came in the excitement we exuded. This was all she needed to feel her peace and joy.

ST(RIPPED)

It was simply that: *service to others* filled and fueled her soul and purpose.

We all filed into the living room to take in the rest of the wonderland then sat, warmed by the fire, and admired each beautifully wrapped present. Grandma smiled big and nuzzled into all 6'4" of my dad. She loved him without measure. The peace and pride she felt in his presence were never hidden. The love around us liquified as we exchanged hug after hug, taking in one another, and relished our presence in our grandparents' home. Everyone's guard came down, and we were *home for the holidays*.

Brilliance Found in Simplicity

I believe it's the underdogs, the men and women who committed relentlessly to their vision, despite optimal conditions, who deserve the real hero cards. The people who, despite their unstable home environment, the less than stellar living conditions, and the obstacles that stood firm in their pathway, figured out a way. They figured out how to continue to listen to the drive, the piqued passion, the voice inside their head that said "even if." They found an imperfect way, but it was the way toward their deeper calling. They built their new reality despite the turbulence, given less-than-optimal conditions, and they turned inward.

I am a true believer that every human born to this Earth has the capacity for greatness. Each of us has a well of potential, impact, and beautiful legacy. It is up to us to identify these unique qualities and evolve them.

During sophomore year of high school, I fully recognized my dream, my vision for my future. And I not only had a dream, I had goals, goals that had been forming since early in my life and were deeply inspired by the family who came before me.

I wanted to become a collegiate volleyball player. And I wanted to earn my way through school with a sports scholarship. I set my eye on becoming part of the two percent of high school female athletes who go on to play at the NCAA level. My want, my *desire* to become this young woman opened the door to my relentless mindset, committed to doing whatever it took to become *her*.

I grew up in sunny Southern California, a hot spot for this sport. The region was full of incredible, talented young female volleyball players. I was lucky enough to attend camp with many of these gals, or later compete against them. These young women were exposed to volleyball starting when they learned to walk. Also, as kids, they all played the sport for fun on the beach, which provided a whole new edge. I discovered my dream and passion for volleyball later in my life, but it was not too late, and I was determined to prove this!

These goals were lofty and, honestly, insane if you consider my experience to date on the path to my dream. They were insane because I had very little exposure to the culture of this dream and little knowledge about what it would take to achieve it. Also, I was an amateur at the sport, embarrassingly so, compared to my peer group.

However, what I did have was a relentless mindset that had been evolving since childhood, an unwavering commitment to my bigger aspiration, and the deep knowing that anything is possible despite adversity if you are committed to the process and evolution. I leaned into the everyday heroes of my life: my Papa, my Nonno, my Nonna, my Grandma Ruby. They, too, had dreams and

ST(RIPPED)

goals for their lives, and they overcame legitimate hardship to realize a better life. These incredible people gave me perspective on my journey, and they gave me the substance to grasp the power of mindset and determination.

I want to call out the powerful impact of the everyday people in our lives. While I also have respect and admiration for professional athletes, well-known authors, successful business leaders, and public figures, I also recognize we are surrounded by inspirational and heroic figures whom we know, and who can shape our lives at a tangible level.

We are those people, as well. It is important to note we often overlook the inspiration to be found in our own family's story. They are the everyday people in our lives, the trailblazers with our own DNA who have made an impact, shaped history, can fuel our greater aspirations.

I think we often get caught up in separating ourselves from grander possibilities due to our limited resources or our backgrounds. Well, I am here to tell you, "You are capable of magnificent things. You have the power to become and to create the version of you that you want!"

We all have the ability to pave a way, to bring an "unreachable goal" into fruition, and to allow our legacy to trailblaze and impact. It starts with dialing in our mind and our vision. When we zero in, it brings us clarity, and clarity gives us the power to embrace the small stackable actions that lead into the bigger desired outcomes.

For example, my dream was to become a collegiate volleyball player on scholarship. I knew early on that this dream would require many different facets of my being to evolve and become better than a certain percentage of my peers, in order to make the cut.

This dream was lofty, but anything we desire to bring to fruition has a foundation, and that foundation is built on a few key fundamentals. If we peel back the layers of any lofty goal and we build on the fundamentals, we find the small stackable steps we can build upon, which will eventually bring us closer to our goal. Homing in on these elements is the key to achieving what we dream. It is what distinguishes those people who make it at the level from those who do not.

I believe, no matter what your goal or vision, these fundamentals hold true:
(1) Mindset
(2) Physical training, and
(3) Nourishment.

Maybe you are wondering how these things apply to you, if your goals don't involve becoming a high-level athlete or anything physically demanding. Please hear me out.

(1) Mindset: When you are able to dial in your mindset with clarity, focus on your "why," and use discipline to maintain your vision, nothing can stop you. Yes, you will encounter alligators in your life, what I call interference, but when you have clarity about what you want, where you want to go, what drives you, and your intended impact, you will always be able to reach your desired outcome, because your mind is locked into your purpose. After all, your body can break or be injured, but your mindset is relentless, if you nourish it.

(2) Physical training: The body is meant to move. It is meant to carry us through demanding parts of life. It is meant to move energy and process. Physical training builds us up through discipline. The need for and benefits of

physical training for a high-level athlete are obvious. But the average person also requires it every day because of its ability to transform the mind and body.

Strength is built and earned. It requires discipline and commitment, but mental clarity and a boost to your energy levels are the byproducts of this commitment and discipline. So how that translates to everyday life is clear. When we put our bodies through this demand purposefully and when we focus our minds to it, we cultivate a level of confidence and resilience that have the power to propel and carry us through life.

No one can take back the hours you commit to building strength; but the grit that develops and evolution that occurs through this process cannot be undone. Our commitment to our physical training (or the lack of it) correlates directly to how we show up in our lives.

(3) Nourishment: What I include within nourishment are your hydration, sleep, food consumed, and social life. Without adequate nourishment, you are unable to sustain a desired outcome. We've all heard the quip, "You can't out-train your eating habits." I would argue you can't out-train your nourishment.

The person who fails to honor sleep will never sustain their desired outcome, because their body will not be able to recover properly, either mentally or physically. Without adequate sleep, injuries occur, fatigue isn't satiated, and the mind begins to function at a lower level and a slower pace.

Without proper nourishment through food, we cannot build, sustain, or prosper. It greatly impacts our ability to recover and flourish. When our food supply is inadequate, it will mess with our hormones and sleep patterns. Proper macronutrient consumption is imperative for us to thrive. It is also essential for nurturing our mindset and meeting the demands of our physical training. These are all connected, so we cannot soar in one area without the others being in balance.

As regards the nourishment of a social life, we all need connection, joy, love, touch, and fun. A healthy social life enhances our mental health, longevity, and mental prowess, plus our sense of belonging and purpose. We cannot overlook the impacts of our connection to others. Personally, I have lived chapters of my life with intense discipline and structure, both in nutrition and physical training, but have failed to recognize the importance of my social life and making sure it was supported while I undertook the other two aspect of my nourishment.

They all have to coexist symbiotically, in order to sustain your long-game goals. To me, mindset, physical training, and nourishment are the non-negotiable foundation for any endeavor, goal, or dream.

We do not get to choose how we were brought into this world or the circumstances we possibly endured in our upbringing. However, there is power in knowing we can write our own story or rewrite it at any time in our lives. So often, we fumble through life, even repeating the fumble, because our lives were, perhaps, tough in the beginning. Or maybe we had success and then lost it due to an injury, a loss, divorce, or a changed career. Maybe we lost our way in the shifts of our age. Regardless, you get the chance to write your story. You may not choose all the characters who make their way in, but *you*, my friend, get to write it, edit it, and evolve it!

Deneke, the Power in a Name

Deneke is the name I was called for years. It preceded me. It set the tone for how people acknowledged or treated me. It freed me. It held me. It also led to being judged before I had the opportunity to prove myself and who I was. To show who this version of Deneke was that I represented.

My father was an athletic director, teacher, high school football coach, and well-respected man who held the line and "took no prisoners," when it came to matters of character and honoring your commitment. With that said, there was a community of parents and peers in his industry who resisted being held to this standard. It threatened their power, and they developed disdain for my father, for the Deneke name, and, in turn, for me.

Deneke is my family name, my pride, and my identity. It represents many years of courage to create the brilliant life I am able to live because of that. *Deneke* was the name people used to get my attention. It was the name I was called on in school, and it was how my peers referred to me. I was not Niccole Deneke, I was only the powerful *Deneke*.

Deneke's daughter

Deneke's sister

Deneke

Coach Deneke's daughter

By the time I graduated, I had forgotten I even had a first name. When I got to college, I started to realize how much of my identity was tied up in the legacy reflected in that time. I was proud of and fueled by the energy packed within those six 6 letters. I didn't mind how it had replaced my first name.

After all, *Niccole* was reserved for people close to me. It was sacred, whenever it was used. In so many ways, this was the name used by people who knew me on a deep level. My last name was rich in legacy, but my first name was *mine*. It was tied only to me, full of so much promise and the deep personal footprint I would create and connect to it.

Deneke represents those parts of my family of whom I was most proud and in awe. They were who paved the path I wanted to trailblaze. The name contained great power and endless possibilities, which I needed to navigate. I had to discover what power was mine to run with and how I would use the possibilities as "leads" to create my own path and build my own legacy.

Once I stepped through the door of owning my identity within my name, I did a hell of a job piquing the interest of those around me. It started as, "That's Deneke's daughter," but soon moved into, "Who the hell is she anyway? Where did she come from? No one expected *her* to step in this direction and make something of herself on the court, in athletics, in community impact."

I was a born underdog, although, with that name, most everyone suspected I was *something* in the making. They could see me bare my heart and share my soul's calling; they knew, behind the scenes, I was figuring out how to work with what I had: a skill set not as advanced as my peers', but a mind, heart, and physical drive that was impossible to break.

They knew me to lean into the power of my name, and to leverage the drive, courage, and truth set before me. I knew most people would try to set the tone for my story, but instead of subscribing to the fear and doubt of others, I leaned into my drive, my passion, and the unknown, fueled

by the idea of what was possible. I set my sights on all the probabilities versus the possibilities. I leaned into what I knew to be true: that my mind and drive were impossible to sate. Unstoppable.
More hurdles, better problem-solving. Here she goes!
Every door closed is a new game plan to refine, a new entrance to be created.

You can hide behind something as powerful as a name, or you can take full ownership of what you bring to the legacy set before you. You can embrace what has been forged and then choose. There is always a choice. You can honor what has been done before, what has been fought for and embraced, while also putting your mark on it. This will cost you, but there is always a choice.

Along with the heritage of my name came expectations, inside and out. From as early as I can remember, I *despised* disappointing my parents or anyone I respected. I carried a very heavy load for disappointing my parents. So much, in fact, that at the start of my freshman year of high school, my mom and dad had to lecture me to stop "being all things to everyone" I could *not* give 100% to everything, so I needed to detach and prioritize and execute.

Let me be clear, my efforts, focus, and commitment needed to be 100% and wholehearted, but I couldn't say *yes* to everything and expect to be less than perfect in all the commitments. I needed to be selective, so I could be the best, most impactful version of myself whenever I did say, "Yes."

This permission was a gift and a challenge. I often took it as a challenge, like, "Watch me!" Let me show you how many things I can be 100% at and impact. I had a mission, starting when I was a small child, to increase my ceiling and never let it remain a limit.

> *"I am just a product of what is possible when willing to do whatever it takes."*
> —NRH

If I had a billboard, this would be the headline of my thought process.

I knew my parents saw me deeply for who I was and who I was becoming. This was a gift. Their guidance was always rooted in love, care, and respect for me. Good God! I needed guardrails to channel the drive that continued to evolve within me. Even if the guardrails were not relevant to what I needed, exactly, I did need structure to prevent me from negatively effecting my own growth, desire, and purpose. I needed a channel for my big, big, deep, deep thoughts and, then eventually, actions.

The expectations I held for myself, my driven mindset, and commitment to what I wanted to accomplish was a challenge at times, I would allow my perfectionism and relentless commitment overtake me. I knew I always had a little more to give. I knew there was always a little more I could muster up and push, which slowly set my bar higher to exceed my thresholds. I became obsessed with how I could expand those limits and become better, mentally, physically, and emotionally. I started to recognize this truth: "The body may be fragile, but the mind and heart united is *unstoppable.*"

My Father, My Model of a True Warrior

I made my way down the stairs, through the kitchen, and out the door to the garage, where I could smell the oh-so-

ST(RIPPED)

sweet scent of my father's classic KIWI boot polish. As he polished his boots, his military fatigues hung perfectly above him, his coffee steamed beside him, and his water was in a tall glass next to the coffee mug.

He was still in his PT gear. Though it was before 6:30 a.m., he had already run five-plus miles on the trail, completed his weightlifting session, read his daily devotional, and rehearsed for the day. This portion of the garage was organized for him to carry out his daily preparations with precision.

Shelves wrapped around the whole twenty-by-thirty-foot garage, stacked four high up into the trusses of the roof. Each shelf held clearly labeled boxes or totes in their very specific spots. My dad and Papa built this shelf project back in 1987, shortly after my parents had bought this house and I was born, after they decided to put down roots in Oceanside, California.

My father always remembered and treasured that visit by Papa to help with this garage project. His parents didn't make it out to visit very often back then, due to their health, so the shelving always meant more to him than just their pristine organization and impressive craftsmanship. The garage was jam-packed with memories of him working alongside his own father to nourish a foundation and atmosphere of stability, organization, and flow for the life my parents were creating for their new family.

I walked into the garage, my eyes sandpapery and my smile warm, and greeted my dad. He paused the boot polishing briefly and embraced me with a welcoming good-morning hug and kiss. His greeting never faltered. He expressed unconditional affection toward us. No matter what he was doing, he always had the capacity to show us love and attention.

While it was early for a five-year-old to be awake, I already demonstrated how I enjoyed chasing the sunrise, just like my dad. I also quickly realized how sacred this time was. It was not only time with my dad, but it was prime observation hours. I could watch how my dad fluidly started his day at his own pace. How he owned what he needed in order to be the man he was in our family, in his career, in the community, and for his *WHY*. I didn't want to miss any of it. I wanted to watch, learn, and be alongside him.

At this age, I already began to want to grow up to be someone who held responsibility like he did, with so much purpose, honor, and ease. I wanted to be the role model he was. I wanted to be strong, loving, dynamic, effective, confident, empowering, faith-driven, and committed to my bigger purpose. I wanted to live "on purpose," to know the direction I was going and to embody it.

After his boots were polished, once everything was dialed in and ready to go for the day, we made our way back into the house to have breakfast. By this time, the rest of the household had begun to wake up. My brother and beautiful mama joined the morning flow.

When I was growing up, it was clear my mom and brother would have preferred to skip the early-morning hangout time. They were more night owls and loved their morning sleep. This was fine by me, because I adored my solo time with Dad. I also learned the power of morning solitude—the quiet, the ease, and the peace that came with waking earlier than most of the world. It was a sacred time, as instilled in me from an early age.

ST(RIPPED)

I think of these early years as a collection of moments that nourished, solidified, and expanded the bond between my dad and me. Later, this morning solitude came to serve as my most powerful time for innovation, reflection, creating, doing, and nourishing my soul.

Thirty-plus years later, as a mom of two, I think back on these moments with my dad, on how seamless he made our time, as he orchestrated his morning, accomplishing everything he needed, but never making my presence a burden. He connected with me in conversation and instruction in ways that were relevant to my age. He was a master at leading and being a role model through the power of proximity. He led by example.

From the breakfast table, we got ready for the day and headed to school. I was in preschool at the time, and my brother in kindergarten. My parents divided and conquered for drop-off. The days when my dad took me to school extended those sacred moments we'd shared in the early morning. I can still feel, see, and smell all the details of this experience.

By the time we headed out the door, my dad was clean-shaven, his hair combed to perfection, his miliary uniform in immaculate order. His boots were dialed to the right sheen, and he had a watch on his left wrist, the slight scent of aftershave, and his skin was aglow. He was the epitome of a Marine Corps officer: tall, strong, and striking in every detail. He was pristine, confident, driven, and organized. He moved with intention and was always prepared, fueled by integrity and honor. He fulfilled this role so well, but he brought an incredible edge to the table, his own unassuming elements of compassion, empathy, love, and embrace.

NICCOLE HENDRICKSON

My dad showed us how to love and respect others through his deep devotion, love, admiration, trust, and connection toward our mother. He adored and loved her with a loyalty I still cannot fully comprehend to this day. A love I have always dreamt of. And he carried this very same love he showed and lived to our mom over to us. He also lacked patience and had other flaws of character, but his faults were far outweighed by his love and dedication to loving and growing us as strong, empathetic, and devoted humans. His faults humanized him.

As the years passed, many of my observations gave me opportunities to join and become more like my dad. I learned how to prepare for my own day, how to attack the day with fervor, and how to show up fully as myself. I learned how "own" the day by laying out my clothes ahead of time, how to truly look forward to challenges ahead versus fearing them, and how to make my bed and stay tidy, because starting my day this way impacted how I presented myself with confidence and ownership. I learned how to scramble eggs and make a beautiful breakfast and how to use these experiences as the precursor to what kind of day I wanted.

I learned to take care myself while always factoring in time to serve others. I saw how valuable a small note to someone can be. Leading isn't forcing someone to do it my way. It is showing them the way so *they* can find their North Star. My own shone bright and true, later in my life, when I fell in love and found my person.

Chapter 1 Reflections

Theme: Rooted. Resilient. Rising.

What parts of your upbringing or background have felt most limiting or challenging to accept? Why?

In what ways have you found strength, resilience, or wisdom through the circumstances you didn't choose?

What vision do you currently hold for your future? What's one small choice you can make today that aligns with that vision?

CHAPTER 2

Why Your Circle Matters

My early years were forged through the power of my family on both my dad's and mom's side. My cousins were my first friends, the sisters I didn't have. My aunts, uncles, and grandparents served as my most dynamic teachers. In high school, college, and during my early adult life, I started to curate relationships with my chosen friends and mentors.

I appreciate how the safety of those relationships I built during in my early years led to the lifelong connections I formed later. My family became my rite of passage to the people I was later blessed to have in my life.

Beautifully creased linens, impeccable organization, books everywhere, matching towel sets, soap and hand lotion to match, throw pillows placed with both intention and purpose, scents that not only penetrated your sense of smell but locked you right into the moment, capturing all of you. The art mixed with personal photos, all carefully curated. Every square inch of her floor pristine. The snacks that lined the countertop were all beautifully on display, chocolate-covered almonds lightly dusted with salt, whole cashews, fruit, and of course perfectly chosen snack napkins to accompany. Her home, not a detail left out. Full of character, items that validated her world travel, humble and ornate at the same time. Everything in its place, however beckoning me to touch the surfaces, ruffle the pillows with a cozy sit, and consume the snacks. This home screamed, "Take refuge and be you. All of you!"

Auntie: silk skin and dainty features matched with a fierce mind and brilliant vocabulary. A stunning woman with a thoughtful heart, intentional spirit, and impenetrable commitment to her virtues. Her embodied perseverance is something I will forever hold dear and thank her for. She role-modeled through her life choices, relentlessly pursuing a path the polar opposite of how she grew up. An unwavering commitment to her marriage, home, and motherhood.

She set her eye on the prize of the life she wanted and stopped at nothing to attain it. Every possible way, she honored it. Like a chess game, she went about her life. This woman was responsible for so many beautiful lessons in my life as a child, young woman, and adult. Any seat at the table with this woman was a vantage point that could never be bought. Access into her heart and impact was earned through integrity, authenticity, and humility. Her love has never been conditional. However, the strength of the bond has always been dictated by the ability to be honorable and open to growth.

I'd say people often mistakenly thought she was hard to win over, that it was difficult to share in her delight, but I argue that is far from true. What she was and is to this day is a woman of her word, full of integrity. She demands authenticity. Come as you are, but you better be true.

She was a devoted mother. In addition to having her own child, she never missed a chance to treat me and my brother. She acknowledged our accomplishments, attended our important life milestones, and gave equal support anytime we needed support to thrive in the trials of life. She remained unconditional and present.

I was keenly aware of her fully vested love for us. The way she kept a pulse on every important person in her life and her circle was impressive. They say proximity is key. The power of her presence in my early life formation. The ability to witness what is possible when you commit to your bigger WHY and stay focused on the legacy you will leave. You will hit hurdles, suffer sadness, question your path, but you will stay standing through hell, when you are clear on *your* guiding principles. No person, obstacle, or illness can be your downfall, when you choose to repurpose your pain and derail.

This woman exuded a tenacious fortitude. I recall wondering how the hell she kept it together and flowing, no matter the season of life she was in.

From her perfectly painted lips to pristine hair, manicured nails, hydrated skin, statement-making eye glasses, with a classic handbag to match her immaculate clothing, she never fell into victimhood. Her mental drive never allowed it. She built her self-respect through her tireless commitment to building and honoring the life she demanded, her legacy. She envisioned it for herself, and pursued it relentlessly.

I see her in my day-to-day and dreams when I navigate trials. I feel into her when my path is obscure. I honor her relentless commitment to her wellbeing every time I apply my skincare routine and bless my beauty process. She was never vain, just full of self-respect. Put yourself together so your excellence is not only seen but felt.

The reality is, in this world, you will command the level of respect that you have for yourself. Wholeheartedly think of the message you want to present, send, and embody. I live for curating my home in a way that makes my family and guests feel seen and valued and that stimulates their senses, just like my auntie did. I work every day to be on top of my game enough to acknowledge those around me the way she always has and does.

To be seen and acknowledged is to be loved on a cellular level that is unmatched.

How does one woman never miss a detail?

This equates to a level of awareness and organization I have found enviable.

As a child, I studied every way in which this beautiful auntie of mine made me and all those around her feel valued. Every interaction. How did she do it? With focus and determination.

I watched how she moved effortlessly in the kitchen. Whether laying table for snacks or a formal dinner, *no* details were missed. My obsession with table linens, silverware, and setting a table started at an early age. While this was modeled to me at home, too, at my Grandma Ruby's house, my auntie helped me understand the why, the how, and the impact of a set table. I learned you always pass the salt and pepper together, even when someone only asks for one of them. They are a pair, as Auntie informed me, so they stay together.

I learned why there are two forks, how to curate the energy of a meal, and to include the honor of a blessing, no matter the religious affiliation of the table guests. She taught me the impacts of lighting and smells and how a platter can serve as a conversational piece. The power of what is around your dinner table, whether art or a piece of furniture. Each can stoke conversation and storytelling, so choose wisely.

During freshman year of high school, I was directing my peers int the gymnasium in all directions. It beautiful chaos.

I locked into a memory my mom had shared from her own high school days, when she had helped to curate the homecoming floats. Thousands of pieces of tissue had to be fluffed to perfection to create unique, vibrant stories on moving flatbeds. It was an art show on wheels, where every person had an opportunity to step into their creative power. This vision is still one of my favorites.

For my freshman-year project, I had to recruit family members, and then distribute tissue paper to several aunts, my Nonna, and my friends. It was full steam ahead for everyone, working together to bring this float idea to life. I was there, wholeheartedly believing in myself and my ability to articulate this vision, get the buy-in, and curate a level of fun where the commitment was so locked in, the vision became *everyone's*! It was a sensational challenge, and I relished it.

My Auntie and Unc lived hundreds of miles away, however somewhere in conversation, they had caught wind that this production was in progress, so of course, they had to be there to witness the magic and, most important, uncontained joy that would erupt when my high school pulled off this production, which had once been reserved only for our rival. *Ha!* Not anymore!

ST(RIPPED)

This element was the *WHY* I was connected to. All these labels were about to be *blown* off. Tides would shift, and belief in something so much bigger would unspool with the reveal of these floats. Daring to push the "this is how we do it" mindset was a feat in itself, but I loved it. I lived for the discomfort and nay-sayers. The fuel was joy and achieving the impossible. The energy to do it was in the pitch to the community, when I encouraged each one of my peers to leverage their assets by just asking for help, to be a part of something so much bigger.

If I learned anything from my own family, it was that we need one another, but you will never receive if you do not ask. The fuel kept coming when each person started to buy in and bring their own creativity. It was never about me. It was about piercing the limited beliefs and being the conduit for change. I could not have desired a better pair of people to validate this plan than my Auntie and Unc.

It was *go time,* baby! They walked in to witness the intricate colored tissue, fluffed to perfection, and the excitement penetrating through the gymnasium walls. Every student knew their role and owned it. Their eyes were big, and their smiles spread from ear to ear. The camera clicked nonstop, capturing every single moment with pride.

There was one theme in every valued relationship that formed me as a young girl: at every table I sat, keen observations were made and a presence was felt and valued. My Auntie was unmatched in her ability to communicate effortlessly but inclusively. She had a way of welcoming our young ears and minds to the table, while also catching up with my parents in a way that made the visit impactful for all of us. I took note of this early on: listening to *every* detail, and watching the body language of all the adults. The table was fortified with love, vulnerability, trust, genuine joy, and laughter. The storytelling was priceless.

My relationship with Auntie flourished throughout my whole life. It started as the love and bond of an aunt to a niece, like any relationship rooted in trust, it evolved into a mentorship and mutually enriching friendship. This proved to me once that wisdom has no age. You forge life bonds, and both people receive, learn, and benefit from them, when both individuals are invested in growth and humility. Auntie has been one of the most influential women in my lifetime.

After high school graduation, most of my peers went on senior trips. I asked to fly to Arizona to spend a few days with my Auntie, uncle, and cousin. I wanted to indulge in sunshine, deep conversation, spa treatments, and a shopping trip to purchase my first classic leather Coach bag. I can still smell the leather and see the richness if this bag; a deep burgundy that screamed subtle statement. To me at that time, this investment was huge. It was a step into womanhood. It was a declaration of maturity. It was me saying, "I value and honor myself, and I take myself seriously." I cannot imagine making this first big purchase with any other woman than my auntie. She was a symbol of class and understated precision.

"Some cousins aren't just cousins,
they are shareholders of your childhood."

The landline rang. (Yes, the landline.) My mom answered and said, "Niccole, the phone is for you!"

ST(RIPPED)

I sprinted down the two flights of stairs and slid into the family room, exuberant. Grabbing the phone from my mom, I said, "Hello!"

"Peach, an affectionate name used between my cousin Andrea and I, what are you doing with your life tomorrow? It's Friday! Let's hit the beach and then you can stay the night."

"*Yaaaaasss*! Count me in!"

(Peach was an affectionate nickname we'd given each other as kids, and it had stuck.)

I knew what this was code for: all-day bronzing, people-watching, and the wing-woman position I played so well for my cousin, while she eyed her crush and interacted with her crew. This weekend, her parents were out of town, and she didn't want to fly solo while they were away.

I always loved how I was the chosen cousin and "friend" for these moments. There was something amplifying about being chosen, something empowering about how we went from childhood friends to teenage partners in crime. I adored how she took me under her wing and how I eventually became the chosen wing-woman. Proximity played a role in this, I am sure, but I also like to believe there were aspects of me that brought out the best in her, just like there were elements of her that freed parts of me.

We rallied in her 1980s black Chevy Blazer, raging to music with the windows down all the way to our beloved beach spot, Tower 5 southside of the Pier. We spent the day in mindless conversation at the beach, bronzing, but never entering the ocean. (This against my deepest desires; I didn't understand why people went to the beach but didn't go in the water?)

NICCOLE HENDRICKSON

We lined our towels up on the lush, powdery sand, with bottles of water on their upper corners. We had our Spy sunnies on, black Reef flipflops tucked to the side, our messy buns in place, and our glow dialed. We sat on our towels, leaning on our elbows so we had the best angles, ease of conversation in each direction, and of course, the ability to keep our eyes on all the people coming and going.

Those were the days. I had a place here as the cousin. Some dared to call me "Deneke's daughter," but most avoided that, since local guys were perfectly terrified of him. They weren't ready to own they were beachside with their coach's prized daughter, though they were scoping me out from head to toe; curious and fully knowing. *Not a chance!*

I was always tall for my age, but my soul was wiser than I could sometimes manage to bear. I was deep, I had a vision for what I wanted, and I was quiet, calculated, and very observant. I reserved the exuberance and intricacies of my personality for those close to me. I was fully aware of my mystery and the way it piqued the curiosities of those around me.

My awareness sometimes got me into trouble. I never missed a detail and that was terrifying at times. While in the action, I was taking it all in and afterwards could recall every minute detail. Then, I would ask questions about why certain friends did particular things, I would connect dots and reveal elements of character that were not always flattering. I'd also started to take notice of how it felt to be noticed. This was fun and dangerous territory.

The smell of Hawaiian Tropic sunscreen for me, Banana Boat for my cousin. Even today, if I catch a whiff of either of those, it brings me right back to being fourteen years old by

ST(RIPPED)

Tower 5 southside of Pier, on my towel, bronzing and observing in my two-piece Roxy string bikini, with sterling-silver rings on my thumb, forefinger, and middle finger. Not a care in the world other than how tan could I get that day.

These beach days were full of so many emotions for me, so many moments of observation and taking notes on my next steps to becoming. They also highlighted where I struggled with insecurity and a need for assurance. Those days were some of my best memories of treasured time with my cousin and shining moments of our solid friendship.

They also represented times when I struggled with my sense of self. I struggled to stand up for what I felt was right or wrong. I was a hell of a lot more impressionable and influenced than I care to admit. I was not leading anything in this time of my life. I was 100% in follower mode at this time. And I started to take notice of this version of myself. It was nauseating. It was concerning. I knew I needed to figure myself out prior to starting my sophomore year in high school, so this follower/observer period was coming to a close.

These were some of the last days for me taking refuge in my cousins while ignoring anything else going on around me. For me not to care any other friendships I either did or did not create. This summer after my freshman high school year was the last time we did what we'd always done, though we both could feel how it was no longer the norm anymore. I had other friends, I had commitments, I had taken notice of the intricacies of developing myself, and I was no longer just the little cousin anymore. This peach had other people and a calling that had awoken in her...

This would impact our relationship, our unspoken contract. I was identifying the official closing of one chapter and the opening of another.

But our bond still reminds me: blood is thicker than water, but give space for growth, celebrate the space, and remember the roots are strong.

"Friendship is the umbrella that shields you in the storm, the strength that lifts you when you fall, and the love that steps back to let your light shine."

2001 was a year of so many firsts for me:
My first year of high school.
The first time I started to see all the cobblestones in my life begin to form a path.
The introduction to my first true best friends.
The first time I experienced the freedom once foreshadowed by my cousins.
The introduction to my chosen soul mentors.
2001 was the year I would explore so many possibilities of choice.
The year I would fearlessly open my heart and discover the beautiful richness and diversity of humanity.
The year that would truly set the foundation for a lifetime ahead.

Prior to high school, I had dabbled in swimming and junior lifeguards, and spent plenty of leisure time building my swimming prowess. In spring 2001, I traded my softball gear for a one-piece racerback, tightly fitted swimsuit and an epic goggle tan. Bronzed legs, arms, and time in the water... *LFG!*

ST(RIPPED)

Swim season was in spring, which gave me time to navigate who was who, which coach led what, and to understand the backstory of some of the athletes. I needed plenty of time to navigate some of the social norms of the swim team, but choosing to join opened a whole new world for me. I had to have it and had to navigate it. The unknown was as deep as the side of the pool underneath the high dive.

Swim practice 1. We pulled into the parking lot, and I had instant flashbacks to my early childhood years. Now, ten years later, I was starting my next chapter of life at the very location where I learned to swim! We all filed in and set our bags down in the locker room. I immediately saw myself as a little girl there a pastel one-piece, my hair down, fuzzy little hairs on my legs, and missing teeth recently compensated for by the Tooth Fairy. I was full of pure excitement to hop in the water and learn.

Ten-plus years later, my heart was beating at a steady, excited pace. I had freshly shaved legs, clean armpits and bikini lines, and was embracing the insanely snug suit, swim cap, and goggles, ready to understand how this flow worked. To be honest, I had never swam in a steady line with others trailing my ass while I followed orders from a coach. I never fully understood how you could sweat in the water.

On this day, I stood before dozens of classmates, many I barely know, all grouped like herded cattle ready to hear the coach introduction to the 2001 swim season. Naturally, I could tell who was already experienced in the crowd, who already swam competitively, and who was eye-rolling the coaches and newly gathered participants.

NICCOLE HENDRICKSON

On the deck, I scanned my surroundings, taking an inventory of who was in my class year. I instantly spotted a few gals with gorgeous smiles, different heights, and a clear familiarity between them. As practice progressed and then finished, we got acquainted, learning who was who and which gals had older sisters, and we quickly made connections to other upperclassmen.

For the whole first week, practices continued to stretch my capacity and kick my ass. But the practices embodied a freedom I could not yet comprehend. The pressure and demand were mixed with epic exhilaration. It is an ass-kicking and a challenge that I learned to crave. Swim practice is a humbling that demanded more and more of me every single day, every moment. It was a life lesson wrapped in 120 minutes, every damn day.

I lived for the exhaustion that swept over my body after each practice. I lived for the time in the water, where you could see hundreds of legs kicking simultaneously and your thoughts ran free. So far, there was no other place, sport, or experience that had given me this kind of mental freedom and demand all at once. There was no other place where I could zone out and in, to protect and unleash my thoughts and my drive. Under the water, I was safe and free. Gliding through the water, pulling with every stroke, I grew capacity with every breath not taken in order to maximize the stroke and time and the power generated in my legs. It was an experience like nothing else. It was freedom! It was becoming.

Swim meet number one: holy moly! The intricacy, intensity, the nerves, the dynamic of dozens and dozens of humans in their suits, caps, plus trench coats to stay cozy in between events. The list—oh, the list! The swimmers who

ST(RIPPED)

were newish to the sport had a general idea of what events they would be assigned to for a meet. But sometimes, I approached the posted event schedule, trembling and praying I wasn't assigned to an event that would humiliate me with my immature skill set.

That was the thing about swimming: it was an individual team sport, a new concept to me. Up until 2001, I had only experienced team settings, where everyone worked as a unit to bring to life the pace and outcome. Swim team was all about what you brought to the pool, and your performance contributed to the team's final outcome. *Yaaaa....*

Little lessons on personal preparation, performance, and who are you when the outcomes are complete. Can you handle the pressure to rise or the pressure to stay on top? These lessons would shape me for a lifetime. This was my first real life experience when I had to open my eyes and shape my thoughts around personal accountability, effort, commitment, and how they impact others. You are not starting and stopping for you. Your commitment or lack thereof will impact your peers.

Who do you want to be?

At meet number one, the start gun went off and *bam!* There she went, all 5'9" of her, my future best friend, Kari. I swear, she didn't breath but three times in the 100 meters she swam. She was ease, power, and peace. She would become one of my soul sisters of my lifetime.

She became the ease to my intensity. It was her perspective I wanted, when my pathway felt foggy. She embraced my humor, laughing uncontrollably and savoring the smallest moments. She was the first to sign on to any unruly idea I had for events and projects, recklessly agreeing to all adventures that pushed the boundaries of our youth. She became the keeper of all my worries, dreams, and secrets.

We forged an unspoken contract and bond instantly. We had no idea the details, but we were *all in*. Our connection grew into a circle to four, two other beautiful women inside and out who each came to the friendship with hearts as good as gold. We became the four young women making differences. We built our friendship with a purpose. We agreed to be difference makers and to hold one another to a sisterhood with rules we had defined.

Two out of the four actually had biological older sisters. We all decided on the terms and conditions of our sisterhood. We dreamed up what we all wanted in a sister, and we forged our bond on those terms. We were known as the Powerful Four. We were a force for kindness, fun, intellect, creativity, and connection.

Each of us had some sort of connection to the town we'd grown up in. Because of a parent or sibling, we were known before we established our own identities. Our family names preceded us, but we trailblazed the path we now walked. We banded together to serve on freshman, sophomore, and junior class council cabinet. We lit up the gymnasium when we attended dances together, shifting the energy as we walked in together. We had one another's backs like a blood bond.

We saw one another through some of the hardest and most triumphant times. We grew in all the ways that teenage years demanded, but we always found our way back *home* to each other. We even had a pair of pants and a journal that we passed among us, inspired by the *Sisterhood of the Traveling Pants* series. We found peace and gratitude

ST(RIPPED)

in our differences. We rooted down in the foundation formed through our initial bond. Time rolled on, life tugged on our bonds, but we followed our heart's desires and remained in contact through the one source—my soul sister, Kari. She remained the glue and the conduit to our friendship.

Kari became one of the most important people in my life.

Isabella Lundy and Jordan B Peterson say it best: "True friendship withstands time, distance, and silence." If you have these three things you have a ride or die.

A true friend: 1. A friend for life. You both grow and evolve, but you rock with each other through it all; not about always being on the same wave, but you respect each other's journey. 2. You don't have to be in the same place. Distance doesn't impact you. Real friends support you from a distance. You want them to win just as much as you want to win yourself. 3. You don't need to talk every day. No matter the space and time distance, you reconnect, and it's like you never skipped a beat.

We all possessed old and playful souls, and our fun-loving spirits set us apart from our peers, at times. This circle of forged sisterhood gave us peace and freedom. Before any of us had a teen's true freedom card—a driver's license—we leaned on our older siblings and parents to help us with our meetups. We were classy gals. Ha! Dressing the part in the early millennium. Cue the low-cut jeans, lace-lined camisoles layered with a second printed spaghetti-strap tank. We all wore a tinge of makeup, some more than others, but never too much, just a little pop that suggested we cared and knew what we were doing. We were mature... Haaa.

Our outings involved endless amounts of talking and vulnerability. We banded together to grow, and we never tore down anyone else. The most beautiful aspect of our sisterhood was the values it was built on. These three friendships were my foundation for how life was possible with friends. They were my chosen family. Each young woman was beautifully different with varied upbringings, but we allowed one another in *because* of these differences, not despite them. Our differences united us. Where one of us lacked, the other possessed that strength to help. Eventually, we all were able to uplevel our inadequacies.

We shared the burden for one another without hesitation. This was a given in our friendship code, the one element that separated our bond from anything else that existed. This platform of trust became one of the most impactful periods of my lifetime. I credit these three women for their safety, trust, and deep love, which I was experiencing for the first time outside my incredible family. These three women are responsible for allowing me to *begin* owning my *truth*, my *"why."*

It was an honor of a lifetime to be friends with them. From coffee to dinner, from breaking rules to endless minutes sweating our asses off on the dance floor, to our sprawled-out bodies and cuddles, crying on the floors of our bedrooms, these three women were an integral piece to my internal matrix flourishing. The love they gave me despite, all of my faults and growth periods, is a love I will anchor to for a lifetime.

One of my favorite memories from this time was....

"As long as I keep dancing.... I love cheap thrills...I don't need no money.... As long as I can feel the beat... I don't need no money."

ST(RIPPED)

The rich essence of my friends was in togetherness with one another and losing ourselves on the dance floor together. Losing ourselves in conversation. Full attention and indulgence in one another's words and hearts.

One of the Powerful Four, Kari remained my anchor through my final teenage years and into my twenties. This tether kept me humble. These roots reminded me where home was. She was my reminder of who I was at my core and gave me the permission to fully step into who I deeply desired to become. The dichotomy between the two never frightened her. It was always, "Hell yes," and we will discuss along the way.

The natural late-teen insecurities that reared their ugly heads never compromised our bond. They just gave us permission to seek curiosity and patience at a depth most people never dare to go or to mirror to each other. We were both rooted in beautiful values and faith, while we freely pushed each other to exceed limits and challenge our commitments, fully knowing we had each other's souls. We could highlight the consequences for each other, so the choices could be thought out clearly and the repercussions could be owned.

This friendship, time and time again proved to be so rare. Permission was always granted to be honest, even when the truth hurt. In fact, we became closer when the truths were cut with the repercussions of reality.

This bond was forged on: trust, truth, and *no* matter what.

There was a dark period of hanging out, calls, and texts.

There were moments when we needed infinite days and hours to fill each other in.

There was some fear of shame and disappointment, only for us to reunite with open hearts and minds.

There was a lot of getting over ourselves and coming back to our roots of what made us unbreakable.

Humility.

Kari became the friend who, if I ever felt myself losing touch with who I am rooted in, would not only remind me but bring me back stronger, healthier, and happier. She trusted me in ways that were gifts of a lifetime. She allowed me to impact her. She would lose her cool, her sanity, and her strength, and lean in. Her ability to see me, truly see me, and mine to see her forged a connection that cannot be severed.

Dare to Fall Apart and Rebuild

What could that look like? What could that do for me, for us?

Free Fall!

Plunging right into our twenties, Kari and I were now crushing Wine Wednesday, and never running out of things to gab about. There we were, two long-legged women, fearlessly emboldened with confidence from each other, ready to own whatever territory we stepped on. There was nowhere we could go that we didn't have a blast and curate a memory together.

From coffee to the beach to the bar to family events to concerts to the gym to falling in lust and love, we were dynamic, unstoppable!

Another Wednesday rolled around. Text flew between the two of us and we settled on our usual spot, The 333, which, at the time, was the classiest, hippest spot around — effortlessly exuding an "I've got it all together" energy. And it just so happened they did a Wine Wednesday promo.

ST(RIPPED)

Well, hell... Count us in! Apps and Wine and a chance to laugh our asses off midweek. *YAAAASSSSSSSS*, please.

We walked in and made our way to two seats at the bar. A 6'4" bartender with a strong stature, golden-brown hair of loose curls, and piercing blue-green eyes, dressed all in black, turned around to greet us while he recorked a bottle of wine. His contagious smile met ours, and he asked if he could grab us a drink.

After the ask and the pour, his curiosity was piqued, and he asked for our names. I introduced myself, and my partner in crime introduced herself, though the music was so loud, he thought her name was *Harry*. We laughed until we cried. That night, she was christened her new name: Harry it was.

We spent the rest of the night messing with this guy's humor and heart, savoring our wine, and always indulging in each other's superpowers. We ended the night like always, rehashing the moments of hilarity and stupidity together before finally confirming the next day's workout time or coffee meet-up. Let's be real: there was nothing between the beach, coffee, and moving iron. Eventually, we decided, let's give hell to a trainer twice a week, challenging him to train the two of us together. There was nothing we did that we couldn't find fun and memory doing together. These were the moments.

My twenties were full of interesting experiences, like anyone's. Some of my friends were falling hard for their man and starting to curate a life together, one that "settled them down." Some were unsure about where to plant their roots, while others were pursuing additional school. Some were playing in the middle ground of life, dabbling in independence and freedom.

NICCOLE HENDRICKSON

Note: your future self will mirror the youthful version of you, so choose wisely. Don't mistake differences for obstacles. Live in awe and deep gratitude of your people. Open your heart wide. Love and let love.

> *Soulmates Aren't Always Romantic— Some Are Friends*
>
> *Not all soulmates are lovers— some arrive as friends and change everything. A soulmate friend gets you like your hearts speak the same unspoken language. There is no need for explanations, no fear of judgment— just effortless connection, comforting silence, and a bond that feels destined. They don't just walk into your life; they belong in your journey.*
>
> —@heartfelt_writing_journey

I believe we have both soulmates in both lovers and friends. There is no denying we are meant to meet certain people in our lives. We are divinely connected, and the degrees of separation to our soulmate(s) are no mistake.

When my college athletic career began to wind down, my role as a strength coach emerged. Without knowing it, my passion for transforming the lives of women was being mentioned around my university. It garnered attention from one of the athletic director's wives, whom we will call Susie. She and I later met at an awards banquet. Susie approached me and asked to train with me, to work with me on both strength training and lifestyle. She also shared how she worked with a gal who reminded her of me, and we had to meet.

Susie was ecstatic about this connection; she raved about our similarities, this colleague of hers and me. We

ST(RIPPED)

both loved and lived in San Diego. We were tall, blonde, and Italian, and we needed to be friends. Non-negotiable!

I giggled and told her, "Let's grab coffee or a drink and all connect!"

This banter continued for months. All of our schedules were insane, so the idea remained just a good idea. Time rolled on, and I nourished the client-coach dynamic with the assistant AD's wife, Susie. I forgot about this friend connection she wanted to forge. However, the message sat with me deep in my soul.

Soon, it became clear to me how much I desired to evolve my friend network in the town where I'd gone to college, because all I did there was work and then head out of town to San Diego. It was too easy to bounce in and out, considering there was a direct flight home from the local airport. I essentially lived two lives, one in Monterey, California, the college town where I worked as a strength coach, and one in San Diego.

One weekend, as I was heading back to Monterey, I boarded the plane, went to my assigned row, and spotted a stunningly beautiful blonde already in the window seat. I smiled and sat down. We immediately dove into endless conversation.

About ten minutes in, she said, *"Wait!* Are you Niccole Deneke?"

I smiled and without hesitation asked, "Are you Andi Bortoletto?"

She quickly said, "Holy smokes, Susie is going to be thrilled and in disbelief we finally met!"

The rest was history. My next soul sister had been found. How could it be that easy?

NICCOLE HENDRICKSON

Our serendipitous meeting was the gift I needed to remind me of how worthwhile it had been to stay the course on the road I was traveling, not to overanalyze but to just be and to stay present in this stage of my becoming. I quickly realized our journeys are so much more than the mission we set out to conquer. This was proof.

Monterey gave me the "container" to see through to completion my once deeply desired goal of being a collegiate athlete. What it really gave me was an introduction to versions of myself whom I never would have discovered, if I hadn't committed to this university. From the connections to the professors in my degree program to the trials that tested my character, from the opportunity to take on the role as a college strength coach to the push to put my craft into play as a young leader. But most important, it was the gift of Andi Bortoletto. If nothing else came of Monterey, meeting her meant gaining the sister I always desired to have.

Andi immediately became the definition of ride-or-die: limitless honesty, unconditional love, and unwavering loyalty. The kind of friend who not only has your back but also holds your heart, always guiding you toward truth and vibrance. The moment we met, it felt like a reuniting, not just a meeting. Her sisterhood became my strength when I couldn't find my own.

"People only throw shade on what shines."

Pay **Attention** to Who is in the Storm With You, not Under the Umbrella

Like over most summers, I headed back to sunny San Diego. I was enjoying life in Monterey, on California's Central Coast, but I still craved the company of my family and felt

ST(RIPPED)

alive and at peace whenever I returned to the golden rays of the sunshine that had captured my soul. On the sand and in the ocean of the beaches in North County were where I felt like myself and in my power. There, I gained clarity and vision for my next steps.

That particular summer was packed with healing past breakdowns with key people in my life. I reconnected with the roommate who had made my life a living hell during the second semester of my junior transfer year. In truth, it was cathartic. To this day, I am so thankful the opportunity presented itself for us to clear the air and put the petty dramas behind us.

She was the first friend to share with me what jealousy and lack of purpose had fueled them to do. It was the first time I sat with someone I considered to be a friend and a pivotal part of my life, someone who called out all the things that were great about me, but then shared how that made them feel certain ways. I was simply a mirror for all the things they weren't and wanted to be. It was intense, eye-opening, and interesting.

She shared how our breakdown had led her to do some further self-discovery and healing. I was thankful for her honesty and our ability to grow in this experience together. I was also thankful for the hard seasons we'd shared together. They'd pushed me to dial in my guiding principles. They awoke places in my heart that helped me see through a different lens. They helped me navigate the power of individual evolution and how valuable timing is.

The breakdown of the comfort zone I'd found in our friendship had forced me to face some fears I had within me. They helped me to recognize how important it was to stay rooted, to stay in line with what I deeply wanted, and not to fall to the pressure of what is convenient. While it might sound brutal, I learned what I *didn't* want to become, by witnessing her choices. That's the reality of life: we observe, learn, become, or evolve based on the choices we make. If her choices were causing the pain I was witnessing in her and led to the demise of our friendship, then I wanted nothing to do with participating in them.

That summer, we let forgiveness flood our dynamic. We put to rest any bad blood, and we opened the pathway for new memories. We rewrote the story that didn't necessarily go the way we had originally intended it to go. This friendship healed, served its purpose, and was put to rest in my history.

This was a key component to the woman I was becoming: forgiveness and growth. This was me living out the valuable lessons I'd observed with my Grandma Ruby. She held the line but always provided room for those in her life to come back in a new light.

These friendships remind us of the power of st(ripping) the layers of our fabric that keeps us from becoming. These friendships also remind us of the power that connection forges on a soul level.

Chapter 2 Reflections

Self-Check: Layers I Wear

Take a moment to identify the "layers" you tend to wear in relationships:

- ☐ The Achiever
- ☐ The Caretaker
- ☐ The Guarded One
- ☐ The People-Pleaser
- ☐ The Strong One
- ☐ Other: _____

Journal Prompt

What layers do I often put on in friendships to protect or present myself? Where did those layers come from?

Action: Nourish the Connection

Send a Soul Note

Text or write a quick message to a friend who's walked with you as you became more of yourself. Tell them what their presence has meant to you—no perfection needed, just honesty.

CHAPTER 3

Values + Guiding Principles

We are nothing in this world without a solid foundation. Our foundation is built on our embodied guiding principles and our core values. We do not get to choose how our lives start, but we do get to choose how we conduct our life as an adult.

I was always intrigued when I observed my Papa. His character was unwavering. He knew what he stood for and was frustratingly good at solitude. Alone was his safe space; however, you could witness how his soul was filled when in good company.

He showed his character in the little things he did. His arm around me when I sat beside him on the porch swing or walked through the apple orchard, where he plucked an apple for me. When we walked to the chicken coop together to grab fresh eggs for my breakfast, or strolled through the garden to gather tiny potatoes for dinner. On the rides to ice cream, where we sat alongside him on the bench seat of his classic Ford F-150, giggling with unrelenting excitement. While sitting next to him, playing cards and learning how to win. It was in the quiet moments of fishing then the

ST(RIPPED)

exuberant, unexpected joy when someone got a fish on the line.

He had zero problems holding school on us and loving us hard at the same time. When he laughed, those noteworthy bushy, white eyebrows raised up and down; he called them his "sunshades." When I learned about his life stories, I was always in awe of his bravery, courage, independence, and ability to find a way. My ears remained tuned every minute I was in his company. He didn't talk a lot, but when he did, his words were filled with lessons, insight, love, and helpful information. Papa's smile was infectious, bursting out when he told a story about something that brought him joy.

He also had remarkable poise whenever we asked him about something tragic or brutal. By observing his body language and cues, I could tell when he was disrupted by pain or sadness, but he never snapped. Instead, he grew still and distant, and his pain was palatable. This is where I learned the power of proximity and holding space for someone who did not need your words, just your calm, patient, humble, and loving presence.

The saying, "Silence is golden," was never more accurate than in the moments when we were alongside him while he was processing. The older I got, the more he let me in, the more trust was built, and the safer he felt with me to handle the magnitude of pain and triumph, plus the depths of his despair and joy. Our relationship reminded me constantly of the power of patience and time. He became one of the most inspiring people of my life.

The bond I forged with my Papa was the bonus to the life lessons I absorbed from my time spent with him. I had no idea when I was young, but the lessons learned while I was in his presence would serve as valuable content in my "instruction manual" for my life as a young woman and, most notably, during the chapters of my life with the love story between me and my husband. The lessons I learned through my bond with Papa taught me patience, inspiration, and, most important, hope.

The Power in Embodying Your Guiding Principles

There are people in this world who embody light and truth. Through their existence, they gently remind you to stay in line with your values and your guiding principles. For me, that was and is my mama.

My beautiful mama was the fence that kept me safe. She was the example of a woman who truly knew her power and impact and how it was rooted in gratitude and loyalty. She has always been loyal almost to a fault. My mom demonstrates kindness, love, and respect *no matter what*. You rise no matter what. You lead with courage no matter what. You know your strength no matter what. You can crumble and still be whole, because the crumble isn't your soul. Serve and be served.

She waited to fall in love until she connected and found exactly what she wanted. She knew what she deserved and would not settle at any cost. She received what she knew she deserved, and she cultivated a relationship that would serve her higher purpose and legacy. She valued kindness, loyalty, deep love, integrity, friendship, and strength.

She knew how to stand at the side of the people she loved while also giving them a wide berth to be who they are and what they desire to become. She had an incredible way of demonstrating dialed-in communication, connection, love, and holding the line. She was compassionate and firm. Honest but open. Relentless in her pursuit to form us into good people, but also very forgiving when we fell short.

While I was growing up, my mother's love was always present. She was deep and true and so pure. Her hugs, the absolute best, were healing and restorative. You never doubted her love and commitment to advocate for us and stay alongside us.

My parents presented a united front at home. They were an undeniable team: there was no playing Mom against Dad, and there was no breaking their bond. However, each of them they did offer us an open ear and heart. Our ability to problem-solve with either one was sacred to each of us. My mother has always had the ability to honor her marriage and bond to my dad while also nourishing trust and confidentiality with both my brother and me. I have not yet figured out how to do this, myself, with my mother's elegance.

My mom was the protective fence that kept us all in line, safe and nourished. She later became one of my best friends, my most trusted resource and confidante. I believe her commitment to being my mom first and foremost is the most important foundation of my life. Her commitment to hold the line, above all else, created unwavering trust and an indestructible relationship. Her commitment to be mom first and maintain a safe place for us to land is what led to our relationship being one of the most sacred friendships I have to date.

My mom's most important lesson was to understand our choices. She taught that you always had a choice, and the choice would lead to the understanding:

"It is always easier to go down than up, so choose your friends, your activities, and your commitments wisely."

To this day, this lesson rings true ten out of ten times.

In my own times of challenge and adversity, I lean into the strength and discipline it took my mom to stand in her power when she was solo parenting. She had the will to set an example and be selfless to a fault, an unwavering commitment to her values, and the strength within herself to never falter to the demands of my father's schedule. She was the glue mixed with the foundation. She was always available and dialed into us despite any exhaustion or personal challenge she may have been battling. She could compartmentalize and feel at the exact same time. She is an angel. She is love.

My Brother, My First Best Friend, a Pillar in Building my Foundation

Since the day I was born, my older brother, Anthony, has been my best friend. I was lucky to arrive Earthside with an instant partner in crime. His companionship, protection, and presence in my life were integral parts of my evolution into who I am today.

During our younger years, we ran in similar but different friend groups, but there was never any question: he had my back, no matter the circumstances. We had an unspoken contract: we were best friends, no matter what.

He protected me and I helped to "own the day" in our daily lives. I kept things on track and dialed in. If we needed to sell wrapping paper or cookie dough or raise funds for a jog-a-thon, you bet, I was the gal for the job. I mapped the neighborhood and sold half for my fundraiser and another half for his.

If we needed to square things away at home—done. I have got this, so we can achieve the end result: freedom. I was the next level of structure for him, and in turn that

ST(RIPPED)

granted freedom for us both. I made sure he was taken care of and protected on levels of his vulnerabilities, while he ensured I was safe and confident in who I was, also giving me permission to loosen up and have fun.

During the summers, we travelled to our grandparents' homes. He helped me overcome fears and limitations in the forest, the great outdoors, and made it cool and fun to learn. He assured me "he had me," listening to all the directions and safety measures our Papa provided for us to thrive in the wilderness. I trusted him and never looked back. I knew, no matter what, he would have it figured out and would never let anything hurt me.

I knew he was good in his skin, that he trusted in the skills and craft he developed over time, and that he took seriously the trust my dad and mom vested in him. In turn, I trusted him without reservation. I always admired his confidence in himself, his faith in his abilities, and his calm. He wasn't cocky; it was cool, collected, and pure.

When we were kids, I can't remember a time when he said he couldn't do something or would not do something and felt scared. He always leveled up when it came to anything outdoors, dangerous, or physical.

I watched him closely, studying his poise and freedom as he launched off a snow-covered hill on his snowboard or when he rushed in to tackle on the field. The way he manipulated his BMX bike. The sheer power he possessed when launching his body into the air to block a volleyball along the net. His effortless maneuvers in the water while bodyboarding and his careless finesse when hauling ass in the desert while driving his quad.

NICCOLE HENDRICKSON

He was easy, he was cool, and he was my big brother, my best friend. His 6'5" body even moved on the dance floor, when he wanted to: put on a good country song, and the man can Two Step, stealing any woman's heart. And that he did.

As time went on, our friendship evolved. In high school, once again he became my wingman. I am sure it helped that my friends were gorgeous and fun, as well. I entered high school at the age of thirteen. [Holy smokes, right?]

Before I started, my brother prepared me for what was to come. He fully trusted I knew how to handle myself intellectually and socially, but he wanted to make sure I understood who was who and how things flowed among the athletes. Also, there was a code of conduct, as we were in the same school where our father was a well-respected and feared head football coach, athletic director, and teacher. *Yikes!*

Just kidding. High school were some of my favorite years of my life. I thrived in the privilege of being Trace Deneke's daughter. My respect, love, and admiration for him fueled my own "just cause."

My brother walked me around the campus and made sure I knew where everything was located and how I could find him, if and when I needed anything. (I went to high school in the era before smartphones, and even the simple flip phone was pretty new.) He was adamant that I know my surroundings, so I would not be worried about anything

Just like during our summers exploring the forests, he made sure I knew the landmarks around our school campus. Then, I could move confidently through this next chapter of my life. He was consistent and strong, and he provided me the needed confidence to become me! He was proud of me and never denied this to the world.

Allowing others to be who they really are, at their core, opens the way to a lifetime of freedom. From an early age, my brother showed me what it was to stand in my values and be strong in my WHY. He reminded me how the temporary discomfort of loneliness will be balanced by fulfillment, plus to always take risks and "go hard or go home!"

Love and Truth, Cornerstone Values

"There is no such thing as 50/50. Love and friendship are built on 100/100, where each person gives everything they have and respects their percentage will look different, but it is always 100%"

—Lina Spano

When love is built on unwavering trust, faith, and commitment, there is an abundance of space to give, nourish, and evolve.

Both sets of my grandparents demonstrated a love and bond that simply seem unattainable in this day and age. When I think about what seems like their fairy tale of love and divine connection, it is truly rooted in a deep sense of surrender and trust. A trust in their own heart compass, a trust in the love forged between them, and a divine faith in their plan, no matter what comes their way. Nothing would defy this bond, because of the foundation it was built on.

One was an Italian immigrant and another, an Italian who left with his family to make a better life in the United States. Connected, they took a leap of faith and embodied a love so pure and so deep, the ripple would have affect us, sixty-plus years later.

My Nonno built his fortune on a work ethic that was second to none. He forged a path that honored his divine purpose of community, love, legacy, and connection. He built his life brick by brick, maintaining a mindset of servant leadership, gratitude, and kindness. Family remained at the center of his world while he built his dream, the successful full-service grocery store and restaurant.

Both businesses reflected the very thing that made his heart tick: compassion and connection. My Nonno was powered by serving, by building something from passion, drive, and the core belief that anything is possible, if you are willing to invest your blood, sweat, and tears, and maintain a level of noble honesty, despite your circumstances.

My Nonna was a northern Italian who fell in love with a charming, happy, and fun southern Italian. She took a leap of ginormous faith and left her family, home, and comfort zone of Riva de Garda, Italy. She believed so wholeheartedly in the love she shared with my Nonno that she left everything behind. This during a time where communication was difficult and there was none of the access or comforts of long-distance relationships like we enjoy today.

She said "Yes" to this dream that my Nonno had been building over the years. She would move to America without knowing a lick of English. She came on good faith, believing in the love and connection between her and my Nonno.

After she married him in her hometown, she moved to Carlsbad, California and started a family of her own. She also supported the unrelenting hours it took Nonno to bring his business endeavors to life. They built their legacy on integrity and faith. After all, that is *all* they had to start with. They knew, if they ever compromised this vision, their lives would never truly progress.

As they built their business, they also grew their family. When all was said and done, they created a powerhouse family of six girls! Through some risk and a lot of faith, they continued to evolve their businesses. They navigated decisions that stretched them, challenged them, and let them down, but they never relented. Their focus remained on their purpose, facilitated by their passion for serving, creating impact, and leaving the world a better place by uniting people through a common cause: the power of community and connection.

My mom and dad both came from parents who demonstrated a high level of love, deep connection, faith, and undeniable honor in their name. The value of your word and name had begun with their own parents. This was passed on through generations, and it became one of the most important guiding principles in the household where I grew up. My dad told me and my brother on repeat: "You have your name and your word. Do not compromise this." While first impressions do mean something, trust and true relationships are built on those two things.

I credit my Nonna for showing me courage, and the power of deep love and trusting your gut. I credit her for showing me deep love that is equal and enduring. I credit her for showing me the power of unconditional love that knows no bounds.

I credit my Nonno for giving me the entrepreneur gene. For the fire and passion to serve and create with purpose. For the understanding of passion and how very powerful it is to lead from your heart, to bring others' superpowers out while you forge your own path. I credit my Nonno for demonstrating what is possible when your heart and mindset are united: simply unstoppable.

I credit him for showing and leading by example what a strong work ethic looks like. He never complained about solving problems. He never complained about a long day at work. He joyfully flipped the switch, once he was in the company of others, and most specifically, when he walked through the doors of his home, where he was enchanted by the love of his bride and six daughters. They were his world, his gravity, and he centered himself around their presence.

I noted this quality over and over and hoped to embody it, as I grew up. I credit my Nonno for showing me how to care for people, and how to treat any and all human beings with dignity and respect. There was never judgment, only eyes for serving and loving. I watched him provide opportunity for those who had suffered many misfortunes or those who struggled with building a foundation. He offered them love, a listening ear, the opportunity to work, financial support, and, most important, unwavering dignity and respect.

Never in my life have I encountered two people who built such successful relationships and made an impact on every single daughter, son-in-law, grandchild, great-grandchild, extended family member, and friend who came their way. These two people set a tone for all of us. They were the example, the beacon of light I leaned into as I grew older. The greatest gift they gave us was their example of how to make someone feel seen, heard, and loved at an unconditional depth.

Love built on trust, truth, and courage is unbreakable. A strong work ethic is a quality that cannot be bought. It is earned. Creating and nourishing relationships in deep gratitude is a superpower we should all attempt to master. Forgiveness and unconditional love. Be fierce and committed in paying it forward. Generosity is powerful; give it energy. There is always a common thread to be found among *all* of us. Seek the commonalities, not differences. Above all, root in faith.

Chapter 3 Reflections

Theme: Choosing how we conduct our lives through our values and embodied principles.

Part 1: Uncover Your Core Values

Start by circling or writing down the values that resonate most deeply with you. Choose 5 that feel essential.

Examples:

Integrity • Freedom • Faith • Growth • Compassion

Curiosity • Service • Connection • Creativity • Presence
Discipline • Joy • Courage • Simplicity • Loyalty

In your journal, list your own 5 core values.

Reflection Prompt

How do these values currently show up in your daily life? Where are they missing?

Part 2: Define Your Guiding Principles

For each value you chose, write a simple guiding principle—a short "I will..." statement that reflects how you want to live that value out loud.

Examples

Value: Integrity → Guiding Principle: I will speak the truth, even when it's uncomfortable.

Value: Presence → Guiding Principle: I will put my phone down when I'm with people I care about.

Create Your Own

For each of the five, in your journal state:

Value: _____ →

Guiding Principle: _____

Part 3: Build Your Foundation Statement

Put it all together. Create a short paragraph or mantra that captures how you want to *conduct your life* as an adult. Think of it as your foundation statement.

Foundation Statement Example:

"I live a life rooted in integrity, connection, and courage. I commit to showing up truthfully, loving fully, and pursuing growth even when it's hard."

Now, write your own.

CHAPTER 4

Becoming is Letting Go

I woke up with an absolute jolt... I just needed to *"Let Go!"* Let go of all that is unknown, the things I cannot control, the worry, and the perfectionism.

As this realization sank in, I began to experience the freedom in this nugget of simple bliss. It was that easy: letting go will open the pathway to becoming whatever I deeply desire to become. I began to understand the power in surrender. It was as if I had unclenched my fist and began to feel the blood moving through it again. The release was a gentle hum of electricity running back through me. *That* is how powerful this realization was for me.

Letting go in order to harness the power of the tiniest seed of faith does not mean forgetting. It means freeing my mind and soul of the things that had taken up residence but no longer served this version of me The becoming occurs when I release the old, release my earlier versions of "what ifs." All of the unnecessary questions that are interfering with what I desire to unravel in my life.

Ahhh, what an epiphany: "Letting go is becoming."

The Early Becoming

From my childhood days through my high school years, the experiences that provided me with the most growth, mentally, physically, emotionally, and socially, were with the Oceanside Junior Lifeguards. I still thank this program for showing me the path to fortitude, friendship, and the strength to overcome so many fears.

This program is about beach safety and ocean lifesaving skills. In it, your daily activities include: running, swimming, beach games, surfing, boat jumps, education in beach and ocean safety, as well as competitions. This program operates for four weeks, five to six hours a day, two or three times each week, for kids aged nine to seventeen. The program includes an incredible demonstration of how to lead up and down the chain of command, how to empower young emerging leaders, and how to hold a high level of responsibility. It was a powerful environment of trust, friendship, respect, and growth.

Before I qualified for the program my first summer at JGs, my anxiety was palpable. All eyes were on me, in the pool, swimming 100 yards under three minutes, then treading water for five minutes, plus a continuous underwater swim for fifteen-plus feet, to simulate going under waves. I told myself, *Test day. Keep it together, Niccole!*

I can still remember rolling up to the Marshall Street pool with my mom and brother. I was ten years old. I hopped into the pool and conquered the tasks. I don't ever remember feeling scared or in doubt about finishing, though. After all, my brother and I grew up swimming countless days and hours in my grandparents' pool and ripping through waves on our boogie boards. When we were kids, it was always a test of how far we could go out together and how long we could tread water out past the break. This is where friendships were nurtured, trust was built, and our fears were conquered. We were driven by the thrill of doing what was forbidden. That was where we found freedom: in the depths of the ocean and at a distance out past the waves.

So, on test day, while I was treading water, I thought to myself, *I got this. I will do this. It will not break me. In fact, I am being made, right now!*

This was my first taste of facing a physical, mental, and emotional challenge and then feeling the reward. Up until then, I had danced, played softball, ridden my bike, and rode quads with my brother, doing normal childhood activities. But nothing had given me the invigorating edge and challenge of Junior Lifeguards. Their program introduced me to conquering fears I didn't even know I had. It was a life experience shaping me into who I was becoming.

On day 1 of our program, a sea of blue swimsuits, sunscreen, and lunchboxes flooded the sand. The energy buzzed as dozens and dozens of kids were dropped off by their parents and assigned to their designated groups.

I was assigned to the sand crab group. After my mom left and the day began, we were briefed, and then it was go time! To this day, I will *never* forget the first drill. It was a run, swim, and repeat conditioning exercise that felt like it went on for hours.

Nothing prepares you for running and dodging waves in a group, with chafing sand between your wet thighs, and trying to maintain calm, cool breaths as you sprint out of the water and follow your peers to the next lifeguard tower, and

ST(RIPPED)

then repeat. You can never know what this brings up in you until it is "go time."

I kept going not because I wanted to, trust me. All of me wanted to stop. I kept going because I deserved to know what not giving up on myself felt like.

This was my first time facing these questions, "Who am I? Who do I want to be, when I am uncomfortable as hell? Far from the Top 10 and merely a part of the crowd?"

"What does this girl do when she feels like quitting? Does she quit? Does she cry? Does she get angry? Does she dig deep? What does digging deep mean and look like to her? What is she thinking? What does her will look like? Does she find a way? Or does she fall back with the others who are barely getting by? Does she study the ones who are excelling? Does she acknowledge pain is temporary? Or does she use it as an excuse? What does finishing look like to her?"

I had *so many thoughts* running through my mind during our first workouts and activities in Junior Guards, just that first day!

These lessons and challenges became essential to who I have become today. It didn't matter which role models I had in my life, my actual lived experiences gave me the ability to dig into who the hell I wanted to be in my life. These experiences gave me the social proof and validation of what I could be, if I pushed myself on all levels, mentally, emotionally, and physically. They taught me what I could experience, what ego meant, and how the hell to set that limiting thought process to the side, if and when I desired to truly learn and evolve.

I also observed within myself my own disappointment, lack, and insecurity. During camp, I learned what it felt like to suck at something and not be a part of a certain clique, because of my lack of skill or prowess. This was the first time in my life when I became curious about why I was attracted to one particular group of kids. What was it about them that intrigued me? What about them did I deeply desire to understand and embody? The truth is, I was intrigued by their physical fitness and their ability to move with ease and power. I also admired their drive and will.

What I lacked in physical fitness, I made up for in gratitude and kindness. I was humble and put my listening and observation skills on high alert. I started asking more questions of my dad. (At this point in my life, my dad was still an insanely fit individual who pushed in his physical prowess to the max.) I asked him how to attain more cardiovascular bandwidth. I studied what these kids ate, and I started paying more attention to my own nourishment and how I felt when I ate certain things.

With every drill, I dug deeper into my mental capacity. I started to become intrigued with pushing limits and what happened on the other side, when you pushed just a little more and a little further. I never died! I just became wildly capable! Fascinating!

It turns out, cramping while running goes away, when you actually breathe and calm the funk down. Turns out you don't swallow so much salt water when you are intentional about your dive into the wave, and when you stay calm and collected when navigating the buoy with several other kids. When you know you've "got yourself," you don't fear what could happen. If you stop short, you only fear what you could've accomplished.

It turns out doing hard things can be fun, can be rewarding, and can be the very things that fuels your

ST(RIPPED)

laughter with friends and rocks you to sleep at night. It turns out, building your self-worth off of the things you are willing to go for and suck at, plus refusing to quit, can be some of the most memorable moments of your life. I 1000% thank the role models I had in my life, the ones who helped me understand the choice to do hard things and what the hard could do for me mentally, emotionally, and physically.

"If you do not bend, you will break. The adaptable prevail, determined, but flexible."
—James Clear

The desire and need for perfection started to rear its ugly head when I was in junior high school and was in full effect by high school.

This is such a weird-ass time for any adolescent. I clearly remember being very bored and annoyed during this period of time. It was the chunk of years in my life when I felt the most out of place, an in-between stage of life. We were breaking out into semi-young adulthood, but, at the same time, we were babies. I know I certainly was.

I was ten when I started sixth grade... That is so young. I was part of the first wave of sixth graders moved into junior high, instead of staying back in a K-6 grade school. My parents gave me the choice to stay at the elementary school where I had been or move over to the junior high campus. Of course, I wanted to move to the junior high campus—that was where all of my people were: my older brother and my cousins, we had to all go together!

I thank God every day I had a good home to return to and that my parents maintained so much structure. The repeated exposure to things far too advanced for my ten-year-old mind and soul could have swallowed me whole, if I didn't have parents who stood their ground on what was allowed and not allowed for my age. Good *gawwwwwd,* I was a baby, asking to do things that I had no business doing. As a mama now, I cringe.

I already had access to things far beyond my years due to being close to my older cousins, and they had protected me along the way, which was a positive intention. Junior high school, though: It was yuck. This was the first time in my life when I experienced a teacher who had inappropriate intentions.

He placed his hand on my shoulder in the classroom, spent and exorbitant amounts of time near me during instruction, and looking at me with gross longing stares. The hair on the back of my neck would rise the moment I sensed his presence in the classroom, and my stomach turned to knots as he neared my vicinity. Forget learning anything, using my voice, I was in full-fledged protect myself mode!

This was the year I nailed my "look," where I used my eyes to say, "You put your hands on me one more time, you won't have the luxury of me telling the school principal. You will get Trace Deneke, and that will lead to a future not to be spoken of!"

His attention and focus on me diminished. Soon, his student teaching days in our classroom came to an end, so I no longer had to deal with him. However, I think of that asshole more than I care to admit, and I feel regret about not saying something to the higher-ups or to my parents. Perhaps I am partly responsible for other young girls being violated by this disgusting weasel, because I didn't say something. This, I live with, and this, I have carried as a

ST(RIPPED)

lesson on why it is so important to have courageous conversations, to use your voice, and to trust your inner knowing.

Between this experience and the blasé homeroom teachers who were riding it out to their retirement years, I was so bored, but also so challenged at the same time. The challenges were in my desire to learn, but I was being suffocated by the start of my perfectionism. During this time, I can recall my focus turning on. I was fully aware of the ways I allowed myself to interfere with my own evolution.

I was caught up in ever-evolving friendship circles, the melding of friend groups, the tight-ass rules my parents held (looking back, I thank God they did), the emergence of my womanhood, navigating the social structure of grades six through eight blended together, and figuring out who Niccole was during these years of development. I needed to root down. I needed to find my gravity. I was free-floating in space, which was not good for me. I needed to find my foundation. My grounding.

It was all so fast. I had nothing defining me yet. I hadn't found my friend group. I was still in limbo, only ever having entertained my cousins and friends, who lived on my street. My school experiences were pretty spread out, unlike those of most of my peers, who lived near one another and had gone to grade school together, before they ended up at our junior high school.

I hadn't found my calling yet to the sport of volleyball. I had an array of hobbies but nothing that spoke to me. I had summers doing Junior Lifeguards and spending hang time with my cousins, plus roots with my family, but I had no tethers I could grasp, in this new setting. It was a bit debilitating. I needed to find my gravity. I was still a little girl, but I was in a young-adult world. Too much.

In seventh grade, my homeroom teacher happened to be a family friend. She became a saving grace, providing me safety and peace. This helped to give me a place to find my footing.

During this year, I started to notice how challenged I allowed my headspace to become during PE. I had been active my whole life. I had spurts of experiences when I was challenged, and I discovered I liked that. But seventh-grade gym class was a whole new world. Now, I was being challenged among my peers, and I had to face them again in the school halls and without a shower. *Ugh.* I swear, all of this contributed to how tough I found junior high.

The timed mile, the interval runs, and the different drills we were introduced to during these classes started to pique my interest in the power of movement. There was something here for me. I started to really identify with the power of moving my body and getting good at it. I started to recognize my interest in getting stronger, my love for competing, and how challenging myself in new ways grew my whole presence.

Growing up, we always had the power of our proximity to greatness. My dad exposed us to high-level athletes and performers, but he never pushed us into anything. He just ensured we witnessed greatness, which might pique our interest; he was always leading by example, showing us what it looked like to refine skills and go confidently in this direction.

While I am not that old, I am old enough to say, "My generation still hadn't launched youth strength and conditioning programs. These were reserved for elite athletes."

We had access to youth sports, but everything was still very basic. Still, observed my dad's strength training and routine. Later, I tucked away my feelings about how running, the group workouts, and competition made me feel into a little place in my heart and mind. This little box stored ideas for my "one day." I used our time together to ask my dad more questions and gain some insight into joining my junior high volleyball team. To try it out.

This was my initiation into something greater. This led to the making of the future version of me. The version I would meet much later. I was still living in my foreshadowing era.

Starting to Find My Stride

"Where are you going, Deneke? You're walking like you are on a mission."

I was on my way to sophomore English lit, that's where. I was not going to be late to class.

My high school had really grown a lot, and now classes were sprawled over thousands of square feet. I had to book it down to the lower campus to my class, which was in an air-conditioned trailer-type classroom. It was crazy, how spread out our campus had become, but in truth, I had always gone to a school with *a lot* of students. And I was quite familiar with our campus by now.

I did not yet know who my teacher would be for this class, but I did know where the classroom was located. I spent a lot of time in this part of the campus, which was wedged on the blacktop, overlooking the football stadium,

NICCOLE HENDRICKSON

baseball fields, and weight room. I had roots in this part of the campus. This was a kind of home to me.

I'd spent years here, chasing my brother on my bicycle, while my dad worked in his office by the weight room, football field, and locker room. He used to freshen up the painted dots and ladders on this paved area by the playing field. He also brought in many high-speed elements to train and uplevel his football team, daring every athlete to break out of their training comfort zone.

So, this area was my zone. It had started as a place where I could race my bicycle and it became the place where I would eventually train my ass off to become someone and something I only dared to see in my dreams.

When I finally made it to the ramp of the classroom and entered the classroom door, I scanned the room looking for a seat. Perfect! There was one right in the middle, fourth from the front! As I squeezed in and sat down, I glanced up to see my gorgeous, 5'2", power-packed, astute, brilliant, blonde teacher, Ms. Shortman.

"Ms. Deneke," she greeted me. "Wonderful to have you in class."

I smiled and began to take in every detail of her and her classroom. I had the feeling in this room that I was precisely where I was supposed to be, literally and figuratively. Not just because I'd been assigned here by my class counselor, so I would fulfill my credits needed to graduate with honors in two-and-a-half years. It was because this would turn out to be a pivotal moment in my life.

This class would change me, my life, and my perspective forever.

I was consumed by my locked-in focus. I tuned out the thirty-plus fellow students and surrounds, because but

ST(RIPPED)

nothing mattered but what was being said to me and for me. The classroom, the prefab trailer, even the class expectations and syllabus were unremarkable. But what spoke to me, what was almost overwhelming was the impact this teacher had immediately on my nervous system.

I certainly had a strong desire to learn, but I also felt really supported, almost like I was the only student in this classroom (though I was not!). How was this possible? I wondered what had clicked for me, different from earlier other moments in my life.

There was the standard whiteboard at the front of the classroom. The teacher's desk was organized with a few decorative items, and she had her Venti Starbucks. (*Phew!* I knew teacher would get me and our shared caffeine affinity!) She was dressed professionally, with some personal touches. Her well-manicured nails were painted and she had a huge ring on her forefinger. She wore subtle makeup with a pop of gloss and heels that tricked you into thinking she was a few inches taller. Her posture, classic beauty, and articulate vocabulary, her wit and million-dollar smile instantly commanded my attention. This was going to be the best year!

Just one year before, I had been consumed by my writing paralysis. During freshman year, when I was driving to school with my dad, I had been unusually quiet and ruffled. He picked up on my unease and asked me what was wrong.

I let out an exasperated sigh and shared my crippling fear of an upcoming "timed essay" I had to complete in freshman English class. I was both terrified and paralyzed. I explained how I would think through my content in advance, but as soon as it was go time, I froze, and all my words would leave me. My desire to deliver combined with my fear of failing had literally led me to freeze and fail. Without my words, I would fail to allow my impact to flow through as my thoughts seemed to leave my body.

For this assignment, we would have thirty minutes, but I couldn't start writing until twenty minutes in, and then I would obsess about writing and erasing, redotting my I's and recrossing my Ts. I was in a cycle of dysregulation, obsessed with a level of perfection that was crippling my abilities.

This behavior was not new. My parents had noticed it before. To their credit, they had dialed into developing a plan to help me. First, they put a Time Out on my relentless pursuit to invest so much time into projects and homework. It was a "Come to Jesus" conversation all through my freshman year.

They would say, "Niccole, you cannot be all things to everyone." Or, "Niccole, you need to analyze your commitments, demands, and aspirations, and then prioritize. They cannot all receive 100% of you at the same time." They explained, while it is possible to give your full heart and attention to the things you value and desire to bring to life, you cannot expect to do it all at once and sustain wellbeing.

The expectation of being whole was such an interesting experience for me. Having parents with a high moral code is one thing, but having parents who expect you to know greatness while first valuing your wellbeing? Let's be clear. My parents were onto something special.

My dad knew the cloth I was cut from; I believe this was a proactive approach to saving me from myself. They had quickly understood how I would hold myself to a standard

ST(RIPPED)

that would break me, burn me out, and become my own demise. My desire and discipline would work against me, if I wasn't fully grounded or in control.

So, there was a snap, and I made a massive shift between eighth grade and high school. I had been waiting my whole life for a moment like this... After taking all the moments, the observations made, lessons learned, and foreshadowed possibilities, I would now live this life! I would live it in all the ways I had vision-boarded. I would live out, brick by brick, the "house" I had dreamt of building for myself, with the house being *my life*.

I had been waiting for a chance to prove myself to myself. This chapter of my life was my kick-off. And it began by acknowledging my perfectionism and my crippling fear of not allowing myself to take action, of not being able to show proof of all I knew and thought and was.

In some crazy way, the environment in my sophomore English lit classroom untethered this piece of my soul. It freed me from my need to be perfect, and it opened my mind and heart to all my possibilities and aspirations, without allowing me to focus on perfection as the endgame. It was the structure that allowed me to be *free*.

The structure of her class was loose but freeing. During every class, we had some assigned free-writing time, and we were encouraged to simply write! Yes, that is correct, just write. She gave us a subject line, a timer, and permission to let it out with only one rule: do not lift your pen from the paper for the whole timed write. And the more imperfect, the better, because there was plenty of room to edit the imperfection into a masterpiece.

This was the first time in my life when I recognized the beauty in the unrefined starts.. There is no such thing as a perfect first draft. In fact, it is foolish to think anything in life has a perfect first draft. That is the lesson here: for any areas in life, the perfect first draft or first rounds aren't "first." What we generally read is the byproduct of the time and effort and commitment that has been invested into honing the craft of writing (or whatever you're doing). Without respect for this process, you will never get past this first draft. Hell, you may not even get a shot at a first draft.

The container created within this English it class, its demands, plus the curator of the coursework gave me some guiding principles for my life ahead. These timed free writes freed my soul, one by one. One morning at a time, I produced a collection of limitations I had stored within me, and then, I would free them. I breathed life into them while also extinguishing their flame.

I learned how to leverage these lessons into all facets of my life. During this year, I not only acknowledged the behaviors that would deter my desired outcomes, but I also put a plan into action that came to shift the tides and became the difference-makers.

This class led to, hands down, one of the most important and influential mentorships I have had in my lifetime. This core class gave me the time and opportunity to grow a profound connection and lifelong friendship. From teaching me how to just write to how to own my magic, Ms. Shortman was a guiding light. In every class, I stepped closer to becoming, acquainting myself with a new piece of territory in my heart and mind.

It was a lot like writing an essay: there is no piece of work to analyze, if you never allow words to be put down on paper. In life, you cannot try on or become the highest version of yourself, if you never allow yourself to live and be. Without using it that, you have no chance to refine your voice. There is no chance to edit or revise, if you never make an error.

This became my year to bring observation into my reality. By breaking down papers I wrote and seeking to understand different literary works, I began the process of asking questions and digging deeper, without any fear.

Throughout my childhood, my ask questions and being curious were always welcomed. But somewhere in the playing-it-safe zone, I lost touch of trusting myself to be curious and to dare to learn and be wrong. Why? I was never punished for these things as a child, but I created this web around me that didn't allow much space to do the asking, out of fear I would waste precious time in my becoming. *Phew...!*

So, this was the year when I learned to love the process. This was the year I embraced the foundation. This was the year I started working on something I was proud of, something really out of reach but tangible, something that felt miles away, something that made people say, "How?"

"Before you can win, you must believe you are a winner. Winners think, look, act, and behave like winners. They focus on the daily process of doing what needs to be done to become a winner."

—Allistair McCaw

I am focused. I have been watching, I have been listening to everything said, I have started to feel what is possible, I have started to bear witness to the physical and mental transformation of my vessel, I have broken out and tested the waters, I have only just begun, I am on a mission. Now, welcome to the fire, welcome to the start, welcome to reality. I am never going to quit, I only just started…

In sophomore year of high school, I found my voice through free writing, and this discovery was the gateway to my discovering the more intricate parts of myself, my inner matrix, my unique wiring. Through free writing, I was able to fully own the dichotomy between certainty and fear.

Writing terrified me to my core, but it also intrigued me to a point where that I couldn't relent. I couldn't let go of my interest and passion for what it could do for me, what it potentially meant for me, and what it would reveal about me. The idea of being a writer and having this skillset refined was both freeing and empowering, in my eyes. It was the first skillset I was terrified of but utterly in awe of.

Writing was one of my first fears that I fully identified and then knew I needed to confront. During freshman year, I had allowed this fear to overwhelm me. I'd allowed fear to ride dirty in the backseat of my head space and to control me in ways I knew, if I didn't address it, would cripple me. This fear of writing, of releasing my words to paper, was tied to the debilitating form of perfectionism that had evolved within me, as a young person.

While writing began to free my internal expression and help me to harness my voice, it was the discovery of my passion for strength and conditioning that revealed my inner warrior woman. The love and interest I found for movement and the science's application to the sport I had fallen for led me to both internal to external empowerment. So, I placed this experience at the forefront of how I would show up in my life. It became my structure, my order for internal to external existence.

ST(RIPPED)

Something clicked for me during sophomore year. I was exposed to my untapped potential, and this wellspring of passion set my soul on fire! This year, I began to fully own my dream of becoming a collegiate athlete. And this year, I decided fear would take the backseat to my passion and purpose.

I started to really find my stride and focus. I created a road map for myself, and the end destination was clear. I committed my time to honing my body into the athlete I desired to evolve into and to developing my mindset into an unstoppable force to be reckoned with. I did this through relentless physical training in the weight room, on the court, and in the classroom. I linked this whole experience together and dug deeper than I ever knew possible. I was a sponge during this phase of my becoming. I used the years I had invested in observing, so I could now "try on" what was interesting to me and leave no stone unturned.

During high school, I learned the power of asking for help, what humility looked like, and, most important, that there isn't just one formula to accomplish a specific goal. The magic is finding *your* way and wholeheartedly believing in yourself.

I also relished my connection and bond with my father. During our early-morning breakfasts together, and special trips to Starbucks, I was able to ask a million questions as I sought to understand how my dad "did it all." And he did it all with so much intention, ease, and passion. I wanted to crack this code. How do I stay united in my purpose and passions, too?

My dad was certainly wired differently, but I saw myself as being one and the same as him; I loved the intricacies of this wiring. I wanted so badly to figure it out.

I already knew I was born for something big, we all are, but how do I figure myself out? How do I dial in my mind-body-soul and live the outcome I deeply desire? How do I navigate my potential and rewire what is not seemingly natural or possible?

I spent the first ten years of my life watching, listening, and studying. Then, I spent the next seven years asking a lot of questions while also keenly observing. This chapter of life was no different, but now, I was bringing my observation and thinking into action.

I learned my dad had been a stud athlete and a mental giant. I learned how he navigated adversity and leveraged what he had versus focusing on the things he didn't have dialed in yet. I learned the power of personal responsibility, what I later studied in the book, *Extreme Ownership* by Leif Babin and Jocko Willink. These were the qualities and actions communicated and modeled to me by my dad, a mindset that we lived and died by.

I learned the impact of patience, hard work, due diligence, a rite of passage, and how to embrace the power of blooming where you are planted. I quickly learned that the more you focused on others, the faster you lost your refined ability and precious time to invest in yourself, doing both a disservice to yourself and others around you. This would be a grave error for any dreams, wasting time worrying about the paths traveled by others.

Studying your opponents is different than shaping your purpose around their abilities. After all, we cannot level one another up if we simply pace each other's comfort zones. Someone has to take the lead to establish the next milestone to conquer. The more distracted you are, the faster your "opponent" can gain traction on you. The number-one opponent is always *you* and your limiting belief system.

"Keep your eye on the prize," my dad would say. This rang true for all I did, relentlessly focused on the mission at hand.

> *"You cannot trust the process, if you do not trust yourself."*
> —NRH

I was ferocious about my vision. If there was a tool I needed to sharpen in order to propel my vision forward, I knew I had to focus on how to overcome the obstacle, not the obstacle itself. Trust me, I was not the smartest kid in the room nor the best on the court, but what I lacked in those areas I made up for with my relentless passion for who I desired to become.

My desire to achieve this mission came with a deep commitment to inspire those around me and to enjoy the process with them. My heart beat for those around me and for bringing as many of my peers to their passion and purpose along the way. I was fueled by the camaraderie and the chance to help those around me discover their spark. The idea of "iron sharpening iron" was at the forefront of my heart and mind. It guided my *Why*.

During sophomore year, I recruited a dear friend to lift with me and discovered firsthand what it looked and felt like to have a fellow female friend uncover her edge and superpowers while moving weight. This connection and witnessing this experience of internal confidence told me I could be a valuable part of every woman's regimen, regardless of whether she desired to pursue athletics or not. Strength training was the vehicle to unlocking potential and securing a bulletproof mindset. It was the "how to" to understand the deepest versions of your limitations and then, the fastest, most effective way to overcome them. After all, muscle is not given. It is earned through hard work, discipline, and commitment. Being wildly capable comes at the price of unapologetically showing up for your vessel. When you give a woman access to this mind-body connection, she is unstoppable. Period.

I initially dipped my toes in the water of lifting simply as a tool to uplevel my performance and abilities on the volleyball court. I quickly realized, though, that this was my initiation into something much bigger. What started as a tool for my collegiate athlete dream became my absolute gravity, the oxygen I needed to evolve and thrive. I was hooked when I recognized my strength and power doing barbell squats. I recognized the freedom I felt when moving a barbell through a beautiful power clean.

I was also intrigued and obsessed by the artforms taking place in this space. This was a world I could escape into and connect with my soul, my inner matrix, and my drive. There was nothing I couldn't solve when I was lifting. This world provided me the edge, confidence, and humility I needed to further open up in my discovered truth as a leader.

Every angle of life radiated the same message: "Becoming is letting go." Letting go of fear, control, false strength, or security...

"No habla español..."

Sophomore year, I had Mr. Olsen as my teacher in Spanish class. This man is solely responsible for my firm understanding of how much better it is to volunteer versus being called out to respond without preparation.

ST(RIPPED)

What happens to your brain and body when you offer to go without being told to do it is a wild trip. It's the difference between showing up or being shoved out. It is allowing your thoughts to roll or your thoughts to freeze. It is truly the most effective way to know how united you were with what lived within you.

When I close my eyes, I can still see the ultra-cheesy, colorful, powerful, linear laminated poster that wrapped around the corner Mr. Olsen's room. It proclaimed this ultimate life lesson: "It is Better to Do Right Than to Be Right." *Well... Now what?* I would think. *Am I doing right or trying to be right...?*

When I snapped out of it, I remembered my answer. "Mi nombre es Niccole y soy hermosa y alta." A big smile spread across my face. *I got this, I am here now...*

Mr. Olsen is sole reason I pursued Spanish. His style of teaching and accountability kept me interested and engaged. I was less concerned whether I would retain the information than I was consumed by *how* we were learning. Why was it working? What could I take from this? How could I implement his leadership and teaching style into other facets of my life? How could I embrace the ability to be chill but confident in my delivery? How could I get the people I lead to embrace the areas that are unfamiliar and also slide into confidence in the areas they have dialed in?

What's the intrigue factor of mastering a skill that will serve you beyond a single skillset? What is the bigger impact? These were the questions I began to ask myself as I discovered that learning Spanish was not the most important aspect of this class. What mattered were the life lessons that unfolded while I was a student there.

St(ripping) me of my comfort, in this case being called out in front of my peers and forcing me either to succumb to the fold of the hard OR sit in the discomfort and refine the areas that are the most vulnerable, screaming to be seen, heard, and to flourish. The reveal is where the power sits. Each reveal forced me into discovering a new part of my power. This class, learning a new language and daring to be bad at something publicly, not only made me vulnerable, but became one of my greatest growth moments.

I quickly realized I could prepare for the call-out, I could anticipate and be ready for it, same as I could volunteer myself. There was just as much sovereignty in refining my response to the call-out as there was in volunteering to go first or whenever I was ready.

Sometimes, "ready" is negotiable. Sometimes, our minds are ready, but our hearts are not. Sometimes, our hearts are open, but our bodies are in a freeze and can't operate to the depth that our mind and heart agree to deliver. Sometimes, our bodies are trained, disciplined, and fully capable, but our heart and mind are not ready for the repercussions of criticism and exposure.

"Everything is energy and that's all there is to it. Match the frequency of the reality you want and you cannot help but get that reality."

—Albert Einstein

Much like writing this book, becoming the college athlete I aspired to be required the same process. I zeroed in on what was possible, I set my eye on the prize, and I became obsessed with the process of arriving there. Not the outcome, but the becoming. That was the prize.

When your sights are set solely on the reward, you will miss all of the lessons, the signs to pivot, and the gifts that have no association with your original intent. The process is the gift, so you have to keep your eyes open, your heart ready to receive, and your mind ready to learn, so you are aware of the distractions along the way that could potentially be detrimental to your desired outcome.

You have to become laser-focused but *not* fixed in your mindset. You have to "bloom where you are planted." However, be careful not to root so deep you fail to allow pivots in your plan. The pivots are the gold.

You see, I didn't fully get that during my high school and college years. I became so locked into what I was doing and where I wanted to go and the version of me that I wanted to become, I fell victim to my own relentless pursuit of becoming. I lost sight of the power of process and presence. I was so enthralled with my becoming and in achieving, I couldn't experience full presence at all times. I lost sight of the joy that comes with the fall, the rise, the undoing, and the building.

I was focused to a degree that was admirable and intimidating. In this pursuit of becoming, I had to be reminded to "stop and smell the roses." This became one of the most critical reminders during my becoming. To pause and appreciate the victories along the way.

Many times, I achieved whatever I was working toward, like a PR in the weight room, a technique on the court, a new training opportunity, or a good grade, and I would simply think to myself, "Good work, Niccole. That is what is supposed to happen when you commit and focus." It was never enough. There was always the next level and the next achievement.

NICCOLE HENDRICKSON

There is great danger in failing to celebrate and acknowledge along the way. It is dangerous not only for you but for those around you. When you fail to acknowledge the small, stackable victories, you not only run the risk of losing out on the rapport you've built with those around you, those who had an incredible impact on your becoming, but you also fail yourself.

The failure is rooted in your mind and heart thinking it's never enough and that you have to keep acquiring in order to be "good enough." You have to keep escalating your existence and taking yourself to new heights in order to be worthy. You never actually fully own the place you are in. If you don't pause to acknowledge and celebrate, you also fail to embody what you've worked for and become. Therefore, you are not familiar with the process and will not be able to replicate it.

I experienced this falter many times in my life, where I lacked full presence and appreciation for what I had become and of those whom I met along the way. These field moments created levels of loneliness for me and were missed opportunities to be celebrated.

I specifically remember working very hard to compete in a doubles tournament one summer. I trained and committed to many meetups with my competition partner. I was so wound tight doing all this training, I missed out on the fun of doing what I loved on the beach, laughing with a friend, soaking up the sunshine, meeting new people, and moving my body in dynamic ways. When I reflected on this, I wondered why I couldn't just let go and have fun at being the beginner I was.

You sacrifice and bust your ass to become, and yet you may have no idea how the hell you did it. No, there is nothing celebratory about this process. You need something to show for your becoming. You need embodiment. Your greatness isn't accidental. It's intentional.

Dialing in, leveling up, pushing limits, and working for something so much greater than your current state require a level of belief, action, connection, and embodiment. The only way to see through a dream that no one can kill is through absolute presence with yourself in the process, not simply bulldozing to the outcome.

The Next Version of You

In order to become a version of yourself that you have never experienced before, you will have to let go of people, habits, and thoughts that do not align with your end state. Many people go through life thinking you simply do this first and then you have a clear path to become... But this whole headspace of clearing a path and then you can do what you desire is a lie. You will wait a lifetime to do and become, if you need "x" to become "y." Those are simply lies and excuses to detour you and waste your time.

Whatever you desire to evolve into or become, you need to do it imperfectly, not fully educated, not fully trained, and not completely prepared. You have to take action while scared, while feeling like you can't. You have to lead your own mind and body by example. You have to dare to suck and be the worst in order to become the best in whatever endeavor you set out to be.

The consistent reps will win and propel your path forward ten times out of ten, versus waiting for perfection and refinement. The failure or the missteps are the lessons that rekindle the fire. There is a clear tie between being completely okay with sucking at something, while also embracing a headspace that believes you will become victorious over your desire to become.

It requires humility.

Find something to strengthen you while also st(ripping) open your existence to arrive at excellence. The dichotomy can exist in harmony.

Becoming Requires Physical Strength

Shortly after the start of my sophomore-year writing revelation, I was introduced to strength and conditioning. The weight room became my personal sanctuary. I discovered my physical body possessed a level of strength and power that nearly matched my relentless mindset. My heart soared here, my body became alive, and my mind spent infinite minutes envisioning my pathway to becoming the woman I so deeply desired to be: strong, relentless, capable, and unstoppable in any pursuit I set my mind to.

The moment my brother walked me into this forty-by-forty-foot room full of its unique sounds, smell, and setup, I was in absolute awe. I was intrigued, fired up, and obsessed. The cranking 1990s sound system was bursting the edges of each wall. The clanking of weights was soothing in their own rhythm. The equipment was established in its place and certainly hadn't been moved since it was delivered decades ago. It stood proud. Earlier athletes had completed many victorious seats on it, and the equipment kept inviting many more, like it had wisdom and power.

Legends had utilized many of the machines, barbells, and squat racks, in order to fulfill their bigger purpose and passion. I would be one of them! This room reeked of passion and grit.

ST(RIPPED)

There was nothing luxurious about this room, nothing that screamed, "You will be comfortable here!" In fact, it was laughable, compared to some of the other high schools in our league, but it didn't matter. In my opinion, the grittiness of this room built true warriors.

Here, I learned the power of becoming despite your circumstances, when you are wholeheartedly connected to your mission. Comfort and luxury don't share the same space with raw and real. This place dared you to level up and tap into the deep interwoven warrior within. This weight room was the proving grounds for becoming the most honest and true version of myself. And this was where I would continue to unravel the layers of my becoming.

From plyo ladders to barbells, I became obsessed with the power and possibilities that waited within me. Strength and conditioning were the combination that opened me up and gave me power, insight, and connection to my body. They provided me a direct pathway to the deepest, most sacred parts of my psyche. They provided me the platform to learn that anything was possible.

Strength training specifically became my way to flourish in every aspect of my life. You give a girl the tools to strengthen and move in order to tap into her internal warrior, and you will never stop her in any facet of her life.

When we have a firm understanding of what is possible within our vessels, then build a solid understanding of how to tap into those possibilities, we can utilize this blueprint for anything in our lives. The body is brilliant, and the quicker you realize the power is in your hands to build or break down, the sooner you can leverage emotion, movement, tension, fear, and capacity within you. Just like building strength in the weight room, this process requires a breakdown of the muscles in order to rebuild them. It requires attention to detail in order to nourish and benefit from the breakdown.

I observed this power building within spaces like the weight room, on the field, and on the court. My curiosity craved deeply whatever was possible for me. How could I leverage this process to become...?

"You risk it all when the open door to greatness comes along..."
- Brenne, musical artist

This moment in my life was the chance to prove myself, to break out, and to dare to become that I'd been waiting for. I would not be held down or back. I would full-force prove anything and everything is possible when you weave vision, belief, and physical action together. I decided then to make it my life mission to show that you can become whatever you want, when you root down and go.

During my sophomore year, I declared I would work to become a college-level volleyball player on scholarship. This would be my MO. This was the identity I was claiming and was going to own.

When you embrace fear and limitations and recycle them, and when you no longer fear the "what if it doesn't happen and you start to welcome the obstacle," this is the turning point in your life.

Through my own trials, I came to recognize that obstacles and limitations are simply a part of the plan. They are intel. They are the fuel to keep your eyes open and not to be so obsessed with one line of thought that you miss all

ST(RIPPED)

the angles of growth and possibility. Trust me, I fell for that trap multiple times.

A fixed mindset will propel you into the ditch faster than you can see it coming. Remaining focused on achieving something specific requires dedicated focus on the mission at hand, but you cannot become so fixed you lose out on the lessons and callings along the way. It is a balancing of two sides of the scale at all times.

The trap attempted to swallow me up when I found myself in situations that tried to manipulate my commitment and relentless work ethic. Like when my ego struggled because I was far from a skilled volleyball player. I was green, fresh to this sport, I began to compete with and level myself up against gals who had played since childhood. But I knew what I had and what I was after. I was determined to close the gap of my skills through humility and learning. I committed to developing those skills while also leaning hard into what I did have.

A mindset that deeply desired to flourish.

A never-say-die attitude that would welcome obstacles and trials.

A heart that asked for expansiveness.

A capacity and base of strength and power, two things I worked on daily in order to refine my headspace and physical body.

A focus that would not be reckoned with.

A vision that was interwoven with my head, heart, and body.

And most important:

A deep spiritual connection.

"I won't let up."

NICCOLE HENDRICKSON

> *"When perfectionism is driving us, shame is riding shotgun and fear is that annoying backseat driver."*
> —Brene Brown

As I was moving through high school both academically and athletically, playing on club teams, the lesson I was quickly able to identify and then experience firsthand:

It wasn't about being perfect or infallible. It was actually about how fast I could recognize that I was falling, that I was out of alignment to my purpose, and that I was people-pleasing and compromising my values. I would do this by saying "yes" to things when I didn't want to, sacrificing my wellbeing for the wellbeing of a teammate, not holding a boundary on the things I needed in order to thrive.

This isn't about being better than someone else. This isn't about casting blame or condemning anyone else's choices. It's about holding myself accountable and owning the stories I've been telling that no longer serve me.

This was about recognizing I had failed to fully understand the magnitude of my wiring and my values, how to carry them out and how to have boundaries, how to honor myself and peacefully leave behind what didn't serve me. It was about doing right not being right. It was about having the courage to go deeper and call out my own lack of knowing and struggles, in order to actually do something about it. I could wallow in what I thought was, or I could actually become it!

You will struggle to become and embody your becoming as long as you're in a state of people-pleasing. When you "live here," you are suppressing your own emotions and preventing yourself from being seen, received, and validated by yourself. You are voluntarily allowing yourself to be a doormat for someone else.

Throughout high school, I came to recognize that the reasons behind playing a sport, joining certain clubs, or striving for excellence varied greatly from person to person. Not everyone was driven to refine their skills in order to become a top-tier athlete or lead an organization; each individual's WHY was unique. As a result, I sometimes felt a disconnect between my level of seriousness and that of my peers.

My people-pleasing took the form of flying under some "radar," so I didn't make my peers in high school feel bad about themselves. So they wouldn't criticize me for wanting something different or more. This was also because I possessed a level of uncertainty within myself, due to me feeling a little alone in my new life pursuit. I had the full support of my parents and mentors, but not of my peers. I was unrelatable in so many ways, it was painful.

Logically, I knew how the endless hours of practice, training, mindset work, and studying I was doing gave me an edge. It earned me something that most of my peers would not sacrifice for. But my heart was still young and cared *a lot* about what others thought and whether or not I was also bringing everyone along with me. Was I inspiring, leading, supporting?

While all of this sounds honorable and inspiring, my willingness to "take everyone's rock and load my pack up" became a problem. The rocks I took on varied, from my teammates' insecurities and lack of work ethic, the attitudes that would create issues on the team, or saying "yes" to help every time a coach needed something. It created a situation where I learned to live with minimal boundaries. I did this in the name of good spirit, and I continued to test my mental grit and physical stamina without realizing the damage I was doing. I was taking the load instead of sharing the burdens. I was trying to lead my teammates and my peers, while assuming all the control and the burden of the load.

This was me proving I could and would. It was my attempt to show what was possible, while I failed to realize how dangerous it was to me and around me. Sure, it was admirable and inspiring, especially knowing the intention behind it, but it wasn't sustainable, and it wasn't making those around me better and accountable, just because I removed their load but never led them to the understanding of how they could individually get stronger and more dynamic in their own lives. I was taking it all from them and taking away what I actually had to give, as well. I wasn't allowing others to be there for me, and I wasn't experiencing the receiving in my becoming.

I had a few things to learn.

Leading isn't doing everything

People don't like you and value you if you play small in an attempt to not make them feel small.

I needed to be courageous enough to own who I was and who I deeply desired to become.

Another lesson before the adulting even started.

As I reflect deeply on this chapter of my life, when I started to compromise my mission, values, and principles at a level that teetered on intense regret, due to my fear of making others uncomfortable with my drive and focus, my fear of being seen at this level, the fear that taunted me if I didn't make it, the fear of not being able to sustain what I set out to conquer, I now recognize how dysregulated my state of being was. It was all catching up with me. The

ST(RIPPED)

people-pleasing and fear of not becoming were leading me down the path of just that: a failure to become.

Following this experience of insecurity around my peers in high school and owning my confidence in my mission came a shame cycle: the shame of allowing myself to be influenced and so easily brought off course. shame around how much I did care what others thought. And shame for disappointing myself and demonstrating a lack of faith.

I recognized this "all or nothing" way of thinking would be my demise, if I didn't snap out of it and figure it out, if I didn't accept what was and dial in what I wanted it to evolve into. The "all of nothing" thought process is the fastest way to lose sight of your end goal and get swallowed in the toxicity of extremes.

I fully recognize how the choices I made were a part of my becoming. I had to endure this. Allowing the shame cycle to consume me was denying myself the privilege of humanity and growth. I would root down in what I knew to be true: I am worthy of the woman I was in pursuit of becoming.

"Look well into yourself; there is a source of strength which will always spring up if you will always look."
—Marcus Aurelius

I had put in a memorable level of work, commitment, and sacrifice, something I will always be proud of. I was at the crossroads where my biggest dream to date met my ego...

Ignorant to what the real world really had to offer, I took a call from a junior college coach who wanted me to consider playing for his team. He encouraged me to refine and elevate my skill set to open the door to better my chances of being recruited. But most important, he wanted me to first provide to his team, to grow, and to evolve into something bigger than myself. My "big" dream now felt so little. Could I do it?

I was a mix of honored to receive a call from him as well as deeply put off... *junior college*? WTF? I had committed four years to my grades, my community, and my academic prowess. How would any of that show its weight in gold if I, Niccole Deneke, went to junior college?

Now, I can laugh and roll my eyes in utter embarrassment at my ego and ignorance. For all I thought I knew, I knew nothing about facilitated purpose and the power of options. Hah! The girl who thought she knew better. Laughable and formidable.

This was my second, but biggest invitation to lead to date. Could I yet recognize that impact and legacy are built on far greater landscapes than simply scoring points with court time, kills at the net, and aces at the line? Was I ready to recognize the magnitude of my calling and soul's purpose? Was I ready to look through a new lens? Or would I wrap myself up in a fixed mindset of what I believed to be true and most impactful? After all, I was barely seventeen years old, thinking I had this aspiration and pathway figured out...

I wrapped up the call with the JC coach, and I sat. Sat in wonder, sat in offense, sat in delight of possibility, sat in fear. For the first time, I was afraid I might actually let my dream go, because my ego was telling me, "Going straight to a four-year university. That is the admirable thing. That is the stamp of who you actually are versus who you are trying to evolve into."

ST(RIPPED)

If I didn't go straight to a four-year, was I weak, pathetic, and without credibility? If I didn't accept this option, was I counting out all my probabilities because I was terrified of the unknown possibilities?

I sat in all of this. I sat with it. I leaned into my most trusted, honest resource: my dad. The man who gave me the outline to dream, to dream so damn big, it made others and, most important, myself uncomfortable. The man who would always tell me the truth about what I saw in myself or what failed to be true. After all, his story was the story that planted the little seed in my mind and heart. It was the catalyst to my dream.

I learned my dad also chose junior college before earning a full-ride scholarship to the four-year university where he graduated. This tiny little detail shifted everything for me. It reframed my thoughts around JC. It helped me see all the options that could open for me. And these went from two choices to multiple ones, if I could humble my ass and allow for a growth mindset.

All the seeds are planted in our lives. It took me seventeen years to figure this out, but damn, I was happy when I started to catch on. Somehow, the option to go to JC became a catalyst to something bigger. It was also another tiny thread that brought me closer to the man I adored. How cool that our paths could be so different, yet similar. I loved this. It was all it took for me to shift my headspace and see possibility and growth versus the option as a sloppy second-best.

Had I marched forward in my ego, I would have voluntarily stripped away my power and opportunity. I would have succumbed to fear, doubt, ignorance, and the path to the least resistance. Hard pass.

NICCOLE HENDRICKSON

Reframe. The power is here.

Days later, I reengaged the JC coach. After I started to attend open gym at his college, I quickly realized this was a whole new level of athletes. Each gal who had chosen to try their time at JC had a wealth of experience to share, which was the most important attribute shared by every young woman present in the gym. Each gal knew they had a little more to give, a little more to be noticed, and an internal burning desire to bring it to life.

This, I could get behind. These women were choosing this path. I would learn so much from every gal I shared court time with.

"Life is not about finding yourself. Life is about creating yourself."
—George Bernard Shaw

As I wrapped up my senior year of high school, I was clear about my physical training next steps, but I was in absolute denial about what I would study at college. I remained unable to unite my passions for wellness, strength, and conditioning with my purpose, my bigger mission to use physical movement, structure, habit-stacking, community building to curate an empire for driven warrior-like women. A place where women could go to build, refine, and harness these skills. A culture where women could embrace their multifaceted goodness.

Here, a woman could be alpha while also in total touch with her femininity and celebrated for it. It could be an everyday networking experience for the woman who didn't just want to talk about the gym at the gym, and then go to coffee to talk about her kids and life. I wanted to create a movement where women were celebrated for their drive but granted permission to mellow out and lean into valuable resources.

Truthfully, I wanted to combine everything I had been gifted through the combination of my upbringing by my mom and dad. I wanted to celebrate the goddess vibe I'd acquired from the beautiful Italian heritage my mom blessed me with, and I wanted to show women we could be warriors, strong AF, mentally dialed in, and dynamic, while also taken care of. I wanted to develop the ethos I'd learned from my father's upbringing and the path he'd forged and then create a blended one for women.

What degree would that be? Insert a huge snarky smile here! There wasn't one, and having to choose a label felt like I was subscribing to being stuffed into a box that was already suffocating to me. Shifting my perception would be key. I needed to get clear on what I wanted from this college experience, so the experience didn't own me. We needed a mutually beneficial relationship.

I continued to repeat the story line over and over that health and wellness were simply hobbies, and while important threads of who I was, the threads did not point to my career path or, most important, a full embodiment of me. When I read this now, though, and when I reflect on saying this out loud to my parents and mentors, I laugh at myself—lovingly, of course. I wasn't ready to name it. I wanted to be outside the box and support it, but that fear was real. The fear of naming it while also getting put into a category.

This is the perfect living example of not being able to see the spectacular forest through the trees, because I was so focused on labeling something while not wanting to be labeled. I was also slipping into the headspace of: if there isn't a label that the rest of the world understands, then it is less valuable and impactful.

In addition, I was fighting against the system that says, "Step one is this, step two is this..." My forever question would be, "What do you do if your life doesn't follow what is presented as the normal steps, the recognizable steps? What if you don't want those to be your next steps? What if you believe there are other options?"

I was so focused on everything I *didn't* want it to be, I failed to describe what I *did* want to experience and become.

There is power in our thoughts, their energy, and how they manifest. I would recognize this aspect of me, a quality I didn't love... When I struggled to name or describe what I truly wanted to experience, feel, and achieve, I quickly went into all the things I didn't want to experience. Only then did I realize I was dumping energy into the wrong way of thinking. I was fueling the fear monster and the antithesis of my desired outcome.

Noted.

When I recognized I wouldn't be able to find a label to describe me or figure out a degree that would fully support my mission, I thought I had to accept what I could commit to a degree and focus. But the *power* was in my hands. I got to decide how I would use it and truly embrace this constant burning fire within me, this fire that was creating something outside the box, something I was deeply proud of. I didn't have to explain to others. I could go inward, refine the clarity, live it, and ultimately share it in the most natural way I knew possible. Leading by example. I would become and I would embody this mission I desired.

I think it is ironic how absolute I was in the power of uniting passion and purpose in order to fulfill my role as a collegiate athlete, but I *could not* see the correlation between my passion for using movement as a tool to my bigger legacy, until I leaned into my circle and my mentors. Then, I was able to put to rest the doubts I had on this pathway. Once again, I was encouraged to think outside the box I opposed being put into. I was advised to have a level of faith in myself that I could pursue the subject matter that lit me up and that aligned with my bigger mission in life: Service and Leading others to harness their inner strengths by living true to their purpose.

I would use exercise, pushing physical limits, expanding one's mindset, and the influence of nourishment and lifestyle to facilitate my bigger purpose.

If you cannot find it, create it.

There are some relationships that require you to shed more than you are quite yet willing, but the becoming is in the letting go, the st(ripping) of what you once believed to be true.

Stepping Into Showcasing Me

Cue long hair, tall body, the start of developed musculature, and a feminine physique. My oldest cousin was a hair and makeup artist, so I was well ahead of my time with highlights (Hello, chunky lights—*phew!*) I was rocking those low-cut jeans, tight tops, and accessories to match. I was already a walking target, being Coach Deneke's daughter and Deneke's sister, but it wouldn't be me if I didn't put my own flair on things.

This commitment to my flair was the start of me taking the observations I'd gathered as a little girl, studying my cousins, and now becoming the version of me that I dreamt of.

High school was interesting. Throughout my whole childhood, I was insulated, being around my cousins, our big Italian family. We were everything to one another. We were one another's number-one support system, each other's checks and balances. We shared the high and lows of whatever particular chapter of life we were in. We forewarned one another, and we wholeheartedly lived out "blood is thicker than water." We simply did not care about many outside friends, because we had one another.

When I entered my freshman year, I was lucky to have my brother at the school, plus my older cousin who was like the sister I never had. We did everything together, and her friends were my friends, my additional big sisters. They were there to make sure I was never alone.

One of the greatest gifts I received from both of my parents and from influential mentors was the guidance to find my way, my voice. They encouraged me to sharpen my judgment and strengthen my character, my power of discernment, and to stand in my values and my passions. As a mother, it can be hard to recognize when we are trying to develop our children in their best interests, or when we are covering up the inadequacies of our own wiring.

When bringing life into the world and guiding their paths, we have to be mindful of how we lead. If we are controlling and overbearing around our children's evolution and calling this leadership, we are failing them miserably. Trust me, I didn't get it until I was in a mother's shoes.

I used to wonder what was wrong with parents who made their kids play a sport they had played themselves,

ST(RIPPED)

forcing them onto that path because it was the one they had gone down. Sure, I know it elicits pride and maybe even reveals a hidden desire to push their child further than they went, themselves. It brings up memories of thing that you, as an athlete, did not fully live out. Now, I understand how easy it is to do this, as a parent. How mindlessly you can put your child into your own sport.

Nothing has lit me up more than when my daughter asks to pepper with me, to play around with the volleyball. But I know we cannot force them to develop in our own image. Like my father, we must provide the power of proximity and allow our children to find their own way. Let your desire to control your children's choices go and embrace who they are becoming. In turn, we can have the privilege of discovering the next iteration of ourselves.

I get it now...

If I had a dollar for every time someone asked me, "Your dad didn't make your brother play football or become a quarterback?"

No! No, he did not. It was no different than how he didn't "make" my brother become a Marine. No doubt, my dad and likely both of my parents were hopeful he would desire to play football, but it was never forced on him. The idea was introduced through the power of proximity.

My brother and I spent our summers around our parents and their careers. That meant we went to the store with our mother and enjoyed the perks of the family business. Or we were with our dad during summer programming for his football teams, where we got to ride our bikes like insane kids, chug Gatorade, give high-fives, and watch the magnificence of his athletes. We ran around the stadium and played with the speed and agility equipment. Most important, we were in the company of some really cool kids and outstanding coaches.

We also got to witness the not-so-great parts of that world, which was a gift, as well. This proximity piqued our interest and opened the door to our curiosity, which was very different than our father demanding we do things one specific way.

Now, let me be clear, we were led by example, by a firm understanding of protocols, but when it came to developing our interests and passions, this was led by our parents helping us to find our passions. Proximity grew our interest and opened the doors for us to find our way. My brother did, in fact, choose to play football out of his love of the game, not my father's.

Research shows, when you demonstrate [aka lead by example] such things as taking care of yourself, having fun, and being kind, your children are more apt to follow this example. Demonstrating is doing and embodying. When you choose to be active, you show enjoyment in taking care of yourself. Then, your kids are more prone to follow and make this a part of their own lives.

The silent teacher is the most impactful one. Lead from a place of helping others find their power, their purpose. This, in turn, will allow you to embrace the st(ripping) of your unnecessary need to attempt to control the outcomes of their choices.

Chapter 4 Reflections

Part 1: The Unclenched Fist Exercise

Visual Prompt

Close your eyes. Make a tight fist. Hold it for 10 seconds. Now... release.

Take a deep breath. Feel the shift.

Let this be a physical symbol of what happens when you *let go*.

Reflection Prompt

What emotions or thoughts did you feel when clenching your fist?

What changed when you let go?

How does this mirror your current life experience?

Part 2: The "Release + Replace" List

* Draw a line down the center of a page.

* Left side, label: **"Let Go Of"**

* List what you're carrying that no longer serves you (e.g., worry, comparison, control, fear of failure).

Right side, label: **"Make Room For"**

* Write what you *want* to feel or invite in (e.g., peace, creativity, trust, joy, flow).

Let Go Of	Make Room For
Perfectionism	Progress + presence
Needing all the answers	Trust in the process
Fear of being seen	Confidence in becoming

Takeaway Prompt

Which Release and which Replace, one from each column, will you commit to focusing on this week?

CHAPTER 5

Passion, Goals + Goal-Getting

*When people who love you see your light begin to fade,
they don't let it go out. They strike a match
and help you reignite your fire.*

During grade-school fall break, when I was in third or fourth grade, I went to the high school with my dad. I had the privilege of hanging out with one of his P.E. classes. The kids were assigned to run the track that day. The group of gals in his class treated me like a queen, feel like the most special little girl. They piggybacked me around the track and gave me all the love and admiration a young girl needed and adored.

They carried this same love and recognition over to the local Friday night lights, where they cheered for the high school team. (My dad's secret was he let me come to get my fix, since I thought I, too, desired a cheerleading career...)

(Insert *cringe*... No offense to all my gal pals and girls out there who loved cheer. But I was always better suited to cheer *you* on, not cheer *with* you.)

I did love interacting with crowds, pulling them together, achieving esprit de corps, but not with a short skirt, sweater, pompoms, and glitter. I wanted to feel something different, a different kind of light penetrating my path, a different kind of hard, a different kind of attention. What it comes down to is this: I had a vision of what kind of girl I was and the woman I would become. I knew already what that image embodied *for me*. My image was of the girl who showed up to one of her dad's football practices, when the guys were having their vertical jump tested, along with their 50-yard dash and their strength and power limits. I was ready to meet my inner warrior.

One of the coaches invited me to "jump," to see how high *my* vertical jump was. *HAAAAAA!* I didn't know what the hell I was doing. But that little invitation and test opened a *whole* new world for me. I was fascinated. Take me into the grungy weight room where weights clanked and bars moved with a paces and intention I had never imagined. I watched bodies move with a finesse more beautiful, in my eyes, than a ballet.

The pace I witnessed while watching my dad's team at football practice and in the weight room was ballistic, it was madness, it was aggressive, it was flow, it was powerful, it was united in communication, it was teamwork, it was grit, it was humbling, it was intentional, and it was proof of getting one-percent better with every rep.

I wanted this!

I wanted to feel and be all of this *plus* be a smoking-hot elegant woman who could articulate herself.

I saw it was 1,000% possible to be a compassionate, sensitive, beautiful, elegant, creative, smart, articulate, strong, impactful, gritty, fierce, warrior all in one. This was the woman I would set out to become. These images began rolling through my mind from the age of eight, and I set out to navigate how to become *her*. This was where my desire began of becoming her…

Never underestimate a woman on a mission. A woman who sets her mind to something that lights her up. A woman who sees something she wants for her life and gets after it. It starts with realizing the power of acknowledging your goals, clearly setting them, and then allowing the ignition of passion from within to fuel the process toward fulfilling them.

Passion Witnessed

"You should try volleyball," said my dad one afternoon while we were talking through my experiences playing youth softball, gymnastics, swim, and dance. "You're going to be tall, you're powerful, and you love the combination of mental stimulation and physical demand."

This conversation captured how I truly felt about softball. Full disclosure: I hated the pace of the game, the hideous tan lines from the layers of your uniform, and the powdery dirt caked into every crevice of your uniform and body. I despised the long, boring practices with minimal movement in any particular direction, the simplicity of the schemes, and the lack of ebb and flow.

Truth is, I will never forget the first time my dad handed me a mitt and played catch with me in our backyard. *This*, my friends, was fire. I had a hell of an arm, and I relished the feeling of the ball hitting my mitt. The more experience I had, the harder my dad threw the ball at me, and I loved it. As simple as playing catch was, I loved the metaphors and lessons for life that I learned in these moments we had together.

"Keep your eye on the ball. Allow yourself to get distracted and multitask. Run the risk of getting clocked in the face with the ball."

"Make sure you have your teammates' attention before you throw the ball at them. Make eye contact—don't assume the other person is dialed into what you're thinking of doing. It is not just about *you* being ready."

"The pace and intensity with which you throw the ball sets the tone."

I mistook my love of playing catch with my potential love for this sport. I have no regrets about the years I committed to playing softball. After all, I developed some connections, learned the early stages of sportsmanship like ego and humility, plus how to use your voice and presence to get into someone else's headspace and distract them by just being good in your own skin. I learned what it felt like to follow rules and not always like them.

I experienced pain after being hit accidently by a pitch. I experienced how to use my body, the power in it, and how your eye truly stays on the ball to make the connection with bat to ball, but it is out of your head and into your body, if you plan to connect all the dots. Overthinking will get you nowhere but struck out!

I learned how to tune out the chatter of the stands and embrace their noise. The noise meant they felt a threat from you in some capacity and wanted to attempt to throw you off your game. Or, hell, maybe they just liked to hear themselves talk. I experienced the power behind the choice to use my body to achieve my desired outcome. (Does this sound funny? Wrong? More on this later!) I learned how to slide into the base you're stealing, at the risk of removing your skin as your body glides effortlessly in the moment, because of the shear force you pack behind the slide. Then, getting trampled by the opponent's cleats and smacked with their glove as they try to tag you out. You either learn to relish the intensity or the intensity will own you.

Participating in this sport helped me understand the power, influence, and impact of group thought. Every sport, career path, extracurricular activity, and club has a culture. There's a way you dress, speak, think, and interact. No matter what independence you possess, there is always a tether or a buy-in that you must share. There is a common thread, and you have to be willing to share it. But after five years playing softball, I decided this team and sport wasn't my space to take up. It was time to find my vibe.

I did find that vibe when my dad invited me to explore volleyball and its community. My early years playing sports had taught me the power of getting curious. How you listen to the inner calling that your heart sings for. And accept invitations even when you know nothing. Never underestimate the power in a sport. Movement is medicine.

From my First Taste of Volleyball... I Was Hooked

When I was twelve, I got a taste for the game of volleyball. I was intrigued. I was hooked. As my parents observed right away, when I discovered volleyball, a brand-new passion was ignited within me. So, they proposed I attend a sleepaway volleyball camp at a prestigious university in San Diego. This became one of my coolest experiences to date, one of independence and self-discovery.

After I was dropped off, set up in my temporary dorm space, and given my welcome bag, I took in every smell and noise, plus the enormity of the gymnasium. Everything was decorated with logos of the school's emblem and colors.

NICCOLE HENDRICKSON

Stadium seating went up for rows and rows, surrounding the vast arena, one I could only dream of playing in. Every coach wore school colors and matching outfits, too. The current collegiate players were volunteering at camp, and they, too, were decked out, head to toe in teamwear: navy-blue travel sweats, crisp white court sneakers, and fitted white tops. They were tall, gorgeous, dynamic, strong, and confident. *This* was a feeling and experience I could get behind. There was something here for me, even if it only served to open my eyes to a whole world that existed beyond the one I currently lived in.

I studied all the other campers as they arrived. The athletic world fascinating, and the culture, even at a youth level, has many telling details. You can quickly identify who is experienced and well-versed in their sport by the gear they wear, how they wear it, and how they carry themselves. There is a healthy dose of arrogance that comes from athletic prowess.

We were all amateurs in camp, but there were levels. There were girls there who had been playing volleyball for the last seven years, which gave them ample time to acquire a level of body awareness around the specific movement patterns volleyball demands. Me, I had body awareness, strength, untapped power, and explosiveness, but I was a newbie, a freshie when it came to this sport. I was not part of the clubs where many of these girls played. Hell, I had no idea the dynamics of these clubs they competed in. I simply had a newly discovered passion for the sport, and I had recognized my internal kindling for competing and demanding my body to move at new levels.

I was here to learn.

ST(RIPPED)

After introductions and a solid period of warming up, conditioning, and team-building, we were broken into groups to do skill work. Holy smokes! There were timers, balls flying everywhere, and vibrant yells of "I got it! Mine! You-you! Good work," with dozens upon dozens of girls running everywhere. I was there, but I was also in observation mode.

"Holy smokes," I said on repeat. "I am here, and I am doing this!"

Up until this point, I had only seen male athletes move in groups like this, excel at their craft, coach, lead, and compete. This was my first experience witnessing and starting to become the female version of all I'd seen, growing up.

I was here, but my mind was everywhere. My experience level was well below so many of the gals' there, but I would not allow this to take away from my experience. After all, it was a skills camp, for God's sake. If I wasn't humble enough to allow myself to suck at a skills camp, then I would be doomed indefinitely. There would be no future.

Somehow, I moved from one court to the next. The university head volleyball coach took notice to my effort, tempo, and grit, but how some of my serving skills suffered. She asked me to follow her to another court, where I had my first experience of what pure calm, collected, and assured confidence looked like in the female form.

She watched me, studied my movement patterns, and quickly noticed my athleticism, but also my sorely untapped body awareness. She provided me a few quick tips, which were second nature to her but life-changing for me. Simple things like: transfer your power from back to forward; elevate your elbow; contact the ball with a firm, flat hand; engage your core; and breathe.

Those ten or so minutes I spent with this woman, learning and gaining a better understanding of my body in motion, were all I needed to validate this calling that had taken root in my soul. It was a full-body experience.

I returned home from this two-night, three-day camp with a whole new perspective on my reality. I had a vision. I had a snapshot of what could be. I had a taste for something I craved but couldn't put a name on. I was going to bring this passion into purpose. I was fully present in this vision.

Actions like vision boarding, building out Pinterest boards, writing about your goals, dreams, and sharing them with friends are all so powerful because the actions bring you into the full "presence" of your vision. They boldly initiate the desire to take action and help your mind unite with the action steps toward your goals.

Once you have a vision, you have to navigate the ability to hold it, own it, and bring it to life. This is where I believe the action begins to happen. The goals you make are the action steps to bringing the vision to life. I believe the goals need to have various timelines with deadlines, e.g., short term, mid-term, long game. There need to be deadlines and defined actions and outcomes for each of these timelines, because, as I mentioned above, life is busy, noisy, and full of distractions. As human beings, we resonate and respond best to structure and accountability.

We also need to understand what is at stake, if we do or do not. If everything we desire is left without a tether, it free-floats, and we are banking on "what ifs" versus "even ifs." When we free-float, there is no timeline commitment, and derailment will paralyze or kill the desired outcome, even for the best of us. When we have structure, we can operate confidently from a place of "even if," incorporating the expected derailments and intel gathered from the process.

When we have structure around our time, we have the ability to navigate the pivots needed when interference happens, because it isn't "if it will." It is boldly a "when it will." Having a plan for derailment isn't "being negative." It is being real and prepared. The best of us get distracted, bombarded, and derailed by accident, on purpose, or unexpectedly. That is why discipline and structure are needed. This is found in our timelines and our measurables.

Seeing Your Goals Through

There are endless approaches to bringing goals to life. In my personal opinion, every approach delivers some beautiful element, a new edge, or a fresh perspective. At the end of the day, every approach is united in one common denominator: *vision*. This starts with what I call a "sparked vision."

I am going to share the united thread I have woven into every fulfilled vision I have lived and realized thus far. My story tells about a few of my key lived experiences, which I hope you will connect to and will give you perspective and, hopefully, spark something within you about the power of your vision, passion, and purpose, which already lives within you and your story. There is no superpower you have to find. It lives within you, my friend. You just need to allow your spark to be ignited!

NICCOLE HENDRICKSON

Vision

We have visions for our life all of the time, they are in our thoughts, feelings, desires, and experiences. They show up from an early age, and they begin to consume us when young, sometimes without our even knowing it. They spark how we show up in our lives, and they often guide our hobbies, how we fill our spare time, and the connections we make, if we allow them to.

As a mother of two, I have validated this claim by bearing witness to both of my children discovering things that bring them joy and elicit a spark within. In feeling this joy, they have built sparked visions for their lives.

"Mommy, when I grow up, I want a ranch with horses, chickens, dogs, and of course a few barn cats. I want to be a cowgirl!"

My daughter's love, connection, and joy for horses started before she was two. She was mesmerized by their beauty, grace, and power. She connected instantly to their presence, and she began to form her life around these magnificent creatures. This joy and spark cultivated her vision for her life. This desire to know everything about them, to experience their magic in her life, to ride and feel the freedom of the world when solely focused on the horses' powerful existence beneath and around her. Early on, she acknowledged how they calmed her, knew her, and embraced her. They have taught her boundaries and trust. They have shown her the power of patience. They have handily demonstrated the power of joy and spark to cultivate a bigger vision.

In Order to Recognize a Vision, We need Presence

For all of us, in some fashion, life is busy and noisy, inundated with lots of opinions, people, and all our acts of "going and doing." There is no stopping the pace of the world, the flood of information, and the pace that seems to pick up ferociously every year. However, there is the power of choice and presence.

We can decide where we will invest our presence. This, my friends, is key. The saying, "Where focus goes, energy flows," could not be truer, when we talk about the ability to be present. We often complain we do not have enough time or energy for the goals we want to bring to life. However, I would argue we need to ask, "Where is my focus and energy going? Where am I putting my presence?"

When I can answer this question honestly, I am able to navigate where I need to refine my presence and edit my energy expenditure. To see a vision through, we need to be present in our lives, our mind, and our vessel.

Bringing your "sparked vision" to life requires both presence and clarity. With presence and clarity, we can move into one of the most powerful steps: *visualization*. This is about taking the time to sit with the feelings, desired experience or achievement you are after.

In your visualization, get as specific as possible: define the emotions, outcomes, and impact of your vision on yourself and the world. Visualize how your physical presence will feel and look, how will you speak, how will you embody this achievement or experience, and how will the people around you see you attaining this achievement or experience.

One of my go-tos for visualization is simply spending two to five minutes grounding and breathing, allowing my thoughts to circulate around the vision. I take a seat on the floor or a chair and feel my feet on the ground. With one hand to my heart and one to my belly, I close my eyes and inhale through my nose for three counts, initiating the breath in my belly. I move it to my ribcage and into my chest, hold for a count, and then slowly allow my breath to exhale out my mouth for six counts. I repeat this four to ten times.

When you try it, with each inhale, bring your vision into focus, not only seeing it, but feeling it and breathing into the desired experience. With each exhale, release an obstacle in order to bring more clarity around the desired achievement or experience.

After a little breathwork visualization, I jot down everything I saw and felt in my journal. Allowing yourself not only to visualize, but to put your thoughts on paper materializes the vision. If you skip the breathing element then be sure to write to the visualizations. At the end of this chapter, there will be guided entries and resources to help bring your sparked visions into fruition.

The next step, in my opinion and experience, is the MVP of the process: identifying and honing in on your *WHY*. Your *WHY* is your North Star. You will have a main *why* in your life and you will have *WHYs* that guide your goals. Please note: these are all interconnected.

At the root of your goals lie your values and guiding principles. When you set about to identify your *WHY* any desired achievement or experience, dig deep. What is it about accomplishing this that is important to you? What will the goal, the experience, or the achievement bring to your life and to those who matter to you?

You will revisit your *WHY* countless times, especially when you hit bumps in the process, when you get busy or distracted, and when life feels hard and too much. Then, you will root down in your *WHY*, which will allow you to align with your mission and vision, "even if!"

A sparked vision needs clearly defined steps of "what will it take?" Bringing our vision to life requires that we clearly outline the necessary resources, support, and time required.

So, fearlessly list out what obstacles to your achievement or experience you imagine you'll have to face, plus what challenges could arise, and what you need that you do not currently have. Let's be clear: this does not bring negative energy to the process. This is calling out and preparing to encounter opposition or challenge and then building a contingency plan. Bolstering your resources ahead of time will give you a smoother pathway to your desired outcome.

After identifying any needed resources, get clear on what it will take. Break the vision down into small, tangible steps, then set timelines, prioritize tasks to create momentum, and identify habits or routines that will support consistent progress.

Last, choose an accountability process. Clarifying and owning your *WHY* and establishing an accountability process are two of the most important elements for bringing a vision to life and holding it. So, establish a system to track progress, but don't overthink this. It could be through weekly check-ins, journaling, or working with a mentor/coach.

Set milestones not only for the accountability to complete each required step, but also to celebrate the process. This is key for sustainability. Surround yourself with a support system that not only holds you to your commitments, but reminds you of your gifts and impact.

Inspired by the Fear of Being Average

Leadership, camaraderie, and inspiring others to go so much bigger than I had ever fathomed possible were wired in my DNA. It is true that leaders are not born, they are made. I made it my business to surround myself and study with as many inspiring, driven, passionate, successful, impactful humans as possible. I lived for the chance to do this in any and every capacity. I desired from my core to be led and to lead.

Shortly after joining class council during my freshman year of high school and ASB my sophomore year, I started pursuing different clubs to learn more about the high school community, how to impact our school simply, and to garner a better understanding of the gap between what was happening in high school and what was calling to us out in the real world, after graduation.

In my head (the old soul in me, who had studied her Nonno and his living, breathing spirit of community and connection and impact, wanted to do this *now!*), I intended to learn about this now, so I knew what I was fighting for, going after, and living for.

Once my life started to click during sophomore year, I knew it was so much bigger than me at this moment. I recognized I had been introduced to my purpose on this Earth. I had gotten my first connection to God's bigger plan for my soul's purpose and impact.

ST(RIPPED)

Holy smokes! Who did I share this with who wouldn't think I was nuts and out of this world?

This realization was big, it was deep, and I would not relent, because I knew I was blessed to have this understanding at such a young age. I tucked this in my heart and my mind and continued on.

I received an invitation for a luncheon at the Rotary Club, an organization with a commitment to improving the lives of youth and in bridging the gap between students and the community. The luncheon was held off campus. There, our names were presented to a group of adult members who had taken it upon themselves to invest in young people's passions and interests. These Rotarians were invested in the WHY and mission of each student-athlete invited to lunch.

I stayed engaged with this club and the community interactions throughout my high school career. It opened my eyes and gave me some of the most transformational moments of my life. Most notable was when I received the Rotary Youth Leadership Award, which came with a chance to attend my first conference, in Idyllwild, California.

There, that I had my eyes opened to how the words we recite on repeat can become either our superpowers pushing us forward or can be paralyzing. I met Jim Brogan, former NBA player, at this conference. Here, for the first time, I wrote my goals down over and over, making me able to see them unfold.

After this conference, I had embodied them. This was the first time I felt the impact and vibration of the things I said to myself and the crippling effects of fear.

NICCOLE HENDRICKSON

This conference marked another milestone in the transformation on my heart. It opened me up to no longer feeling alone in my deep desire to live out my mission and my bigger goals. This felt not only normalized, but it was encouraged as the norm. I was intrigued, and I put away more ingredients in my arsenal. I was inspired, and I was lit up. The fire had been lit now was stoked.

Chapter 5 Reflections: A Woman On a Mission

Theme: Acknowledging your power, clarifying your goals, and igniting the fire to pursue them

Part 1: Declare the Mission

Prompt

➢ What is the mission that's stirring in you right now?

It doesn't have to be polished — it just has to be *true*.

➢ My Mission Is:

Part 2: Define the Why

Behind every powerful woman on a mission is a *why* that pulls her forward when things get hard.

Prompt:

➢ Why does this mission matter to you? What deeper truth or desire is it connected to?

➢ My Why Is:

Part 3: Set the Flame

Now, get clear. Choose one goal that supports your mission and makes you feel a little lit up inside.

✶ One Clear Goal I'm Setting Is:

✶ Timeline:

I will begin by _____ and I'll complete this step by _____.

NICCOLE HENDRICKSON

PART II

EXPECT THE UNEXPECTED | ST(RIPPED)

"*Relentless* means demanding more of yourself than anyone else can demand, knowing every time you stop, you can still do more."

—Tim Grover

NICCOLE HENDRICKSON

CHAPTER 6

The "St" in St(ripped)

"Adversity introduces a person to themselves. What you do in hard moments is who you are."
—James Lane Allen

One Tuesday, after finishing my college dance class, a chosen elective that kept me connected to the inner wild and femme free spirit that lived within me, I headed up the quad, wearing my black terry-cloth Juicy Couture pants, patent-leather black flats, a fitted T, my messenger bag, and sunnies. I was on a mission to get to my next class, located at least a football-field away.

En route to class, I stopped in the commons area to grab a snack and coffee. When I caught the eye of one of the most gorgeous football players at our school, I flashed a smile, but was thinking I needed to hurry up, and wow, I felt kind of weird. I couldn't name the feeling, but I wasn't right.

I sneezed, and holy smokes! My body nearly collapsed. What was happening? My back went out, and the pain was excruciating. I was so disoriented, and the flood of darkness that came over me was something I had never experienced.

NICCOLE HENDRICKSON

I knew I needed to get out of the commons area. I needed to get out of sight of all these peers, this handsome boy, and the commotion.

Somehow, I made it to the bathroom just up the way, where I dialed one of my teammates and asked her to get the athletic trainer asap. To my utter dismay, they came for me with their cart for carrying injured athletes off the field. They brought me to the training room, the place I had once considered a comfort zone, but now was a place I came to loathe. Here, we had to make some decisions on how I would get help.

I was losing feeling down my left side. I was nauseous, I was hot, and I was not well. I was quickly declining in my physical stature, and my mind raced: all of this lead-up and preparation, for what? For this? To be taken down by a sneeze? What in the actual hell was my body doing?

After listening to several calls talking to the training team, I was transported by my mom to the emergency room. No way in hell was I taking an ambulance, I was not dying. Well, maybe my soul died just a little. My mind was traveling into a dark hole fast, and my body had decided it would take its own course of action.

What was happening? Where did this all go wrong? What a damn disappointment. For a body so well-trained and a woman with so much control over her body to succumb to absolute debilitation from a sneeze... I mean, really, a sneeze?

I knew this doesn't just happen! I was not naive. Something was missing. I was missing something. I believed in having a united front between my heart, mind, and body, so I knew there had to be a disconnect somewhere.

ST(RIPPED)

We made it to the emergency room, only for them to give me a painkiller that did little to nothing. (Fast forward to the wealth of knowledge I have now, after years of formulating an understanding of my anatomy and wellness modalities to support the vessel.) To think: had they tapped into my nervous system, to breathing and to additional medical modalities that would have helped to bring the inflammation down, like dry needling, flossing, heat and ice, or e-stim therapy, maybe I would have been set up for recovery in a much different way. By the time I left the emergency room, I had had X-rays and been given so many general approaches to this injury, my mind was whirling, racing at a pace I could barely keep up with.

All I wanted to know was: how do I get back to what I was doing? How do I reconnect with the mission I set out on? *Who am I now?*

I was injured. What? I don't get injured. And a back injury... This was derailing to say the least. This injury would do a few things:

(1) It forced my eyes open to the reality that what I thought I wanted and what I was actually seeking to accomplish were going to require a hell of a lot more sacrifice, focus, and humility than I had ever imagined.

(2) Who was I really, behind the energetic presence I had become so comfortable with?

(3) What I wanted my power to look like and what it actually was... I was st(ripped) of it, and this would call upon me to find a level of resilience and knowledge I had not even begun to scratch the surface of. What would I do now?

As the days went by, the injury progressed negatively. I could barely recognize the woman in the mirror. I now had a foot drop on my left side, I couldn't walk normally, and I couldn't engage the left side of my body. It was atrophying at an alarming rate. The pain progressed, and the physiological deficiency escalated. The formal diagnosis was terrifying: lumbar disc herniation at L4-L5 with disc bulge and rupture; lumbar spinal stenosis at L4-L5 and L5-S1; left-sided L5 nerve root impingement; left-sided foot drop; and S1 nerve involvement with additional radiculopathy. But even more paralyzing was the mental weight and emotional toll that came with the injury and its aftermath.

I looked into the depths of my soul, and for the first, I did not actually know who I was looking at. I could not connect with the broken-down, unevenly-presented body, the crushed soul, pain-stricken vessel with grayish-toned skin looking back at me through my eyes, the eyes I once looked through and saw nothing but endless possibility.

Just like that, one sneeze changed everything. A sneeze. What had I done? Where did I go? Weak. I was weak, and in such a level of pain I had no idea could exist in my body or mind. It was not the pain you feel from slicing your finger with a knife, not the pain of breaking something and being mended. It was nerve pain, relentless pain that radiated through my vessel like a constant pulse of agony, taunting my senses. No matter what I did, I could *not* escape it. There was no medicine, nothing to escape it. It was the pain of being st(ripped) of every possible morsel of strength I'd ever known. I was literally a living, breathing firecracker of nerves, deficit, and pain. There were times when the nerve pain came second to the darkness my mind was feeling.

I was broken on a level I couldn't understand why I'd deserved it. I quickly slipped into being a young woman whose plans were talked about and set into motion and then completely derailed. I wasn't who I'd envisioned myself to be or what I proclaimed. I felt pathetic.

As the days rolled by, I'd had enough. The pain wasn't subsiding. The decline was occurring physically, but I realized I had a choice and I had better make it quickly.

"No... *No*! This cannot be happening. This is not how I go down. This is not the end of the story. The plot of my life can twist, but no one else gets to decide, *I Do*!"

This situation, this st(ripping) of everything I thought to be true, would be my launching point. Whatever I thought I was just scratched the surface of who I would step into becoming.

The combination of all the modalities prescribed to me were placing me in a hazy phase. Appointment after appointment attempted to place me in a category of humans I refused to relate to; I refused to succumb to the diagnoses and fear. *NO*! The answer was, "NO!" I would not allow any of these white-coated, vanilla-based, fixed-mindset medical professionals to decide my path. I would not accept their diagnosis as my end state. I would simply thank them and gather the intel. I would use the intel to fuel my next steps and learn better questions to ask. I would learn more about my body and things I could and would do to come back, and the comeback would be one for the books. The comeback was personal, and it would mark a milestone met in my life, my story.

By the time I was in motion with a couple of physical therapists, a trainer, and was devouring literature to better understand what had gone wrong, I was in a mindset that was impossible to sate and would have been impossible to reach, had I not experienced this derailment. This derailment, this st(ripping) of what I thought was my power, would only initiate the opening of my eyes, heart, and mind to who I would become, leave behind, and embrace next.

"You have the power to change your beliefs about yourself. Your identity is not set in stone. You have a choice in every moment. You can choose the identity you want to reinforce today with the habits you choose today."
—James Clear

In this process, doors were slamming in my face, but bigger entrances were opening at the same time. It accelerated spiritual growth. It was a level of attention to detail I didn't know could exist. It was a shaping and nurturing of a relentless mindset that I'd thought I had, but I had only begun to scratch the surface.

It was a fierceness I yearned for, while, simultaneously, a surrender that I didn't know I could succumb to. It was humility. This would be my story, the story of not how badly do you want something, but how diligent are you willing to be in the becoming of something. Of someone who is so much bigger than a college athlete on scholarship, when completely st(ripped) of all the known and comfort zones. The "goal" would be the afterthought; this process would be everything. The endurance it would require would be my defining moments.

While I still wanted this accomplishment, what became evident was I really wanted the knowing that I could overcome *anything*. I wanted to embody my becoming. I recognized resilience is not given, it is earned, and I would build my truth and live it.

ST(RIPPED)

Nothing would be given, everything earned: sweat, drop by drop, tear by tear, blood, discomfort, naysayers, humility, and all the odds were against me. That is the comfort zone I would come to know, not a place of ease and assumed reward, but the validation of a resilient mindset and a body honed to overcome any defeat. I would not let up. I would not wait for permission. I would exhaust every level of possibility. I would get my ass handed to me and reconfigure a new plan. I would *NOT LET UP.*

I would embrace obstacles and anticipate instead of fear them. I quickly understood the biggest shift I needed to make was leaving the mind space of "what if" and fully owning the mind space of "even if!"

This injury made me question absolutely everything I knew to be true. And it kicked off the renovation to my headspace that I needed, in order to navigate derailment.

* Step one: Deep audit of me. My thoughts. My belief system. My actions.

* Step two: Invest time in understanding my weaknesses.

* Step three: Commit to Finding a way that breathed life into me.

This required surrender of every cell in me in order to navigate the st(ripping) of who I knew Niccole Ruby Deneke to be. It required me to dissect all that I thought myself to be and all the plans I had made in order to nourish that version of me. If a sneeze could shift it all for me, then what would happen if something more tragic came about? This was a horrible moment for me, revealing what actually was. It was an unveiling to the darkness, a darkness I could choose to explore or run from.

I decided to head boldly down this trail and seek to understand how something as meaningless as a sneeze could be the thing that opened my relentless mindset to refocus on more than becoming a collegiate athlete with a determined mindset. It was so much more than this, and I knew it.

I knew the moment I stepped foot into the ER, this was something so much greater than a life-altering injury. It was insight to depths of despair, stress, and nervous-system dysfunction. To this day, I wish I knew then what I know now. I wish I had access to the incredible doctors and practitioners whom I have met over the years since. I wish for this, but I am equally grateful I didn't, because the trail I have traveled in order to arrive at the state of being I am in now is a direct result of learning to *first* trust myself, while I was also learning to surrender and trust the process.

It is important to note, as a strong, limitless, mutifaceted, driven female, we do not always want help. We do not want to believe a derail such as a life-altering injury can take us off course via something as simple as a sneeze. But the truth, is the sneeze is so much more than a sneeze.

To refuse to acknowledge the depths is to refuse the greatness you proclaim to want to harness on the other side of the trail you must navigate to get there. The sneeze was s(tripping) or purging one identity that I had believed held it all for me. Without that sneeze, I would've never had the derail that put me on a far better "trail" than I ever could have asked for.

The trail has been tedious, but it was scaled for what I am wired for and meant to share. My hope for you—or

ST(RIPPED)

anyone close to you—who has faced an injury or illness that's altered the course of your dreams or quality of life, is that you hold onto this truth: **it is never too late to rewire your nervous system, transform defeat into triumph, and step boldly into the vibrant life you deserve.**

The derail, the st(ripping) of what I thought to be my power, pathway, and focus, not only revealed a surrender I wasn't aware that I needed; it also provided a beautiful gift of leaning into the strengths of the key people who impacted my life as a child. My Grandma Ruby was a pillar in leading a life built of strength and resilience.

Strength is often built and honed through repeated physical activity, which demands that you respond to the stimulus and tension provided. Internal strength is built through similar demands and requires deep self-reflection, awareness, empathy, and humility.

The compounding of challenging moments in my Grandma Ruby's life produced a woman of deep strength and unshatterable will. You could place her photo in the dictionary beside the word *determination*.

In her early forties, my grandma was diagnosed with cervical cancer. She accepted a trial treatment that would either work with residual health havoc, or it would not and her life would wrap up shortly, leaving behind five children and a husband whose existence was nothing short of a miracle. With cancer treatments being new and unfamiliar, every possibility was simply an act of hope, with some science blended. Her tenacity, fearless faith, and commitment to living sustained her through the process.

The treatments were unfathomably reckless, compared to today's treatment modalities. The treatments' poison was distributed mindlessly into the body, and it wreaked the havoc, leaving other health deficiencies. Not only did she lose her hair for the rest of her lifetime, but her thyroid lost function, and her kidneys became less than optimal, causing ongoing day-to-day health issues. Her optimal function went from a hundred percent to sixty-five, at best. But she was alive and would own her sixty-five percent, making it the new 100%. Where her body lacked, her mind, heart, and spirit soared past 100%!

There was no stopping this woman. Where there was committed will, there was an unbelievable way. The st(ripping) of her health only encouraged her will to find a better way to enjoy her life.

Fear Will Trip Your Becoming

I spent years refining my process and embodying the details of my yearned-for identity. I overcame the st(ripping) of one aspect of my dream: that sneeze that took me out, the one that changed the whole trajectory of my collegiate volleyball career. I overcame the adversity of training, the missed playing time, and the shattering of what I'd believed was the exact recipe for my desired success and my longed-for journey to achieve my bigger vision.

I clearly saw the power in surrendering. and I was the underdog who rose to my desired occasion. Fast forward to when I was in the company of the team I had longed to be a part of. I was with the coaches I had I deeply desired to be mentored by. But those, along with the uniforms, the schedule, the training, and the whole experience, were unraveling in front of me.

I was in it, and I was also observing it from a detached viewpoint, almost like I wasn't living it, but rather watching what I had envisioned for this chapter of my life. I was too scared to fully own it, because, God forbid, it might be taken away again. I might lose it, and maybe this st(ripping) wouldn't be a build-back as I had done before. Maybe it had all happened accidentally, and the next round couldn't be replicated.

Holy hell, the doubt cycle became crippling. I began to wonder whether maintaining and honing my edge was even sustainable. Was I even tuned into what my vision was anymore? Or was I merely going through the motions?

Here's a real question: have you ever worked so hard for something then overcome an obstacle that took you away from that desired achievement, gotten back in it, and then failed to fully allow yourself to reengage 100%, out of fear of losing what you have?

I don't think I am alone in this experience. I believe the fear of "letting go" in order to become the next desired version of yourself is something crippling for most of us. It occurs in our relationships, during the growth in our careers, and affects our commitment to change. I think the fear of actually having the life we want or the relationships we desire or the success we yearn for and the goals we set out to crush, becomes a state more focus than the actual process of owning and embodying the person we desire to become or the goal we have worked for. The fear interferes with the actual ability to be all in.

The fear takes us away from our full presence and ownership. The fear keeps you one foot out, "just in case." This will crush your becoming every time. Your body-mind-soul will eventually acknowledge this disconnect and this fraying in your attempted embodiment.

We have to figure out the "strip" to the ripping, the breakdown before the build back in order to become. I believe we set out to accomplish and achieve, meet the person we want to be with and attain the career we desire or the life we want, and then we get into flow. When we are derailed, we have the option to quit, to make an excuse that it wasn't really for us. Or, we have the option to boldly embrace the st(ripping), embrace the build back of said needed process.

Then, there is a next level to the st(ripping). It's the embodiment and ownership of the build, the strength and resilience we discovered in the process. It is fully owning this next evolution of you and releasing the old. For me, this is the piece I struggled to harness for years. It wasn't until years after my first injury, which st(ripped) me of what I believed was my power and edge, that I realized I was evolving. But I was also refusing to allow the previous versions of myself to be fully st(ripped), to be let go.

This showed up in my mindset. This was the disconnect I felt when experiencing a level of fear around not being able to sustain the work I had put in, that maybe attaining my dream of becoming a college athlete, which I had worked so hard for, was all just luck. This showed up in allowing me to believe my coaches had a lack of depth and were not supportive of my commitment to become. I allowed the naysayers around me, like my peers and some family members, to cultivate doubt within me. As a result, I began to overtrain, and my unreasonable demands for perfection reemerged. It also manifested in flare-ups of my pain during college and into adulthood.

These painful flare-ups were subconscious reminders from my nervous system that I hadn't fully released the trauma or the stories that went with it. After my first injury in college, I realized the amount of effort I was expending to remain detached from my comeback meant I was not

ST(RIPPED)

letting go of previous versions of myself. I was resisting stepping into any new chapters of my story out of my fear of being unfamiliar with the version of me whom I was actually becoming.

Let's be real, most times in life, we set out for one thing, and what we become, who we meet, what we learn, plus the unexpected often end up being so much more than we ever could fathom. This is the "light" that is discovered from darkness, if we allow ourselves the gift of being open in the process versus fixed in our mindset.

I bore witness to glimmers of this, but I sure as hell was not equipped for it yet. I was so focused on reaching a specific goal that I created a lot of stress for myself—physically, mentally, and emotionally. I couldn't let go of the identity I had tied to becoming a college athlete, even though that version of me was stripped away after my injury during freshman year. Life was calling me toward something greater, but first, I had to release the pain of not "making it" the way I had imagined. I was being called to so much more in life on the other side of this derailment, but I had to let go... Let go of the pain tied to not "making it" in the ways I thought it should look.

"Your competition is the attitude, habits, discipline and the choices you make on a daily basis."

What felt like a lifetime of creating, studying, researching, testing, and pivoting amounted to only a fragment of the time I would commit to this dream. It was a mere "taste-tester" to what I deeply wanted in my life.

For a fragment of time, I began to experience the fruits of my labor and focus, the evolution of my mindset, and the courage and commitment that served as proof of what is possible, when you set your mind to a state that deeply aligns with your purpose and passions. When you unite your physical efforts with the deep calling inside of you.

The pursuit for excellence, evolution, and impact served as simple beacons of light for the unknown darkness that awaited me. The unknown elements of my ego and the real questions: "How bad do you want your dream? Have you truly considered what it costs? Have you identified all the parameters? Are you clear on what your dream actually is? Do you know why you want to bring this dream to life? Can you sustain it, once brought to life?"

The answer is "*No!*" I had no idea the full magnitude of what I'd set out to do. I only knew it was all possible with my relentless, gritty, never-say-die attitude. I knew I could sustain what was to come, because I had become something from nothing but a mindset that cared zero fucks about interference. However, I was blissfully ignorant of all the forms that pushback could materialize as. I had failed to consider that the derailment came in more forms than I had fully acknowledged.

What I did know: I trusted in myself deeply to navigate any and all pushback. I was devoted to the "becoming." I saw only possibility, never impossibility. I would be victorious despite my naivetés. I had to be: it was the only choice I would allow myself to make. The only path I would allow my mindset to travel.

For this headspace, I thank my Papa, my Grandma Ruby, my Nonno, and my dad for modeling what it looked and felt like to stay the path, despite opposition and defeat. To stay in line with my purpose. To welcome obstacles in

ST(RIPPED)

the name of growth. To know light is always found through the darkness.

I would not break in the st(ripping). I would reemerge. I would listen differently to my body, my soul.

Fast Track to Freedom

All the tight-ass timelines I held and the power in my level of organization were admirable. I was a walking level of dialed-in, yet confined by my own parameters. My move to Colorado helped reveal the freedom I sought to experience in my day-to-day.

I had spent a year or so on a slight detour, pausing my pace of life to tend to my brother's healing after unexpected open-heart surgery in December, 2009. I took refuge in the comfort of my family, and we navigated the aftermath of his health crisis together.

I was in the early stages of my new life in Colorado, which I had been so certain about. Moving away from "home" wasn't a new experience for me, but this was a new version of seeking freedom and a mission to dial that in. I came in "hot and confident" when I moved to Colorado. I was a mission to explore and create a life, not to allow life to create me.

I had actively decided I would seek out what I needed and wanted, instead of waiting to be introduced to it. This required me to st(rip) elements of my identity. I had to leave behind my need to have things perfect, dialed in, and known before I arrived. I deeply craved the chance to figure it out along the way and to see what would happen if I showed up and allowed myself to evolve based on the unexpected and the "to be determined," in order to explore who I became in the process of the unknown...

NICCOLE HENDRICKSON

I was on a mission to foster as many new connections as possible, to seek new perspectives, and to navigate my new landscape through a multitude of lenses. I explored new coffee shops and boutiques, and I mixed in the known with the unknown. I went to places that sparked my interest while also challenging my comfort zones. I got lost in the city and drove to new spaces to explore what the culture was like in all the areas of the new state where I lived.

I wanted to form an opinion based on my experience, not the opinions of my boyfriend at the time and his circle. I was determined to know my city for when friends came to visit. I was determined to commit to getting lost and embracing it as valued time versus lost opportunity. I intended to let go of my need to have it all understood and figured out and to embrace what unraveled along the way. It was one of the most freeing and exciting times of my life!

When you are new somewhere, don't fear the unknown or the loneliness that can accompany you in the process. Give yourself the gift of endless opportunity. I am a huge advocate for courting your own aspirations. The best way to do this is to allow yourself to be new, alone, and in discovery mode.

When people move somewhere new, so often I've noticed how they start with a level of intrigue and excitement and then fail to court the aspirations they had about moving, so they find themselves lonely and disappointed in their move. You can make magic anywhere. You have to allow yourself the freedom to st(rip) comfort zones to discover what's available on the other side.

Chapter 6 Reflections

To be *st(ripped)* **is to ask:**

- ♥ What have I outgrown but still been gripping tightly?
- ♥ Where have I been cracked open—and what light has started to come through?
- ♥ What truth has been revealed beneath the image, the pace, the noise?
- ♥ What strength am I only now discovering in the aftermath of release?

CHAPTER 7

Grit, Perseverance, Determination

One summer, my Papa opened up and shared with me all about his honor receiving the Purple Heart. His pain and pride were palatable. I became obsessed with every detail. I wanted to know all about the *WHY* he had received this, who he had been in that moment, how he sustained, what the medal meant to him, and why it meant so much to me. My questions and curiosity were endless.

Somehow, knowing all this flooded into my deep desire to embody his excellence, courage, and fearlessness. Holding my name in a way that would support the strength, fortitude, and integrity of his lifetime achievement of courage and grit was my sacred duty.

To this day, I do not understand why he chose me to share all of these stories with and then, to give his medal to. He has three sons, a daughter, and a dozen grandchildren, so it meant the world to me that Papa wanted me to have this medal, which recognized his sacrifice, bravery, and strength. I will never forget his story and those experiences he shared with me.

As a member of the famed 101st Airborne, the Screaming Eagles, my Papa experienced his first combat on June 6, 1944, known as D-Day. He and his unit, the 501

ST(RIPPED)

Parachute Infantry Regiment (PIR), jumped into France at 1:00 a.m. on June 6. Shortly afterward, his unit conducted another combat jump into Holland, as part of the infamous operation, Market Garden, also known as the Bridge Too Far. Thousands of British and American troops were killed in that ill-planned operation.

My Papa's last combat engagement occurred in the Ardennes at Bastogne, Belgium, in the Battle of the Bulge. Papa was wounded on December 27, 1944. He was sent to the rear area for immediate medical care and then to a harbor on the coast of France. Finally, he returned to the United States on a hospital ship and anchored in Baltimore, Maryland.

He chose wisely when his heart fell hard for my Grandma Ruby.

She was a woman of strength, faith, independence, optimism, and patience, a shrewd judge of character with firm boundaries and unconditional love. Their love story will forever be one of my favorites. Oftentimes, I dream of it being a plot for the next Nicholas Sparks movie. Their love was the real thing.

Their love story threaded its roots throughout my whole being, from my childhood to well past their Earthside existence. Their connection, love, respect, and commitment were built on genuinely finding love right where they were. It was good enough because it was built on a foundation of truth, openness, and unwavering commitment to always grow together and fight for their deep-rooted love and commitment, *no matter what*. It was a love built on, "Yes, I love you, all of you, and I will only commit to knowing and growing in your love."

NICCOLE HENDRICKSON

That focus was something I tethered myself to. I came back to it multiple times in my life. It was my gravity to fight against all odds and the distractions of life, the persuasion of evil, and any flare of doubt.

When my Papa was stationed at Fort Bragg but not involved in training events, he and his buddies spent the weekend in Baltimore. During this period, Baltimore was a bustling city with the most significant military harbor on the East Coast. Papa and his fellow airborne buddies would take the train from North Carolina to Baltimore to enjoy the city's great seafood, dancing, and cheap beer. On one momentous occasion, Papa was asked by one of his buddies to tag along on a double date. Unbeknownst to him, he was about to meet the 5'9", breathtaking classic beauty, Ruby.

Limitless. My Grandma Ruby was simply limitless. I always credit my determination and desire to find a way to her. They say this generation of men and women had no choice but strength and resilience. I disagree; there is always a choice. However, most members of this generation chose wisely and embodied a degree of tenacity that is as rare as someone holding a million dollars. My Grandma Ruby would be my life's pillar of hope, perseverance, and faith.

Her roots were in Virginia; she was raised in a holler or small valley that runs up the side of a mountain. Her father worked in a coal mine, as did most of the men who lived in Virginia hollers. She was the oldest of four children who graduated high school in just three years and was the star basketball player for her school.

In the holler where she resided, she lived near an aunt and two uncles, both of whom were in Europe, fighting the Nazis. Grandma told me she was always very close to her father. She was ten years older than her next sibling. She spent much of her free time with her father, while her mother raised the other three younger children.

Living in a holler limited her social life and opportunity to grow. Her world was small, the opportunities were few, and she craved freedom, independence, and more possibilities. She was on a mission to see the world at the first chance she could. The world, in her eyes, was outside the tiny home town that stifled her dreams.

The first chance she had, she took a job in Maryland, where she could explore and redefine her path and purpose. She shared a deep bond with her father; he was a mentor, a safe place to dream, a truth-teller, a devoted man to his faith, and an ambassador for her to expand outside the world while he worked very hard to provide for her and her siblings.

I can't help but relate to the power that comes to a young woman when she has her father's unconditional love and support. This bond she shared became a living teacher for generations to come. It was her place of gravity for the instability ahead. It served as her accessible power to pull from, when life presented her with health challenges, lack of resources, and uncertainty.

"What others say about you is none of your business. What others fear about you is not your burden to carry. What others do in an attempt to derail you is a warning call to who you 're keeping as company."

—Niccole Hendrickson

Harnessing Your Grit

During my sophomore year in college, I was able to show off the relentless work I had put in behind the scenes, not

NICCOLE HENDRICKSON

just physically, but mentally and emotionally, as well. The young girl who showed up on campus in the fall of 2005 was not the same young woman who returned in 2006.

I knew this was not only my one shot to get myself noticed by potential scouts for four-year college volleyball; it was also my opportunity to show myself who actually lived within me and who was also semi-fearful to be *fully* seen. This was the year I allowed myself to experience myself while also revealing my fullness to my peers and coaches.

This was my *becoming*.

This year was about leading in the direction I *knew* I would go, in order to arrive at the next spot to facilitate my bigger mission of impact, not where I *hoped* I would go. Hope and dreaming were for my earlier years. This was now calculated action.

The dialogue between me and my teammates. So did the dynamic between me and my head coach. This man went from, "This girl has a level of potential and interest" to "This girl is going somewhere." It was only a matter of where and when I decided; but there would be no interrupting me.

There is a palpable energy experienced when you go from the headspace of "I hope" to "I will." This isn't to say I wasn't living in some elements of my "I will" presence. However, sophomore year, when I first set out to make this mission part of my reality, it became wildly clear to me that I was still in the infancy of my becoming. I believed in myself more than most people could ever fathom, but I was still living with levels of uncertainty that my body could sense. I was grinding myself down in ways that didn't support the bigger path I so deeply desired to have a shot at traveling.

ST(RIPPED)

My grind was an over-compensation for the time I needed to actually evolve into this version myself. I believe God knows our bigger plans, and our vessels also know what we truly can handle. While I put in admirable amounts of discipline, focus, commitment, integrity, and sacrifice during high school, it was clear I wasn't quite ready for what was to come on other levels. So, naturally, in college there had to be some sort of derailment to snap my focus into where it needed to shift, in order to properly prepare for whatever my story was ahead.

While we can all choose to believe, to view our derailments, and accept our stories in different ways, I am here to vouch for what happens when you actively choose to pursue the endless possibilities to be found in the surrender required to build or rebuild your truth in resilience. I choose to validate the power that occurs in the st(ripping) of your being.

There are popular sayings like, "There is beauty in the breakdown," "Greatness emerges from darkness," and "You have no idea how strong you are until you are fighting for your life." They are popular for a reason. When we are st(ripped) of what we believe our power to be, there is endless opportunity to meet versions of ourselves who are packed with determination, strength and resilience. My first introduction to this st(ripping) was in my initial injury.

For me, it was challenging at times to make up for the years I didn't have of volleyball skill development. However, every skill I lacked I made up for in: strength, explosivity, leadership, commitment, and tenacity. I clung to my grit. I had to *accept,* though, that the lost time was something I could never get back. Acceptance was essential to my ability to propel into the next chapter of this dream. I had no choice, and it would require absolute humility.

This season on my college team, we also got access to a conditioning coach, which was a welcome home feeling for me. This was a space I thrived in. Plyo ladders, cones, fields, bands, stop watches—*Hell Yes!* I was in my zone. These were the moments I lived for. I had been studying drills like these for years. With my dad's workouts, I had experienced my own body move through these drills prior to being a part of this team. So, this was my zone of comfort, thanks to being behind the scenes with his high school football team. This was the edge where I had begun my own sheer fascination with strength and conditioning when I was fourteen.

It had started with curiosity and moved to my commitment to a plan that incorporated drills like this as a necessity to my *becoming*. There was something so beautiful not only to watch but to experience my own body move in an elegant but explosive way. I loved who I was when I trained in this way. I was limitless! With each call out/cue of the timer, from the synchrony of feet shuffling to bodies moving, it was elegance and power all in one. To give your all-out effort with the lightest touch and the most power possible, it was simply freeing.

The mental focus and the unification of mind to body were two things I committed to perfecting. This was an area where I thrived. I became intrigued about how much more effective any athlete could be on the court or in the weight room when they were dialed into their body. The mind-body connection was essential to executing any desired outcome.

ST(RIPPED)

During high school, I had been introduced to the power of visualization. I used this skill to bring my hopes, dreams, and goals into mini-realities. However, I honed this skill during my early college years. While I early in my recovery for my back injury, I used the power of visualization to see my body moving in the ways I wanted and needed it to, even though it wasn't quite possible yet. When my left side of my body was not firing fully, I sat in deep thought on what it would feel like and look like to move it.

Eventually I took the visualization from getting my body to fire and flex to actually moving it in the ways I needed to, in order to execute movement patterns for hitting a ball, passing a ball, and blocking a ball. I would see myself and imagine feeling these parts of my body doing what I needed it to do. It was exhausting and defeating at times, but it was also a powerful distraction from the nerve pain I experienced with the injury.

The mental space occupied by nerve pain is unspeakable! There was only one way to counter it: by replacing those thoughts with something else productive. I would slide in and out of what was productive and the pain. The scoreboard started with barely getting by with a "productive win." Sometimes it was tie. But I practiced this diligently until I eventually had landslide victories within my visualizations with only hints of energy going to the pain. This was a victory.

We can decide either to identify with the pain or repurpose it and identify with the fuel and resilience it provided for us. I chose the latter.

I would go on to earn a starting position on my college team, following my rehab. I stepped into a stronger role, too, not only as a leader on the court but as a valuable asset, skills-wise. While my volleyball prowess was still emerging at this stage, I was living out the fruits of my labor in the weight room, conditioning, and lifestyle. I was mastering the skills I later realized would serve me in my life, not just in the short stint living my collegiate-athlete dream.

As I wrapped up my season with my JC team, I was just warming up for what lay ahead: the Junior College Sophomore Showcase. This was where potential recruits for four-year universities got one more shot at being noticed and recruited. This was my first goal: to get an invitation there. Next was to show up and make an impression. While this event served as a milestone, I sincerely remember only going to the showcase, working my ass off, and heading home with my parents, knowing I had left nothing behind on the courts that day. I gave every piece of my heart to the drills and every piece of my soul to the hours that were demanded of me. That had to be enough.

The coaches who attended the showcase came from all over the U.S. A couple of coaches were very memorable. They spent a lot of time watching me play then commended and scrutinized me. I pinned their images in my mind. Once I was done at the showcase, I left those images hanging in my memory before I moved on. I thought to myself, "Our worlds will collide at another date. When or for what, I am not sure."

Weeks later, I was presented with a few options. By now, I was no longer uncertain about where I wanted to focus my four-year degree: I knew exactly what I wanted out of a program. I was also still teetering on a deep soul aspiration to attend a university that bled their colors. Part of me dreamed of going somewhere that was all Friday-night lights and school pride to the Nth degree. A school that lived and breathed their alma mater.

I was also up against options to play volleyball versus how far I really wanted to go in my degree program. When I think about it all now, I wish I had given myself more opportunities to explore different programs, because there are thousands. But there is also a more certain part of me that truly believes and knows I ended up exactly in the spot that my higher calling wanted me.

> *"So it goes... All the pieces fall, right into place..."*
> —Taylor Swift

Naturally, I Tag-Team my Becoming with Exploring. Unpredictable Exploring.

During my sophomore year of college, I called in a lot of transformation, which was tied to a lot of testing my capacity and the intricacies of how I was wired. Also, this was the first time in my life when I allowed myself to be in a full-on relationship.

Fawk me, I had no idea what I was getting into when I fell for a guy who was also a collegiate athlete on a mission to see through his own next steps. One with a past and a name for himself that didn't fully align with me, but, needless to say, our youth called us to make some decently illogical choices.

These choices have made it into this book for one reason and one reason *only*: there are thousands of other women in this world who have either walked this similar path or will be tempted to walk a path like mine. I am hopeful they will read this and go the complete opposite direction than the

NICCOLE HENDRICKSON

one I travelled for four-plus years. This is my take, my story, and my red flags to learn from. Hoping yours isn't as interruptive as mine. Got it?

I believe that every moment lived, every hurt felt, every element of challenge experienced, every obstacle presented, and every hurdle barely cleared is a chance to learn something remarkable about yourself. I always hope and pray that we remain safe as much as possible. I pray there is a guardian angel watching over as much of the process as possible.

One Thursday afternoon post-match, we were wrapping up practice, and my teammates were brewing up our weekend plans based on invitations we'd received. This weekend, we committed to a house party thrown by one of the football players. This was not the norm, to be honest. We rarely gave the football team our time or attention. And during this particular season, the guys who played were not our favorites. Now, the basketball team and the water polo guys, *they* were a blast and so kind. It certainly helped that one of my cousins played on the water polo team, and we were great childhood friends.

We competed on Friday night, as well. On Saturday, we had a slow post-game recovery, and then my firecracker Texan and I did what we always did: meet up that afternoon to scour the racks at Forever 21 and nab our newest outfit for the weekend. We got ready together and rolled to the party that night.

It was at what seemed be some rich kid's parents' house, because the set up was over the top, and the amenities were like hanging out in the game room of a hotel. Of course, there were drinks and games and no shortage of noise and stupidity.

ST(RIPPED)

That night I was greeted by a guy, who we will call Joe. Joe made his way back to JC after making some immature choices while he was on a full scholarship freshman year at a four-year school. This should've been my first and only red flag. Apparently, though, I was just beginning my era of, "I can lead this one to greatness too!"

The night I met him, I stayed occupied by hanging with my friends, having drinks, and not allowing myself to get pinned down in conversation with just him. Before the night was over, he asked for my number.

Texts began to fly, but I didn't commit to hanging out with him for weeks. I also didn't run. I didn't tell him thanks but no thanks. I just dragged him along for some time, doing back-and-forths over possible hangouts, until finally, a month or so later, I agreed to meet up with him for a beach run.

That initial run led to a chase I found nearly impossible to sate, but I did give in to more dates until, eventually, I was his girlfriend. I think his relentless pursuit of me let him into my heart in some way.

As I look back, I see how the failures in this relationship revealed so much about me, as a young woman, and the things I still needed to address. Sure, I liked a healthy dose of distraction to keep me on my toes. But little did I know this would be a distraction that cost me a lot of mental and emotional energy. This distraction came to imprint my life forever.

The next red flag was that my brother and dad despised this guy. Well, I knew better, of course. But this conflict added stress to my life that, later, was detrimental to my health. And this wasn't because I needed their approval. But I trusted these two men with everything in my life, They always had my best interests at heart. While most saw my dad as scary AF and my brother as intimidating, I knew them and had bonds with them, so I had forged levels of trust that no one else was privy to. Our bonds gave each of us the ability to speak with one another in ways most siblings and father-daughters could not.

Despite all that, I 100% bypassed their opinion and ignored everything they knew, felt, and shared with me. So, I went for it. I disregarded all my red flags and belief in my family name and reputation. Somehow, I knew better, and I chose to participate in a low that was hitting some sort of high for me at the time. Somehow, walking this scary tightrope of a dynamic, I found a level of safety, because I knew there was an expiration. He had been signed and moving on to his four-year. I had been signed and moving onto *my* four-year at the end of summer. In my head, this was temporary and short-lived, so why not?

With this relationship came character-building and tests. I had never experienced being disliked by someone's family. I had never experienced such an intense amount of discrimination by someone's friends. I had never been in a situation where grown adults saw me as a threat to someone's future. I had never experienced both despising and relishing the push-back at the same time. It was a time of mental and emotional chaos, to say the least. It was walking into a fire that was going to burn, but somehow, I subscribed to this mayhem voluntarily. And somehow, the pushback from each of our circles also fueled the dynamic between us. This guy had something I needed to fulfill within my *becoming,* and there was *no* turning away from it.

Every month was a step in the wrong direction. But I did discover more intel about myself. The closer the two of us came to our launch points to college, the more intense everything became. The intensity brewed in the cold, hard truth that we were not meant to be together or stay together, yet we were tethered in some sick way.

I never faltered in my training, my academics, or the focus needed to keep me well, but somewhere in all of this, the part of my brain was faltering that typically maintained a level of discernment for my heart and emotional wellbeing. I was being swallowed by the nonsense this guy's family was spewing.

During our time together, I did earn the love and respect of his mother and one sister, but his father feared me. I realized his fear wasn't about whether I was going to interrupt his son's chances of being recruited again, because I is attached to him and not strong in pursuing my own objectives. No, his paranoia was flipped 180 degrees. He knew I would not give up my own aspirations. He recognized that my work ethic, drive, and focus were three things nobody, not even his son, could deter me from.

His father's fear was that his son would give up on himself and meld into my world. The father's fear revealed just how deeply broken his son had become. Despite their playing with my emotions, still my fortitude outweighed the psychological manipulation. I saw this in how the father acted, in the mean things he said about me, and his complete lack of accountability to encourage his son to be a man and own his own display of manipulation. He never had the courageous conversation with my boyfriend, saying, "Hey, son, this girl is going somewhere with her dreams, as well. You need to back off and own your pathway." Instead, he worked diligently to tear down my character and try to show his son I was not a worthy person in his life.

Meanwhile, my boyfriend was trying desperately to lock me down in unbelievable ways. He shared his desire to get me pregnant and have me pause my path to my aspirations, trying to convince me to stay in this relationship. But we had this timeline for departure, as I'd planned, that would put thousands of miles between us. And we each had college contracts binding us for our sports

Once I arrived at school, I knew I would have intense demands on both my schedule and emotional state that would put a semi-protective cocoon around my being. But I carried the weight of this nervous-system blowout into my initial year at the university after I transferred. It was a shock to my system to finally have space from this dynamic and to reflect. It was very messed up to realize I was in a relationship with such a narcissistic man and desperately wanted out, yet there I was, yearning for that very relationship…

We received big news that broke just ten weeks before I was due to report to school and move into my off-campus housing: *New head coach and staff hired to lead the women's volleyball team into a new era.*

Holy smokes, this was thrilling and absolutely terrifying. I was thrilled, because the coach had an intriguing résumé, but I was also terrified, because I had not been recruited by her. This could mean a lot of things. I was also a junior transfer, which meant I had privileges that most first and second years did not.

Soon after the news broke, my email inbox began to blow up. All of our onboarding materials came via email, including a training program. As I read over this program,

ST(RIPPED)

my heart flared with excitement, and I developed a little more interest in this new coach. Her levels of expectation and organization, I could get behind.

I set to work on this program, learning the lay of my "new land." I was also introduced to my roommate. Worse, my dorm-room roommate.

"Roommate? Wait, *what*?" I had off-campus housing with a friend all set up...

New coach, new rules, new plan. *ALL transfers, for their first year, will report to the dorms and be on campus*! Are you serious right now? I was nineteen years old and not going to live in a dorm with a group of gals in a twin extra-long!

Here's the deal. Many kids yearn for this. Heck, if my kids choose a traditional college route, I hope my kids they'll start their higher-education journey this way, living on campus for their first couple of years. But for me, this ship had sailed. I had gone a different direction for my first two years at college, and I had *no* interest in sliding backward in my life. I was already an old soul with a dialed-in routine, and I most definitely *did not* want to share my space with a bunch of immature, out-of-control, hormonally freedom-driven kids. Shared common spaces, sticky kitchen floors, fire alarms pulled in the middle of the night, and smelly-ass trash were not on my list for a desirable living experience. *AGHHHH!*

But there was no escaping this. This was my reality. I was introduced to my dorm room "winingmate," who was also a junior transfer and my teammate. We were both pursuing the same major and both from beach towns in California, but we grew up on opposite sides of the state. She was a driven, uptight, anxious perfectionist. This would be fun. But, we would become friends, though, and navigate together all these waters we had not anticipated.

The team we had been recruited onto was stacked with seven seniors. These women were tightknit, unruly, and ran the program, bonded by their carelessness and mean-girls vibe. The previous coach had allowed them to run amuck and get by with minimum accountability, which was clear if you looked at their team record and personal reputations. I really hadn't heard about this reputation during my recruiting trip. The more interactions I had with the team, the more I wondered what on Earth I had committed to.

As the days rolled on, I quickly realized how many the shifts were happening very, very fast. The university had been in the process of moving from DIII to DII. The new conference we were joining was competitive, accountable, and demanding. The new staff had come in to clean up shop and curate a legit program. In my naiveté during my initial recruitment. I didn't catch all of the dirty details, but it is also quite possible I could have never known, because it was guarded information. Like it or not, I had signed, and this is where I would be for at least this year.

The previous staff had secured a spot for our team to compete in a tournament held in Hawaii before the season kicked off, and to be honest, this was *all* the seven seniors cared about. They could care less about the actual season ahead; it was all about going on this trip and playing in this tournament. They felt entitled to this opportunity, and nothing would rip it away from them. At the same time, the team knew it could be taken away at any given moment. The tension here was unnerving. This tournament became the carrot dangled before their eyes to guarantee a faster buy-in to the new program flow.

ST(RIPPED)

The seniors' bonds deepened, and they developed an "us versus them" mentality. But the gals' deficiencies cleared up to survive and present an annoying unified front to the transfers like me, who were just joining their team, along with the new staff. Let's state this right away: the ring leaders of the seven seniors were not fans of mine. In fact, I was their worst nightmare: a driven self-starter, fit, dynamic, a leader, structured, strong, disciplined, and kind. They loathed me!

Even though they knew I was not recruited by the new staff, somehow, they grouped me into the nightmare they were living. To be real, I didn't care for them. I was never disrespectful, but I would not cave to their deception, either.

It turned out the real reasons they despised me began when I refused to engage with their dishonesty. It was true, outside of them being my teammates, there was nothing about them that caught my interest.

I was walking a fine line during my transfer year. Just eighteen months ago, I had come back from a life-changing injury, and now was *no* time to engage with activities or people who would distract me from the entire reason I'd ended up at this particular four-year university. I would not relent for them, their likes, or their patronization. I simply focused on reentering a blend of my observation phase of life, as well as staying in line with who I had become, post-injury-1. This environment would either grow me or dampen my spirit.

"A cheerful heart is good medicine, but a broken spirit saps a person's strength."

—Proverbs 17:22

NICCOLE HENDRICKSON

New Season, Determination On

Prior to the start of the next school, we all met up on campus to train, condition, and dial our team dynamics. It was a shitshow to arrive at any sense of being a team, but we did it. We slowly started letting go of the previous year's toxicity, which had included the old practices of our previous coaching staff and a major lack of structure.

It took a slow and steady build to unite us all on the common ground we walked and to find the similarities in our *WHY*, while also temporarily letting go of our differences. Ultimately, that sealed the deal for us to become a real team was everyone realizing how special it was to put on matching uniforms. In appreciating the common language that we spoke on the court. In recognizing we could push one another to new heights and enjoy the experience, because no one was pushing alone for something singular. The team required all of us, not one of us. It was also recognizing the power generated when we ripped off our ego-driven masks and dared to learn something new about one another.

Every single person came to realize they had a teammate, a sister, in every other athlete. This was our chosen sisterhood, at least for the season. We needed to live by this code in order to attain the end goal we all wanted: a trip to Hawaii and a fall season competing and living out an element of the passion we all possessed, in one way or another.

To the credit of our staff, they held the line initially and fostered a positive transition. It was clear, though, that they were biding their time until this crew graduated. In the interim, they did their best to bring organization and dignity to the program.

ST(RIPPED)

When we were six weeks into pre-season training, conditioning, and team-building, I found a decent flow with my dorm-room setting, practice, team dynamics, and prehab routines. I was sore from the volume of workouts we were doing but not unfamiliar with the grind. I was dialed into the possible role I would play on this team, court-wise, and I had established my voice and leadership role among my unruly team.

I had also earned the reluctant respect from a handful of gals, including some of the senior seven. They were wary of me and loved to hate me, but they also knew it was their own baggage and laziness that had brought on these feelings. As they began to know me, study me, and spend time around me, they had no choice but to recognize my actual intentions which, unfortunately for them, were golden.

At one midweek practice, the first of two that day, we were running passing drills on both courts. In round six of this drill, I had just finished my pass and sprinted to the net to retrieve the next ball from my teammate. These drills, when everyone was dialed in, were truly my favorite. They were like a choreographed dance. Each athlete moved with power, grace, and focus. Every athlete matched, wearing their team swag, and used their voice to call out their role, with the gals around them listening and ready to respond. To this day, the chaos and synchrony of these drills fills my soul with a flood of memories.

I was up. I squatted down to retrieve the ball in a passing form, and I never made it back up. That was it. Just like that... My back. It was out, and I was down for the count.

Fuck my life.

NICCOLE HENDRICKSON

Here we go again.

This time was worse than before, because I knew *E-X-A-C-T-L-Y* what was happening and what I was up against.

The once-serene mayhem of passing drills, shuffling footsteps, and high fives became the sounds I wanted to flee immediately.

My coaches rushed to me along with a couple teammates. I let them know I needed the trainer right away, plus a minute to gather my pride, my focus, and my grit. I slowly crawled on my hands and knees to the other side of the court, so practice could resume and I wouldn't be more of a spectacle than I already was.

There were nine million things going through my mind and heart, but the number-one thing was: "You are not alone, Niccole." I kept praying for peace and release of whatever control I thought I'd had in my life up to that point.

The athletic trainer came quickly to my side. One of the perks of a four-year campus was a setup conducive to high-level athletics and taking care of its athletes. As he crouched down beside me, I looked him in the eyes and said, "This is not good. I just made a comeback from an injury like this, and now I am sidelined for another season! I need ice, connection to the e-stim unit, and something to start getting the inflammation down.

With a calm, even tone, he replied, "You are going to be okay, Deneke. Let's get to the training room." There it was again, the ring of my last name and the reminder of who the hell I actually was, how I was wired, and all those who'd come before me in my life to grant me this opportunity, to remind me that Denekes are not only resilient, but they are built in the darkness.

ST(RIPPED)

Somehow, with my familiarity of the pain, the knowledge of my previous comeback, and the calm presence of my new athletic training staff, I was good. I mean, I was not *good*, but deep in my soul I knew, "God not only has a plan for me, but whether I like it or not, this st(ripping) of my newly refined strength, drive, and current role is the start of this chapter's plan." There was only one way out of this, and it was to surrender and trust myself to trust the process.

My focus and commitment to my purpose was dialed, it was in action, it was a force to be reckoned with. My fear-stricken vessel that had encountered this initial injury in 2005 was not the same vessel meeting this version in 2007. The young woman who faced this new st(ripping) was calm and well acquainted with who she was becoming. She was confident in her mission, and she knew that rising from her own ashes was not only possible but astonishing, when done with grace, honor, and unwavering commitment to her values.

This round of my st(ripping) proposed a whole new reveal of my character. This time, the stakes were higher. This time, I was under a different microscope. This time, I had to battle some control of the staff and my own way of doing things; I was under a contract with the university, which meant they had a say in my recovery treatments. This was one of the most stressful elements of my comeback. In this moment of life, I recognized a bigger lesson for my future: my medical sovereignty was an absolute priority to me.

The take down of my presence was apparent physically, but this time, my mental and emotional wreckage were initially minimal. I had the comfort of knowing what was possible on the other side of pain and after the st(ripping) of what I thought was my power in this chapter of my life. This time around, I turned inward immediately and sought clarity on what was being asked of me to surrender and edit this round. Where should I seek a level of alignment that I am missing?

The shedding of this next layer required absolute diligence in my trust in something so much bigger than the present moment. I had committed to this university for a college athletic opportunity on scholarship. I had to readdress my will and commitment to holding this as my truth. I had to dig deep into my soul to find out if it was worth fighting for, because God knows, the circumstances (the dorm, the small school, the team, the setting) weren't my top choices. But they sufficed simply because I was able to fulfill a dream, this aspiration that had brewed in my soul and my entire being since I was fourteen years old.

I was left to ask myself, were my fire and passion enough to keep me at this school, in this program, in an environment where I had no points of contact for my healing? I was not sure. But I did know one thing was for sure: I had bloomed where I was planted in every previous chapter of my life, and this one was no different. I had work to do, and mulling it around in my mind was getting me *nowhere*.

I leaned in to my athletic training staff. I utilized the cold-therapy tubs, heat, e-stim, and every referral on their contact list, while I waited to be seen by their spine specialist. As I made slow strides in my recovery, I also stretched my resources list by taking it upon myself to find a yoga practice. I needed a place to breathe, to find a flow that worked internal to external. Flexibility wasn't something I needed; I was flexible and overly mobile. I needed to find a space that gave me internal peace and slowed me down. And it needed to be a space outside of my campus and team.

This injury was a cue for me to do a deeper dive into myself outside of this dream. During this time, I discovered my first boutique fitness experience. This was a fairly new concept, one that was common for yoga, but not for fitness as a whole. I was not only intrigued, but my interest around this business concept piqued my entrepreneurial spirit. Noted.

In discovering this studio, I started to create a little life outside of the one where I was rooted at my university, with my team. In this outside connection, I started to learn a little more about me and about a potential part of my future. I kept this place to myself and allowed the curiosity that had been piqued to calm the chaos brewing inside me from this derail, this st(ripping) of me once again.

In many ways, the awareness of what was available outside the walls of campus breathed life into me in ways I didn't expect. It was another healthy dose of distraction, this time, though, the distraction was an ominous reminder that my purpose was so much bigger than why I chose this university. So, I must not allow this derailment to take me from the bigger things that lay ahead of me. Noted.

Chapter 7 Reflections

Theme: My Grit Mantra

Prompt:

Choose one word from this list that resonates most with your journey right now:
   Resilience | Grit | Humility | Tenacity | Courage | Determination | Surrender | Leadership

Then complete this mantra:
"When I feel behind or broken, I remind myself that I lead with _____, and that is enough to keep going."

Challenge: The 1-Week Grit Practice

Pick one small action to take daily for the next 7 days that reflects your chosen word.

Example: If your word is *Grit*, maybe it's showing up to move your body each day, even if just for ten minutes.

My action will be:

CHAPTER 8

Falling Back into your Vision + Foundation

"Trusting yourself in a world that's disconnected is an act of rebellion."
—Matt Gottesman

During the summer after my senior year of high school, I was tempted by the hoopla of emerging adulthood: the parties, the alcohol, the long nights, the inadequate sleep patterns, and the *almost* freedom. I engaged with boys who had no place on my pathway. I found myself in situations where, *thank God*, I had my older brother to call upon; he rescued me from stupid choices more than a few times.

My brother would look me in the eyes and ask, "Niccole, was it worth it? I am all for you pushing limits in life, but please, do not get yourself killed!"

This came after he'd nabbed me from a house party where there was a shooting. I don't even know how I'd ended up at places like this. To this day, I think my social EQ gave far too much leeway to the people I was hanging around with. I trusted my circle of people too much.

I think we all had a desire to push some limits and *no* idea the magnitude of where we'd end up. I attended a few parties despite hating every minute of them. The party scene literally grossed me out: the smell and the whole vibe. But in so many ways, this was my stupid attempt to normalize myself among my peer groups, to say, "Hey, I am like you. I do these things, too," even though everything about it was a full-body cringe and out of alignment for me. Parties were not my idea of fun or my idea of letting loose, but I wouldn't give myself enough credit to listen to my inner knowing and requests.

Truthfully, I made choices I thought I *should* be making, in order to be accepted and embraced. This was eye-opening. This was also terrifying. This would serve as a defining moment for my life. Recognizing this about myself was alarming. I thought I had grown out of my people-pleasing, but damn, I sure was living the role with excellence.

I dumbed down my passion and drive, after recognizing these parts of me were hard to relate too. I created internal conflicts that wore down my alignment with my greater version of myself. I entered a little chapter of self sabotage. I allowed *my fear* of becoming to interfere with my actual becoming. This was in response to some of the people closest to me making me feel bad for my drive and passions, which they saw as impossible, but which I saw as an opportunity to evolve and grow. I was failing to acknowledge my process and own me. Noted. I had some growing up to do.

Here is the deal, my desire to fit in, is no excuse for my reckless behavior. Running in friend circles that didn't share my values was proving to be compromising to my bigger mission. I saw it as the easiest way to navigate doing what I wanted while also not making those around me feel bad about themselves or make me feel like an outsider. To *not* belong. It turns out, you are not for everyone. This was one of the first signs that I needed to understand this concept: I won't be for everyone and that is okay. I needed to dig deeper into a sense of the self I wanted to align with and fully grasp what that would both require and embody.

It was odd to be my age and both self-aware and self-discovering at the same time. Most days, the "Olympic games" occurring in my head were almost too much. The complexity of my thoughts and feelings needed a place to come out and play. This is the stage of our lives when we seek independence but scream for the structure and safety of our parents to help see the guardrails. In this chapter of my life, I learned that my *becoming* required *me* to set the guardrails and hold them.

I had to edit my actions and recognize there would always be "alligators" in my life. There would be temptation, there would be the path of least resistance, and there would be proposed shortcuts. There would be pushback and naysayers. Demise would be dressed up as glamour. There would be plenty of obstacles to challenge my values. All of these things would fall into the category of life's "alligators," sometimes nipping, sometimes chomping, and sometimes along for the ride, but always present. My personal mission was to learn how to tame them and, most important, embrace them.

I quickly realized and accepted: I would fall, I would be tested like any other human, I was not infallible. I would rally in my foundation and recognize the importance of having values and guiding principle. Life required me to embrace this and become, despite it.

Trust Yourself. Decide

My JC campus, Palomar College was sprawling. There were classes held in buildings and in add-on trailers, stacked high into the warm hills of San Marcos, California. Because I was under eighteen years ago, the adult age, I was put through the ringer in order to be approved to start college. You would have thought I was signing up for the armed services! I had to laugh and groan as I waited to submit my permission slip from my parents to the admissions office. A permission slip…! This makes me laugh still to this day.

While I waited, I scanned my surroundings. The school was in a massive expansion phase, and at that point, I was a part of the expansion. Plus, I, too, was in an expansion phase. The construction felt relevant to my period of life. I had chosen this place, the intermediate option, to refine my skills as a volleyball player, to nail down just who I wanted to be, academics-wise, and to explore the endless options at this new juncture of my life.

After submitting my permission slip, I made my way over to the athletes' academic advisor headquarters. This office was, of course, tucked away in the athletic buildings, the one area I was very familiar with by this time. It was the spot I had visited over and over to finalize my decision to attend this JC. And this was the part of campus where "my people" would hang out.

It was the end of summer, and the inland heat was intense. In an effort to keep my cool, I walked briskly but not intensely. Still, I arrived in a full-on sweat. The surrounding facilities were full of the many fall athletes. As I scanned the area, I thought to myself, "Damn! My options have increased. This is not high school anymore... We now have some men! *This* I can get behind."

I threw a small, coy smile to a few of the athletes whom I assumed were football players then made my way into the advisor's office. I didn't give anyone much time or space to explore their curiosity about me.

The office reeked of sweat, men, chew, and old musky building yearning for a carpet change and open windows. As I made my way inside, my last name again preceded me. Before I could even introduce myself, the advisor extended his hand and said, "Coach Deneke's daughter. What a pleasure to meet you. Your dad is the man! That guy takes no prisoners!"

"Ha!" I thought to myself. "You have no clue!" First and foremost, he wouldn't put up with your disgusting office and sloppy attire, chew-lined teeth, and sleepy teenager-like presence. But all that aside...

I smiled and kindly replied, "Yes, sir, he is quite the man. It's a pleasure to meet you." Once again, my last name introduced me. I would set my first name in motion later.

We sat down and outlined my schedule for my projected two years at the college. I was already clear I wanted to do my degree in kinesiology, exercise science. I had no idea about the ins and outs of that, but I did know I desired exposure to everything, so I could decide where my emphasis would be and how I would use it.

When I exited the office, there were several other athletes hovering like carefree vultures. This time, though, I was less interactive and more, "I'm on a mission, don't waste my time." This wase a comfortable vibe for me to operate in; it kept me focused and out of trouble despite the endless opportunities around me. I'd get done what I needed done and get noticed later. Engage later.

I headed to my coach's office. Messenger bag in tow and sunnies on, I climbed up the stairs to the head volleyball coach's office. By this time, the location was second nature to me. This area was one of my comfort zones. I had been here dozens of times, setting my future in motion, gathering details about the season ahead, and solidifying my plan for my role.

School was about to start, and our season was days from kicking off. The tempo we trained at wasn't anything more challenging than the pace I'd put myself through, leading up to this point. But the heat was unrelenting, and our gym was old and *hot*. The biggest adjustments were the ever-evolving personalities, leaving behind what was, and embracing what is.

At a junior college, each athlete is there only a maximum of three years (if they take a red shirt), so the turnover is intense, and the chance to establish connection and esprit de corps comes fast and furious. It develops at a depth granted by the participants.

I came in with my notetaking and expectations, and so did everyone else. The goal was to unite everyone in their *WHY* for being there and to build off of one another. This season's team was packed with experienced gals, reckless mentalities, and a little too much carelessness. I was wired, a little like a pulled-back bow string ready to release its arrow. I thought, well, this should be interesting.

Weeks into this new setting, my coach decided we needed to do a massive audit of my form. It turned out that during this whole volleyball journey of mine, not one coach before this had thought anything of my footwork. They had

ST(RIPPED)

simply let me be. In my naiveté around volleyball, I had never thought anything about it, either. My focus had always been on the things that had led me to this point: strength, conditioning, power, explosivity, mindset, and leadership. I'd allowed everything else to continue to develop, to flow.

I spent my early weeks of freshman year studying, dialing in my classes, practicing, and adjusting to campus life, new faces, new professors, and simply who I was becoming in this whole process. After all, I felt I was living part-time in the dream I had set out for myself.

This in-between feeling and experience occurred during an interesting time gap in my soul. It was as though time slowed but then picked up along with the intensity of becoming. This was the slow-burn time when distraction could easily have become my enemy. Not only was I living out the prerequisites of my larger aspiration, but I was living the next test around whether or not I really wanted this bigger dream, this next step where my purpose and passion united. It was a time of mixed observation and living in my becoming.

> *"I have a hidden and inarticulate desire for something beyond the daily life."*
>
> —Virginia Woolf

One of the beautiful things about staying local in a JC for the initial two years I was at college was that I could keep my job at my grandparents' café in Oceanside, California. I had worked there in some way or another since I was ten years old. When I started school, I didn't know my exact schedule yet for training, school, and competing, but they let me know I could work whenever I was available. And that worked for how I was wired.

Any opportunity to keep structure, make money to save for whatever my future held, have freedom, and, most important, continued to play a role in our family business. It was ingrained in me. I had held jobs since I was ten, between babysitting, the family grocery store, and the restaurant. I never worked because I had to, though. It was because I wanted to. I valued freedom, security, and responsibility.

From my earliest memories, the family grocery store was an important part of my mom's life and, in turn, in ours as well. My mom chose to work there and play a role in carrying out her father's legacy. She was not only loyal but passionate about working there. The store held many sacred moments, including my mother and father meeting, when he stopped in for some groceries and beer, as a strikingly handsome, strong, second lieutenant stationed on Camp Pendleton.

He was mesmerized by her breathtaking olive skin, long black hair, rich brown eyes, and a smile that always met her eyes, so he took a shot on asking her out. Their love story began there.

The store had been our Nonno's dream, his legacy, the family meeting spot, our source for food every day, our babysitter during the summer months, our first job, and one of our greatest life teachers. The grocery store introduced us to people from every walk of life, which let us witness how our Nonno demonstrated not only superb customer service, but the power in treating every human with dignity and respect. Every day, he demonstrated the power of paying it

ST(RIPPED)

forward. It was in this store, inside and out, where I witnessed how "love and kindness know no divide."

Service was at the top of Nonno's list every day, and he did it with passion. The store was a center for connection and learning. It was a living, breathing opportunity to refine real life skills. I learned my most useful math skills there, plus customer service, why we rotate the stock on the shelves, the differences in the quality of meats, how to shuck corn and make a killer sandwich or salsa, and the best presentation for produce. The store provided me my first insights into the best-selling libations, the illogical kickbacks from liquor and cigarette sales, the rampant hidden habits of gambling, and the power of never underestimating the quality of connection. The breadth of customers showed me how we are all connected, no matter where we come from, no matter our fortune or misfortune, the color of our skin, or our language spoken. We are all one when we choose to see we are all human. We all need to eat and provide for our lives in some capacity. The store was the ultimate teacher.

As kids, this place was our launch point to freedom. It was walking distance to one of the most beautiful beaches in the world. Most kids attended camps during the summer or hung out at home, playing video games. Not us. We headed to work with our mom. We headed to work but knew, after a few short tasks over a few short hours, we could grab our boogie boards and walk left out of the store, ten feet to the stop light, cross the Coast Highway, and *boom, baby!* The beach was four blocks down.

Our Nonno gave us the chance to do a little work and, in return, shop the shelves for any food we wanted to devour at the beach. Eventually, those snack choices turned into cash, then into a real-life schedule with a paycheck. Who knew you'd be lit up by contributing to your Social Security starting at age fifteen… ha-ha!

By the time I was in high school, I already had a résumé and a savings account that I'd filled through my commitment and grit. It was not only empowering to make money, but the responsibility gave me a level of pride and capacity that served me in the most expansive years of my life. I developed an understanding through these responsibilities that molded my very structure and being.

Eventually, I shifted from working at the store to helping at the family restaurant. Intermittently, I was a busser, a hostess, and eventually a waitress. There, I refined my superb customer-service skills.

Let's be real: people have a true affection for their bacon, eggs, and coffee. The way to most people's hearts is a warm smile, hot coffee, and kindness. I learned quickly how fast you could increase your wages when you were "on it." I used this chapter of my life to test my skills of efficiency, capacity, compartmentalizing, and customer service. After all, I was raised to give it my absolute best, no matter if I was taking the trash out or competing on the court. This job was no different.

The restaurant was a cornerstone in my life. Working at the café gave me insight into how hard a kitchen staff works to provide us the luxury of a hot meal. I developed a whole new appreciation for how much work the dishwashers do, too, to keep the whole operation running.

This café was my sanctuary and place of empowerment for so many reasons. I grew into a young woman there. I found my stride in life there. I practiced sharing my dreams there. Every greeting at the end of the table was an opportunity to use my voice and to dial in my tone and body language. Every interaction gave me a shot at learning a detail about the customer sitting before me. It taught me to pay attention to details within each interaction, to provide better service. It was a weekly reminder of how far remembering someone's name can go and how fast you can influence someone's day, simply by being kind and gracious. For me, serving each customer was a chance to live out the power of first impressions.

The restaurant was more than a café. It was a guaranteed reconnection with my family every week. It gave me the time to laugh and build memories with my cousins. It also was a chance to experience directly the pride and love my Nonno felt every time he came in, with his huge smile and warm hug. He beamed when he saw me every Sunday.

"Nicci baby!" he said with exuberance and love. (Note: he was the *only* person I allowed to call me *Nicci*.). His smile would reach his eyes and touch my heart every time I saw my Nonno. His genuine smile was a reminder rooted deep within me how powerful expressed gratitude was.

A Healthy Dose of a Distraction Reminds You that You can Achieve and Live at the Same Time

The summer before my sophomore year of college was pivotal. I was coming off of months of rehabilitation from an initial back injury. I was recovering physically, emotionally, and, most important, mentally.

I had spent my first year of college losing the footing I thought I had firmly established in order to find a new approach to my training, preparation, mindset, and lifestyle. I spent my freshman year derailing myself from who I thought I was and fighting for the truths I deeply desired to build and live out for myself.

During freshman year, I was st(ripped) of all the versions of my being that I thought were my power. During this derailment, I discovered how truly capable I am, mentally, emotionally, and physically. During this time of absolute derailment, I always had a few constants: my family, my faith, and my job at the Harbor House Café.

While I laugh typing this, you may have raised eyebrows, wondering how in the world does a breakfast-and-lunch café play such a significant part in my revival. The comforts I found in my role at this café played a much larger part in my wellbeing than I ever imagined possible. During my absolute breakdown and st(ripping) of myself in 2006, I recognized the power to be found in the stability of what you know.

Here I was in a chapter of my life when everything I had dreamed of, worked for, and believed to be true was crumbling. However, I found great comfort in knowing that, every Sunday, the regulars would be there for their coffee, chicken fried steak, club sandwiches, classic burgers, and French toast. I knew they would greet me with the same level of dignity and respect, despite my dreams crumbling before my eyes gave me peace and consistency.

It gave me the fortitude to keep going, to dig deeper, and to nourish a safe haven that became my secret spot to take refuge in, while I rebuilt the structure for the truths I would live by. My role at the café each weekend gave me the space I needed from distraction to home in on the pathway I needed to stay on, in order to: get back out there and live out my mission.

ST(RIPPED)

My mission was more than healing or a comeback- it was to embody tenacity and show the world my strength in motion.

Each Sunday, there was always the glimmer of possibility I would be greeted by a handsome, eye-catching gentleman, as well. That kept it fun! Let's be clear, I was not on a mission to meet my match or to have my time taken, and I certainly was not going to allow anyone, especially a man, to take me away from the dream I had set and owned since I was fourteen! If the last year had taught me anything, it was that I could, *needed,* to live a little and still reach a level of desired excellence.

At this point, I needed to live a little. It was essential to my wellbeing! It had been a grind, and I had been so damned tunnel-visioned about building myself back, I had lost touch with all the parts of me. I had lost touch with what it felt like to laugh and let go of control. I'd lost touch with any reality outside of the one that put me into full "go" mode on the court and in the weight room. I'd lost touch with a young woman who loved to dance, grab a good coffee, sit on the beach, and cruise the coast with her windows down, singing "Promiscuous Girl" by Nelly Furtado. I'd forgotten how to have fun and live, because I saw no other pathway other than the one that led me back to the place of my deepest hopes, dreams, and goals.

During this building-back of my truths, I did a lot of forgetting. I needed to strike a balance. I was even beginning to be bored of my tight-ass, rigid personality and inability to let go. I needed some pep to my step, a little added magic. An interruption to also prove my capacity was expansive.

NICCOLE HENDRICKSON

There is nothing like the first taste of lust and infatuation and a glimmer of the feeling of desire to interrupt your flow.

One sunny Sunday around 11:00, there was a chatter of energy making their way to the café's front door. I was busy grabbing the food that was ready at the kitchen window, so I didn't catch the details of all the guests, but I knew a vivacious crew had come in, based on the laughter and energy up in the front of the restaurant.

As I made my way back behind the counter to grab additional condiments for my table, my fellow waitress gave me the quick details through a huge smile. She said, "Party of six, table eighteen. I will start them off with some water. And by the way, the guy at the end is not too bad to look at, either!" Without even glancing over at the table, I was overcome by a rush of heat. My cheeks flushed slightly, and I smiled back at her before thanking her and saying I would be right over.

As I approached table eighteen, the three people seated facing me watched me with large, curious eyes. At this point in my life, I had been training intensively to make a comeback and attain my ultimate goal: a scholarship to a four-year volleyball program. I was in my full height, 5'10", strong as a disciplined athlete, poised with my posture dialed in, and tan. While our dress code at the café was less than flattering, my physique was apparent through my unsexy shorts and teal Hanes T-shirt. The no-show socks and Nike Frees displayed my athletic prowess and trained physique. I kept my makeup simple, but always wore a little pop of mascara, bronzer, and gloss to do the trick.

At the table was one guy with his back to me, but I quickly noted his strong, straight posture, broad shoulders, and built arms that were no doubt a byproduct of time spent in the gym and outside, doing physically demanding tasks. He was tall with dark hair and olive skin. My heart slightly skipped a beat.

I greeted everyone with a cheerful, "Good morning and thanks for your patience." Then, I scanned the table and my heart stuttered.

Butterflies overcame me when I locked eyes with the guy at the end of the table who had turned toward me. *Oh my!* It was the "tall, dark, and handsome" I had spotted with his buddy at the gym the other week. *What the hell were they doing here? How was this happening?*

I had just told my fellow waitress about seeing the most eye-catching man at the gym the other day. The odds of ever seeing him again, let alone talking to him, were slim to none. But now, this freaking guy was in my grandparents' restaurant, the Harbor House Café, at my table, locking eyes with me as he ordered Farmer's Brothers coffee. *What the hell was I going to do now?*

I told myself, "Pull it together, Niccole. You're at work, not in a rom-com. This mystery man doesn't even know your name, and his friends are all sitting there, wondering when you are going to take their drink order." In an effort not to embarrass myself any further, I quickly pulled it together and shared our weekend specials, took their drink orders, and retreated to behind the counter. I realized I needed a quick moment to reel it in, so I pretended we needed more orange juice from the back room and headed through the swinging door.

When I rounded the corner into the cooler, I let out a gasp and repeated, "How is this happening? Get it together, Niccole. Holy smokes!"

NICCOLE HENDRICKSON

As I made my way back through the swinging door, directly in his line of sight, I avoided locking eyes with him again, but I felt his curious, penetrating gaze follow every move I made. As I quickly passed into the galley to finish preparing their drinks, I knew my pulse had not fully recovered.

I played it safe when I delivered their drinks. This was not the moment to show off and do more. I had to keep my recklessly beating heart under control, my flushed cheeks at bay, and my witty mouth in check. Sass was fine, but I told myself not to dish out more than I could handle. I knew this group would not be forgiving with their replies, so there was no need to set myself up for a crew I couldn't recover from quickly.

The struggle was on. I had to maintain a level of service with all my tables, including table eighteen, while also avoiding the urge to hover and overdo it. The demands of the restaurant helped to steady my pulse and focus, but my mind was still reeling. I had to get more information about these people. I needed to know how I could see Mr. Tall, Dark, and Handsome again. This couldn't be left to chance. But there was also *no* way I would be taking the lead on this one.

Time rolled on, and their breakfast was served. I had a steady flow of customers in my section, plus my fellow waitresses needed my help as well. I knew my Nonno's expectations when it came to keeping the people happy, fed, and served, with the tables turned over, so this was no time to slack just because my irresponsible, hormonal heart was begging me to be distracted by the jaw-dropping presence of this man.

ST(RIPPED)

As I began to clear plates off table eighteen, the friend sitting to the left of Mr. Tall, Dark, and Handsome asked, "Do you happen to work out at the 24-hour Fitness off the 76?"

Holding a stack of used dishes, I grinned and replied as if I didn't know they also worked out there. "I do. That is my training spot!"

They looked at each other as I left the table to put the dishes in the bus bin and return back to gather more.

The same guy said, "I think we saw you training the other day." He glanced at Mr. Tall, Dark, and Handsome [TDH for short] for validation.

At this point, Mr. TDH hadn't said much verbally, only with his eyes, smile, and focus on me. Finally, though, he confirmed, "It *was* you. You were on the treadmill when we walked in." His voice was strong, deep, and smooth, which sparked curiosity in me. I could not deny it.

I quickly shot back an abbreviated explanation about how I was recovering from a back injury and that that gym was my spot to dial in my rehab and training in preparation for my next season.

Mr. TDH's eyes grew big. After looking me over from head to toe, he said, "Let me guess, you're a volleyball player?"

I smirked and replied, "That's a good guess. Gold star for you!"

He guffawed. "Gold star, huh?" His eyes creased as he smiled.

I smiled, too, and walked away. The building curiosity, tension, and intrigue on both our parts was palatable, and I had to get the hell away from this table before I said something reckless and promising.

Briskly, I went behind the counter to get their check and see them out. I didn't want this to end, but I needed them to get the hell out, so I could focus and gather my irrational hormone-driven emotions. I thanked them for their business and said, "See you around."

After they left, I was a puddle of smitten curiosity and disbelief. What was this was... *infatuation*?

"No, Niccole, you do not allow yourself to be affected like this," I reminded myself. "Put it in a box, and store it away with everything else you don't have time for or allow!"

But even I knew how much I needed to make time to let my structured, rigid being have fun again. *Ughhhh*, oh my gosh. I did not have time for this!

I spent the rest of my shift with a ridiculous smirk on my face and a joy for how I could still get butterflies and feel all mixed up. It was clear my structured, no-fun, no-distractions mentality needed a revamp. I had come alive in a way I hadn't felt in months. I had rekindled a piece of my fire that I didn't even realize had dimmed. And even if it was over a stupid man whom I did not know, and even though it was reckless to allow myself the wandering, curious thoughts, I was still so damn happy to recognize I hadn't fully lost my internal spark.

By this point in the summer, I had started training with my team again, in addition to my own workouts and daily rehab. The JC was a two-year program, so, by this time, I had a whole new crew to work with. The new team included a sassy, minimally-mannered firecracker from a small town in Texas. This girl was either going to be my demise or my best partner in crime. Or maybe both! *We will see*, I thought to myself.

ST(RIPPED)

She was reckless, diligent, driven, and beautiful. She had a mouth like a sailor and a beauty that captivated you. She would be the spice and disruption I needed in my routine, and I was thankful. My head coach purposely paired her with me. At first, I was annoyed and saw the distractions coming, but I also quickly realized my coach was asking me not only to lead but to be led in the way of, "Chill out, Deneke!" Noted.

My JC head coach was one of the best gifts in the realm of coaches. He was the perfect balance of intense and fun. He was a brilliant volleyball mind, very assured of himself, and patient, but he had no problems snapping into gear when you were out of line or busting limits that would compromise your future. He was also a father to two girls at the time, married, and a testament to what it looked like to be a man "good in his own skin." He was clear in his *"why,"* and he committed wholeheartedly to his mission: giving young women a solid program and platform to excel at their affinity for volleyball.

He was a hell of a lot more relaxed than I ever would be, but his mentorship and approach were welcome in my life, after my previous coaches. He was also the perfect coach to help me make a comeback; I know now for certain this coach was a quality man who saw my gifts and potential at a deeper capacity then I ever gave him credit for. It wasn't until over a decade and half later that I fully appreciated his impact on my life.

He was certainly strategic in pairing me with the Texas firecracker. He did this in a way that empowered me to my duty, to keep tabs on her, lead her, and refine her, It also opened doors to shifting my dialed-in, no-room-for-much-flex routines. I needed some malleability, and this gal would certainly challenge me for it.

We started training together, going out at night when we could, shopping, and navigating team dynamics. Later, we would be wing woman for each other. I had a wild Texan teammate helping to rekindle the very fun fire I was reintroduced to, when I ran into Mr. TDH. Thanks, pardner!

One afternoon, as I was starting my solo workout at the gym, I felt a heaviness I couldn't shake. My body ached from the increased level of training I had embarked on for the upcoming season. I was tired, and I was tense, with a little underlying fear about what my body could handle as I added volume and tempo. I was just blah, but I was there, doing what I knew would funnel my clarity and recalibrate my focus: movement.

As I was lost in my thoughts on the treadmill, step after step, thought after thought, I was interrupted by a tall—taller than I remembered—handsome, strong man who stepped onto the treadmill to my right. *Holy smokes! It is him*!

The dragging heaviness morphed into so much nervous energy, I wasn't sure I could handle it. I quickly gathered myself when he said, "Look who it is. Not at the café but on her treadmill. I hoped we would run into you again!"

I allowed the slight curl to my lips to form a smile and replied, "Here I am, in the very spot you first discovered me."

The back-and-forth flirting picked up until it ended with his friend annoyingly reminding us that we weren't the only ones in this gym and the point of their time there was not to flirt. They were there to actually lift and get a workout done.

ST(RIPPED)

Mr. TDH invited me to join, flashing me a smile. I laughed and quickly turned down the invite, dismissing him so he could catch up with his needy lifting partner. I stayed on the treadmill for a bit longer to keep my distance and give my irrational, fluttering heart and uneven breath a chance to stabilize. *What in the actual hell was that about?* It was the distraction I had called in, but damn! I hate when I do this: put an ask out and receive it. After all, I'd already been gifted my firecracker Texan teammate, and that friendship-teammate dynamic would be enough of a distraction, plus new real estate to navigate. Not this, too.

Irrationally, I slid into my default, over-the-top headspace. My thoughts were quickly going down a path, rearranging all the logistics in my life to find or create another training spot, another space where I could take refuge and not be interrupted. *Seriously, Niccole, you are insane. There are more hours in the day than the training hours when you see this dude. Do not go and switch your whole life to avoid him and a distraction you asked for! Besides, Grow Up! You can't run or rearrange your life every time something threatens your desired tempo and proclaimed peace. You must learn how to enjoy your life while also embodying a level of focus and bringing your bigger aspirations into fruition.*

That was what this was *all* about: a test on how to exist in this desired duality of carefree, fun, spontaneous, and also structured, successful, and unapologetically dialed in, pursuing my bigger hopes and dreams. It was clear the all-or-nothing principle would be the death of me, if I didn't navigate the bow strings I constantly pulled way too tight and never found full release.

I was done way before I ever pressed stop and stepped off that stupid treadmill, but the extra minutes I spent walking gave me time to gather my senses and dial in my plan. I would lift and take care of myself, like I did every other time I was there. I would get after it and not allow interference. It was simple: do me and, most important, BE me.

As I'd expected, they wrapped up their workout before I did. I could sense their presence making their way across the gym to where I was working out. The friend conveniently went to fill his water, while Mr. TDH made his way over to me. He smiled, said something innocently flirtatious, and asked for my number so he could ask me out.

Just like that, here we were. I was in the real-life moment I had dreamt of creating and living. He asked me out, he asked for my number, and I was validated in my victory. They left, and that was that. The dopamine hit was solid, and really that was all I needed to perpetuate a headspace I'd wanted to rediscover. Just the invitation to get me the hell out of the over-the-top headspace I was swirling in.

I was nineteen years old, and I hadn't given in to any derailing social. They decided that this stud muffin, six years older than I was, would *not* be the person whom I allowed to rob me of my bigger mission. It was clear to them I was welcoming a distraction and was walking dangerously close to my line of focus, to the opposite side of the tracks, with a guy who did not belong in my current chapter.

What they found to be dangerous was why I was intrigued by the possibilities of this dynamic. I also thrived on being told no at this point in life. For me, it was, "Bring it!" I was welcoming just enough distraction to validate how capable and determined I was.

ST(RIPPED)

Just like in high school, there would be nothing to deter me from filling my mission. No party, no invite, and sure as hell not a guy. This was me validating what my parents believed was true about me and proving that their fears could be silenced. Not only could I handle myself, I would stay focused to a level that would be intimidating as hell for the gorgeous man I was currently hanging with.

This little six-month stint was simply a live-and-living experience to remind me I could be focused *and* fun. They were not independent. Rather, they were a healthy, coexisting duo that relied on each other. This butterfly-inducing dynamic was the eye-opener I needed in order to remember to live and feel passion while I also achieved. Losing yourself while building yourself will lead your soul down a dead-end driveway that doesn't belong anywhere in your story of triumph and living.

Remembering Why, Rooting into my Foundation

In late summer, 2011, at 4:15 a.m. MST, I was heading to work in Broomfield, Colorado. My eyes were blurry from the overwhelm of tears. My heart was pounding with uncertainty, my palms were sweaty as I gripped the steering wheel, my stomach was in knots from drinking too much coffee and not eating enough food, and my voice sounded muffled as I dialed my dad and burst into hysterics.

Just like during my childhood, my father met my hysterics, my pain, my uncertainty, and my inopportune call (it was 3:15 a.m. back home) with calm, compassion, intent, and unconditional love.

When I finally formulated the words to communicate, I said to him, "What am I doing? I don't know what I am doing here… I left my whole life and created a new one in another person's world, and I don't know what I am doing, Dad!"

He met my upset and ambivalence with full acknowledgment. He responded with love and clarity. "Niccole Ruby, I have been waiting for this call. It is okay. You are okay. When we follow our hearts, it can still be very scary and lonely. But it doesn't mean it was the wrong decision. It means there is a lot of discovery of who you are, in this next chapter of life, and you are discovering her while also learning what it is to fall deeply, madly in love.

"That is scary, because it is deeply vulnerable and exposing. You have to trust yourself. Just because there is uncertainty doesn't mean your original instinct and drive were wrong. Now, the deep discovery occurs. You must stay in line and true to you, sweetheart. Trust yourself and stay true to Niccole Ruby!" Then he added, "I love you. You are strong, beautiful, and a force. Do not deny the world of you. Be you. Trust in God's plan."

I hung up the phone, sat with this conversation, and for the first time in weeks felt my feet back on the ground.

It is that simple. When life is unraveling, going so fast, exposing blind spots faster than we can comprehend and respond, we have to remember the power is *always* within. The residual impact of taking a pause and returning "home," going inward, and remembering your vessel is smart and your heart speaks to you.

Taking a simple pause to reconnect and *listen* will open doors to clarity that no professional therapist can touch. While I am not suggesting we do not need professional help at times, I am saying the answers always begin within. They begin with a pause and with listening to what your mind,

ST(RIPPED)

heart, and gut are trying to articulate to you. The answers are in the returning to baseline.

I wish I could tell you that, after nearly forty years on this Earth, I don't still need this reminder. But I do. And every time, it is just as eye-opening, mentally freeing, and physically rewarding.

Trust your vessel. Trust the undoing, the st(ripping) of your thoughts, the reveal. Do not fear the darkness. Fear the denial of facing it.

Remember: just like building muscle, we have to break it down to build it up, to refine it. The road to greatness, to deep connection, to growth, and to harnessing the desired experiences will require a breakdown, a shedding, and what I believe is the perfect term: a st(ripping). What is revealed in the "breakdown" amplifies the ability to build even more effectively.

Chapter 8 Reflections

Theme: Unmute Your Magic

Letting go of people-pleasing. Reclaiming passion. Becoming unapologetically *you*.

Part 1: The Role I Played

Complete this sentence:

"I've caught myself playing the role of _____, so I could be more accepted."

Examples:
- The chill one
- The non-threatening one
- The supportive but silent one
- The less ambitious version of myself

Part 2: Red Flag Realizations

Check off any of the following that you've done to make others more comfortable. (No shame—just awareness!)

☐ Downplayed my success or goals

☐ Avoided sharing something exciting out of fear of being "too much"

☐ Agreed with things I didn't believe in

☐ Hid how hard I work or how deeply I care

☐ Apologized for having big dreams

☐ Sabotaged myself to stay small

Answer this: *The one I'm most ready to stop doing is:*

Part 3: Permission to Shine

Prompt

If you were to fully **unmute** your passion and purpose—what would that look like this week?

One thing I can do this week to live louder is:

CHAPTER 9

Becoming Happens in the Darkness. Leverage It.

"I believe, I believe we can write our story...
I know, I know I was born for this."
—The Score

The Comeback, Round 1

The words of one my doctors lived on repeat in my head: "You will need to establish the strongest core of any of your opponents. You will require a level of training that is unrelenting. This will likely flare up again. Have a plan, Miss Deneke."

This was personal. I would be the force to be reckoned with, not only on the court, but, through my mental grit, to a level of strength and conditioning that would far surpass any expectation. I might experience flare-ups, but I would *not* live in a dialogue with victimhood. I would recycle this pain and utilize the intel to guide my new path, just like I did during my sophomore year of high school, when I decided I would no longer accept the fears associated with my inability to allow my words to exit my mouth and deliver my message.

ST(RIPPED)

My injury may have led me on a detour during my freshman year of college, but I would not become a discarded byproduct of it. There was always a choice: I could succumb to the fear and the pain, or I could navigate a plan to recycle the pain and formulate an idealized plan.

When my initial injury took place, what was revealed in my thought patterning was alarming... My thought process was bombarded by haze, overwhelm, doubt, fear, unfamiliarity, and derailment. I was exposed. I was raw. I didn't recognize the feelings in my body and the thoughts in my mind. Perhaps this was a revelation of my subconscious? Perhaps this injury was a desperate outburst of my nervous system to reveal what lived deep down in me?

While I felt it was my body that had let me down, I later learned it was my mind-heart-body that lacked clear communication and understanding of their needs. My system was screaming at me, and I had ignored its warning signals. I'd taken advantage of my grit, determination, and physical prowess. But my lack of true appreciation for my vessel and acknowledgement of its needs had led me to burnout and debilitation.

I wouldn't know all of these details until later in life, but the intel I gathered in the fall of 2005 was: I am not subhuman. *Duh*, right? The body is fragile, the mind and heart are unstoppable, however, *the body will speak for the ignored heart and mind*. The whole vessel needs to be nourished. This derailment and complete st(ripping) of what I thought was a large part of my identity revealed a pivotal opportunity to redefine how I viewed and lived out my life. It forced me to get clear on what my power really was. On who and what truly dictated it.

This injury facilitated my headspace into a clearer, stronger, empowered, tested, open, st(ripped), and humble place. While the st(ripping) of all you know and believe to be true is revealing and devastating, it is also freeing. There is freedom at rock-bottom and weakness.

When you lose what you thought defined you, when you lose what you thought provided comfort and power, you begin to see your life differently. When you cannot access the same pathways to achieve a certain state of existence, you are left with two choices: 1) accept defeat and wallow in what was and what is, or 2) recognize what you do have, work with what is possible, introduce yourself to the parts of you that have always existed but were left untapped, take ownership of the areas in your life where fear usually takes the lead, lean into help to develop these areas, and, last of all, free yourself of the fear of losing something. Live like anything and everything is possible when you are open to whatever lessons life can teach you in derailment.

Move from a "what if" to an "even if" mindset. A steady stream of power can flow through your mind and heart when you have nothing external to pull from; when you realize that, *all along*, the power lives within you and the "mustard seed of faith," which you always have access to.

Freedom Found in Rock-bottom and Weakness

The body is brilliant, the mind is sharp, and the neuroplasticity of the nervous system gives the human experience so much power. It is up to us to tap this power.

Freedom is in the bottom, rock-bottom, without anything. While this sounds insane, hear me out. When we are working toward something, once we arrive at the level of expertise, success, love, happiness, strength,

ST(RIPPED)

empowerment, and comfort that we deeply desire, the challenge shifts from working to achieve it to navigating *how do you* maintain it?

If success or achievement of something is your goal, sustaining that feeling will never come to fruition, because it is short-lived and without sustenance. The sweetness, notoriety, and recognition that comes with succeeding are fleeting and short-lived. They are temporary and a never-ending chase. When a sports record is broken, the person who held it prior becomes an afterthought. The same will be true for the current athlete who holds the new record. Do you lose yourself when you are beat or passed? The answer will always be yes, if you are not tied to and invested in the process.

The fear of losing someone or something, like a feeling or a status, is a hell of a lot more stressful and strenuous then the path to actually attaining it, believe it or not. Once you arrive at the destination you desire, you now have to test if your process, mindset, and surroundings actually support the life you deeply wanted. The goals you worked so hard to achieve, do your habits sustain them? Given the trials that will come with sustaining and maintaining your goal, does your mindset embody the thought processes necessary for you, in excellence?

In my case the answer was "no." I was so focused on achieving the goal of becoming a collegiate athlete, when it was st(ripped) of this thought power, I lost who I was. I realized this would become my storyline, lived over and over, if I didn't establish a better respect for who I became in each of these processes. I was no fool. I knew this was just the initiation into what the future held for me. With that said, no matter what, not only do we need to have a level of respect and trust in the process, but we need to grasp our evolving identity in it and trust the version of us in that process. The growth that occurs and the alignment with our guiding principles while in a process of achievement are where the value lives.

This initiation to life happening opened my eyes to a 100% understanding of how people lose themselves in life-altering events. I came so close to just giving up on something that not only lit my soul up, but was a part of my formation. The end state: earning a scholarship and competing at the NCAA collegiate level was not my goal. The goal was becoming someone against the prescribed odd and staying on a path in the face of adversity and challenge. It was finding a way and trusting there is more than one option, despite the paths outlined before me.

Finding a way doesn't mean it will be the "way," the pathway that is familiar to everyone else. It would be the way that was divinely crafted for me and my purpose.

> *It is not the critic who counts; not the man who points out how the strong man stumbles, or where the doer of deeds could have done them better. The credit belongs to the man who is actually in the arena, whose face is marred by dust and sweat and blood; who strives valiantly; who errs, who comes short again and again, because there is no effort without error and shortcoming; but who does actually strive to do the deeds; who knows great enthusiasms, the great devotions; who spends himself in a worthy cause; who at the best knows in the end the triumph of high achievement, and who at the worst, if he fails, at least fails while daring greatly, so that his place shall never be with those cold and timid souls who neither know victory nor defeat.*
>
> —Theodore Roosevelt

ST(RIPPED)

It felt like an eternity, the year that stretched me, tore me down, exposed me, and grew me the most, but it proved to be only the warmup for what life had in store for me. I had come to learn this is how the st(ripping) process works. Each derailment, each loss of strength, power, and all I believed defined, in the end only gave me deeper insight into who I was on a cellular level. It pushed me to face who I was in real time, who I was under pressure, and it exposed me in ways I don't believe I could have done without the forced unveiling.

Once again, I had a choice: whom would I choose to reveal in this next comeback? I had fresh ground to build upon after experiencing back injury number two. It was the start of a new season and a new version of me. St(ripped) of the first comeback leading to the reveal of my next-level build.

The seven seniors moved on and the new staff evolved, recruiting more athletes and preparing for our next season. I lived on my own and was in full go-mode for school. I had completed a couple of fitness trainer certifications that gave me the ability to teach at the small boutique studio I had discovered the prior year. My world was broadening in ways that were both healthy and stimulating enough to keep my vision big. I was not only making my comeback to this college-athlete dream, but I was in motion, setting stones to my future endeavors. I was recognizing this growth within me while also noticing the unique experience of becoming and observing in my life.

When I took some time to go home for the summer, I discovered my love and passion for beach volleyball. It became an incredible asset to my training and preparation for my indoor season. I was alive and invigorated that summer. My skin was sun-kissed and my body finally tuned for the sport I loved so much. My skill set evolved due to the volume of reps and the change of scenery.

I reported back to my university early, so I could settle into a routine that would fit my training needs and the demands of my degree program. I embraced this reentry as a fresh start and made a conscious choice to release the weight of the previous year, so I could go into this one with a whole new perspective. After all, I was a whole revived version of myself, so that seemed fair.

The new coaching staff greeted the team with an upleveled approach and commitment. They expected our team's camaraderie and high level of leadership would be second to none on our campus. The staff had worked diligently to overhaul our operations and team experience. This included some impressive things, like new uniforms, swag, and finally, a new gym. They implemented protocols that fostered deeper connection and communication. They made strides to level the program up from a variety of angles. You could see and feel the changes. But there was also still an absence in strong character and leadership. Those deficiencies would come back to bite us in the ass.

Once pre-season was in full swing, we were a well-oiled machine compared to the season before. The team didn't lack its petty drama, but the desire to unite and be something bigger than ourselves was stronger than the desire to combust and destroy one another. That was a win!

Throughout the summer and preseason, I was called upon to play leadership roles, I felt the call to duty, and I also felt I was put on a unique path in this role well before the season started. I was keenly aware of what was happening, while also trying to navigate my path as a

ST(RIPPED)

student-athlete who was making a comeback to meet her own aspirations. I quickly caught on that I was walking a fine line.

There was no doubt I wanted to earn the position of team captain. I wanted to pave the path of leadership and mentorship amongst my peers, too. I wanted to accept this call to duty from my coaches, and I also wanted to be a peer in my peer group. So, I wanted my role as teammate, as well.

My coaching staff curated an in-between role for me, and I quickly had to navigate this, reminding them I was still a player, that I was on this team, earning my place as I made a comeback in the sport after derailing injuries. This would be my season to see it through. I would walk alongside my teammates, leading them while also in the trenches with them. I asked the coaches not to pit me against them by painting some picture that I was not in this with them.

This was a growing chapter for me. This was a moment in my life when I needed to remind myself, "be here now!" I had to advocate for myself with my team and my coaching staff. My head coach and I had a great relationship to start. She fully recognized she had a relentless workhorse in me. She knew what I was after and my standards. She knew my values and commitment to excellence. She watched me make a move into this four-year for specific reasons.

She knew what I was up against the season before, and she knew I would stop at nothing to see my mission through. She was strategic and spent time learning about all of us, so, in turn, she could use it to grow the team. In my case, she could use me as a valuable tool in her tool box. She would end up playing me like a fiddle.

NICCOLE HENDRICKSON

Her presence in my life was the best example of who I would *never* become as a mentor. Her own insecurities and weaknesses robbed her of the ability to be in her power as a leader. She used my drive and relentless commitment only to cut me off right before I had a chance to showcase it and develop on the court. She treated me as one of her athletes one moment, then quickly switched my role to almost a junior staffer. She would say one thing and do the complete opposite, because she fell victim to her own inability to hold the line. She succumbed to the pressures of parents and her own emotions.

She would speak into me with love, respect, and inspiration in order to get my buy-in, commitment, and belief to a turn around, and then she'd take it away from me on game day. She played her staff against me while she addressed me as a trusted confidant and mentor.

This was all it took to confirm I was truly done with college volleyball: one toxic, poorly handled situation between me and the coaching staff. That moment left a lasting impact on me and made me lose faith in her way of coaching.

We were on the road for our next series of matches. When we checked into our hotel, it was late, and we had to get to bed asap. After everything was settled, I sat in my bed, starving and thirsty. So, I made the grave error of going down to the lobby to buy water and a snack without asking permission.

In all fairness, I could have shot a text message to notify my staff, but I didn't think twice about it. I was twenty years old and an adult; I did not think needing water and a snack warranted a ping to ask for permission. I was just going to take care of myself and go to sleep afterward.

ST(RIPPED)

One of the assistant coaches spotted me, but instead of confronting me right then and there, he decided to make a spineless, cowardly move and snitch to the head coach that I had been out of my room after curfew without asking permission. He said he wasn't sure what I was doing, despite it being blatantly obvious: I was getting water and a snack.

The next morning, he made a spectacle out of me in front of my team using demeaning words. Not only was I punished by his taking away my starting position, but so was my team, given a new load of conditioning drills. As a result, any ounce of camaraderie among us evaporated. The conflict burnt out our bodies before we even began to compete that weekend. The coach's attempted "power" move did nothing but diminish the trust within the team.

The truth was, naturally, the team was annoyed that my choice had led to their punishment. But sadly, the coaches' immature handling of the situation tanked any miniscule belief or trust we had in them as our leaders.

I had myself together enough to hold it down. They knew, "Deneke won't compromise her path." They could attempt to cover up their ill-equipped leadership skills by pitting me against my team, but this wouldn't cover for their lack of qualifications to lead us and then the implosion of leadership that happened within, with the staff falling apart and us on the receiving end of their immaturity.

After getting our asses handed to us the next morning, the team headed off to get their breakfast. My coaches all sat together, filling in our head coach on their idiotic choices to punish us. I pulled up a chair and took a seat at the table beside them. They squirmed awkwardly, their body language riddled with guilt.

NICCOLE HENDRICKSON

I looked each of them in the eye, apologized, and took 100% ownership of my choices. I went on to tell them how disappointed I was in their disciplinary choices and the impact it would have on our camaraderie and our bodies. I went on to tell them, while I hoped and prayed there isn't a next time, in the event there was, to come to me first. They came to me for everything else, so it appeared, in this situation, they had made a deliberate choice not to.

It was clear to me their actions were an attempt to assassinate my character, and I would not allow that. I would rather forego this chapter of my larger aspirations rather than stand by and watch my own character be shredded.

Then, I scooted my chair out, gathered my own breakfast, ate, and made my way back to my room to prepare for the madness that lay ahead. My legs were toast from the conditioning, and my internal rage ramped up to a level 10.

Without a doubt, this experience shaped me in ways I'll carry forever.

> *You will teach them to fly, but they will not fly your flight.*
> *You will teach them to dream, but they will not dream your dream.*
> *You will teach them to live, but they will not live your life.*
> *Nevertheless, in every flight, in every life, in every dream, the print of the way you taught will always remain.*
> —Mother Teresa

ST(RIPPED)

When I transferred to CSUMB as a junior, I entered right into my degree program. The coursework actually excited me.

I chose this particular school because of its new exercise science program. One of the deciding factors was the recent hire of a few prominent professors who had left larger universities to grow and evolve incredible wellness labs in order to conduct research and write grants. They had a personal mission that was inspiring to the students, as well. Studying with this faculty would uplevel the opportunities of the students who studied under them. I, too, was intrigued to have a shot at learning at their level and in small class sizes. I didn't know it at the time, but two of the three professors would become lifelong mentors of mine.

I was bombarded by so many responsibilities at this point in my life, I didn't have much time to wallow in what came of my first season with this team, the reinjury of my back and the challenges posed by the seven seniors who held onto their toxic energy throughout the season. I moved out of the dorms and into my original off-campus house. I was on a mission to revive my vessel and, once and for all, put this derailment behind me.

I established a pretty solid flow in school and discovered my keen interest in the science behind my passions of strength and conditioning. I started to involve myself in more of my coursework at school. I began to live in a beautiful phase of my educational becoming. This year, I recognized you can be both devastated and blessed.

My injury derailed my volleyball plans, but it secured opportunities for my future. This injury st(ripped) me of living out the potential of my physical prowess temporarily, but I was in the perfect environment to find out why and how this had happened again. It would become a part of my true north, my bigger impact. My true north was helping people down the road using an internal to external approach. The injury fueled my fire to study the power of mindset and the ability to be in temporary derailment while also evolving into something unstoppable.

I was no stranger to pain and distraction. I quickly recognized this st(ripping) would be more detrimental to my future than the first injury, if I didn't stay focused on my *"why."* At this point, I had fulfilled part one of my dream: obtaining a scholarship to a four-year university. Whether I completed the athletic part or not didn't take away its being a great achievement. I recognized the power in this. I also recognized the possible dilemma here.

I was faced with adversity, and now it was time to truthfully answer my soul's biggest question: "What do you really want, Niccole? What is it you are really looking to accomplish, to become? How bad do you really want this vision? What are the costs, and what truth are you building in this st(ripping)?"

Derailment does many things. The most important thing it does is forces you to answer that very question: *"What is it you truly want to become, and how badly are you willing to walk in the darkness to become it?"*

The darkness: let's dive into this. So many of us are afraid of the dark. Some literally, but most of us are afraid of the darkness that presents itself in many aspects of our lives, within us. The darkness found in our relationship with ourselves, our habits, our actions, our mindset, and our hearts. We are terrified to recognize the darkness that lives within us. It is in recognizing our darkness, however, that we can discover and find our light. There is no shame in our

ST(RIPPED)

darkness. There is only paralysis to our becoming, if we avoid a deep dive into our darkness.

This chapter of my life demanded I face the dark. It asked me to confront pieces of me that no longer could stay dim and abandoned. My mind, heart, and body were demanding a united front. They demanded a deep dive into all facets of my being, in order to coordinate "Operation Heal and Rise."

The strength required of me this round was not as simple as rehab with the PT, relentless hours in the gym, and recovery with the team of practitioners who'd helped me see the multiple modalities to healing my physical body. This st(ripping) required a full internal tune up. It required an exposure to how I was wired and how I would articulate this wiring in real life. How would I live out the boundaries necessary in order to live in fluidity and the peace I needed in my vessel?

I had already lived out the chapters of life when I'd take on everyone's rock in my pack. Now, it was time to face the fire of living out my purpose, my true north, while operating in opposition to the circles I lived in. I needed to navigate how I would stay in line with my values, my becoming, while also coexisting in the world of opposition. This would be simple, if I was clear on my purpose.

The off-campus house where I so deeply desired to live, the one I swore would be my space of independence and resemble freedom, turned out to be a hell hole that only bred stress rather than alleviating it. One roommate was a teammate who decided to forego the rest of her college career and spend her extra time curled up with her boyfriend. Another was confused about whether or not she would attend college, while she was attending college. She was simply riding the wave of independence, living outside the confines of her parents' house, while skipping class, shopping, and taking advantage of having roommates who bought groceries and supplies.

Those two were the polar opposites of how I was living, I was simply a rent-paying contributor of supplies and amazing products. I was out of the house a ton, between training, practice, school, and a side job.

While I thought I was clear on my expectations and the ground rules for respecting shared space and my own bedroom, it turned out this was just an invitation to use whatever I had. One small thing layered on another and another, until I finally came home to find things missing in my room and my laptop used and broken. Honestly, I'd had enough.

The entire environment was chaotic, and the energy of the house was detrimental to my ability to focus and exist in the power I needed to heal, study, perform, and simply be. While this was no doubt an emotionally taxing chapter, it kicked off my full independence era, the one I had craved the most: living alone, doing me, and trudging the darkness without distraction!

"Character cannot be developed in ease and quiet. Only through experience of trial and suffering can the soul be strengthened, ambition inspired, and success achieved."

—Helen Keller

My season ebbed and flowed, though the ebbs started to dominate the flow. I became increasingly more curious about what awaited me outside the walls of the college campus. I dove deeper into certifications, and I grew in

ST(RIPPED)

specific areas of my passion for strength and conditioning. I started to see more clearly what freedom could look like in my adult life.

I was eager to evolve and tired of the immaturities around me within the team dynamics at this level. I was living this crazy dichotomy: yearning to be present in my young adulthood and college life, while also deeply desiring to ride the wave of growth that was naturally unraveling in my potential career space. I started to dive deeper into student research.

Opportunities became available in my degree program and through my professors' connections. I realized this aspiration of being a collegiate athlete would be a stepping stone to my next endeavor, the next evolution of me. At the time, I was powered by this realization. I was carving out space for my identity to flourish.

As the season progressed, I turned twenty-one that October, and I made the decision this would be my senior season. I would put a peg in this aspiration.

I decided to end the poor working dynamic between me and my coach and the unraveling power dynamics with the team and staff. I decided to put myself in the driver's seat to my next level of aspiration.

I had reached finality in living this portion of my dream. I had done it, and I'd lived it out. I'd had fun, and I'd learned things about myself that no other path would have exposed me to. I had not only made it, but I'd made a comeback from two different chapters of derailment, but my passion for this achievement was wearing thin. I wanted many elements of it, but what I didn't want far outweighed my drive to keep going. My gut said I was done, and I needed to honor it.

NICCOLE HENDRICKSON

My heart sang for the sport of volleyball and to play doubles on the beach. It sang for me to pursue this aspiration. But it also sang for me to be a student under the wing of some of the most brilliant minds in exercise science. At the time, I was being offered different options to stay connected to the sports program and assume the role my coach kept trying to put me, in as a student athlete. The truth was she saw something in me that I already knew existed, but I tried diligently to take my life one step at a time. She, on the other hand, selfishly tried to have me in both roles: athlete and coach, which compromised my chapter as a student-athlete.

I saw what was unfolding, and I needed space to navigate it. I needed to wrap up this part of my dream. This also meant walking in the darkness, to put to rest something I had allowed to define me for so long.

In the darkness, I allowed myself to feel the hurt and disappointment of my unraveled reality. In the darkness, I discovered the next evolution of my purpose: using my drive, connection, leadership, and passion for strength and conditioning to create a program that would bring out the emerging qualities and skills in each of the athletes on the team. I would graduate in spring 2009 and then become the strength and conditioning coach that summer, to prepare the team for the 2009-2010 season.

As I wound down this chapter as a student athlete and paved my path to graduation, I started to feel a level of finality to this chapter. I was ready to welcome the next phase of my life, and that included the purchase of my own pup. I spent my down hours searching the Internet for a black Labrador puppy. I was determined to add this friend to my life.

ST(RIPPED)

I found a listing for puppies for sale: *Mama is a yellow Lab and father is a Catahoula.* This grabbed my eye. But I thought who in God's name would breed a Lab with a Chihuahua? I gasped. Of course I needed to look at the picture of the puppies. I quickly realized I had misread the listing. It was a Catahoula, which is a medium-sized dog bred for hunting and herding.

I replied to the ad and convinced one of my buddies to come with me to meet the puppies. I knew I was crazy for making this choice, but I already had my mind made up. I was getting this little companion. Two months later, I brought the little, black, furry bundle of love home. I was completely in over my head and so in love with her tiny stature at the same time. We were going to navigate the next chapter of life together.

The peace of her presence was steady in the unpredictability ahead. She was love and responsibility, and I was her home and source of comfort and friendship. She was all ears to listen and all snuggles while I pulled late nights, finishing my senior projects. She was my trusted companion as I began to map out my plan ahead as the women's volleyball strength and conditioning coach.

This next endeavor would be my shot to try out what I believed were the necessary elements to close the gaps. This was my opportunity to lead by example, but also to lean into the intel I had on each of these women who'd previously been my teammates. It was my shot to lean into the evolving mentorship I had with my professors, to test out theories within science. But most important, to lean into the power of mindset, connection, integrity, and ownership.

This volleyball team would become a force to be reckoned with. They would bring a level of attention to themselves not because of their record of wins and losses, but because of their character, their discipline, and their efforts to connect with the community. They would walk with their posture strong and chins high because they'd earned it! This was my shot to prove a warrior woman lives within all of us, and she is only built through grit, discipline, surrender, and truth.

This team would remember me because I'd empowered them with tools, not holding them hostages to their power. They would know how to access it at any time. I would begin to live my higher calling. I would give everything I had to see this through. In this chapter of my life, I came alive. It was one of the moments when I legitimately felt, "I am exactly where I am supposed to be, living my true north!"

When I was programming, running the workouts, and pushing each athlete far outside their comfort zones, while helping them see the full-circle impact on their athletic presence on the court, it was a view into my own soul's higher calling. It was the first hit of what embodiment felt like: living out the unification of purpose-times-passion.

While I indulged in this chapter of my career as a strength coach, I also worked for a wellness publishing and production company. This commitment was short-lived but jam-packed with some of the most transformational moments in my early twenties. I quickly identified three things about myself:

- A 7-4, 9-5 job would *never* be for me. Period, non-negotiable.

- Dialing in systems, creativity, innovating, and connection were alive in me. Suppressing these aspects of my being felt like I was sealed in a glass box. Anything in life that elicited that feeling would spark me to find a way out of the commitment immediately.

* I would publish a book one day.

As I have reflected over the last fifteen years, I have come to know a combination of fierce focus, determination, and perseverance, as well as the repercussions of not waiting it out long enough. The desire to make a move, take action, and go for it have never been pain points for me. The pain that I have come to know is *wondering*.

As time rolled on in, my body began to reflect the weight of inner struggle; the quiet tension of wondering if I was patient enough, if I had truly exhausted every option in the stage of my life, or if my relentless drive was causing me to miss something deeply valuable in my journey.

This thread of doubt, questioning my path, my choices, and the way I was chasing my biggest aspirations started to manifest in unexpected ways. It began to reveal itself in how I was showing up, both to myself and the life unfolding around me. Stepping into the role of Strength Coach, **I was reentering a phase of people-pleasing, of downplaying my superpowers to protect the possibilities against derailment.** I was starting to become a victim to my own story instead of the warrior I had known myself to me. I was suffocating myself with past versions of my being. It was dark and unfamiliar, and I needed to get a grip on who I had started to evolve into.

It was time to initiate a self-inflicted level of st(ripping), a deliberate deconstruction of what I thought defined me. I knew I had to reverse engineer the journey that once shaped me into the college athlete I aspired to be. This time, I would leverage the lessons from my injuries and the unexpected shedding of the identity I once believed defined me.

Now, I wasn't being st(ripped) by circumstance. I was choosing to release whom I had been in order to step into whom I was becoming. It was time to leverage what I knew to be true about my previous experiences of losing what I thought were my power and impact, and it was time to own the strength that I had not only discovered in my resilience but was built in the process. It was time to be the curator of my life, not a witness to it.

Making the decision to wrap up this college athletic career I had once so deeply desired was one of the most impactful choices I made for myself. Advocating for my next steps and the role I wanted to play was key for reigniting my clarity, my purpose, and the value in what is created in the darkness. Stepping into this form of my power, which I found when treading in a darkness I didn't sign up for, gave me the confidence and ability to actively pursue this next st(ripping). This was me saying yes to shifting and releasing this element of my identity, to leaving behind what I thought defined or didn't define me. This was me finding my strength in the lessons learned, experiences I had, and the woman I was becoming in the process, not just the outcomes.

We all have the power to create this experience in our lives, to harness the strength discovered in this process of breakdown and to build. Instead of waiting for the breakdown in order to address change, instead of waiting to see if you burn out "this time." Instead of purposely sabotaging your relationships to test the waters of possible change or instead of being a victim of your own circumstances, take action. Purposefully lead yourself into surrender to experience the growth on the other side.

Here's how:

Start by coming back to the root of "what drives you?" Who are you at the core? What are your values and guiding principles? How do you want those to radiate in the way you show up in the world?

Next, address the thought patterns, people, and activities that are adding and subtracting to your ability to live out your purpose, your *"why."* Address whether or not you're true to your values in the process of living out these patterns. Be honest with yourself.

Next, tune into your stress, rest, and presence in your life. Your nervous system's health is a key indicator of your ability to build or sustain. Living in a state of conflict with your vision of life, including the stress of not letting go or not acknowledging all parts of your needs and healing, will be detrimental to your nervous system and, in turn, the quality of your desired life.

Perpetuating burnout and avoiding your needs, the inner voice speaking to you will weaken your nervous system, which, in turn, will leave you frustrated that you haven't moved on to the next state of your desired existence. Staying in a cycle of high stress and never addressing the alerts your brain is providing you will numb your ability to properly think and navigate through your evolution.

This was me. I spent months in my healing and needed therapies to heal my original back injury, but I didn't fully address the thought-patterning that was cultivating deep-rooted psychological stress and, in turn, keeping this loop open, perpetuating the strain on my system. We have to close the loops and address the healing needed in order to become, to let go. The self-inflicted st(ripping) must embody the nervous-system work.

Next, analyze your physical regimen. Have you lost track of this element in your life? What are you doing for movement? Are you holding your vessel to a standard of health and strength?

No matter your goal or your drive to evolve, this piece is imperative for your ability to sustain anything in life. We are meant to move. We are meant to leverage the power of our vessels. This requires strength and resilience that is built, nourished, and sustained in the act of physical activity.

Movement, a dialed-in strength regimen, requires you and me to own our process. You cannot outsource the building of your strength. *You* have to do it, in order to embody it, this commitment. This demand on your body is imperative to invoking change in your life. The self-inflicted st(ripping), in my opinion, is deeply rooted in this physical work.

We do not have to wait for a life-altering experience to st(rip) elements of our identity that no longer serve us. It is not necessary to become a victim of our own circumstances in order to address needed change. We do not have to wait for anything. We can choose to actively pursue the discovery of our power and strength by allowing ourselves to release what once suffocated us, including our thought patterns.

Choose to actively pursue your st(ripping) in order to embody your evolution.

"Talk about your failures without apologizing."
—Brene Brown

ST(RIPPED)

I think many of us wrestle with some choices and experiences of our past. I think we hold onto these things deep in our subconscious, and they inconveniently rear their ugly heads when we arrive in chapters of our lives that embody the elements of beauty, worth, love, and the success that we have dreamed of, worked toward achieving and becoming, and earned. We wrestle with them now because we never gave light and addressed them when it happened.

Most of us bring this baggage with us. We allow these things to later define us and steal the power in the becoming. We allow all of the unacknowledged doubt, sadness, disappointment, and pain to make their debut because they have to, at some point of time. We have shoved all this back, ignored it, and bypassed its warnings because we feel bad. Then, we pass it on to someone else close to us. We close up but we never close the loop. The end result is detrimental to our current life.

We shove it down and store it away until we can't anymore, until some part of our vessel says, "Enough!"

There are always consequences to our choices and actions. I also firmly believe in the power of choice to do something productive with a learned experience. I am not suggesting we run around and make fools of ourselves, compromise our values, and be careless, knowing you can always learn from your consequences.

Instead, I am suggesting, if you live your life on eggshells, in the fear of failing or disappointing, you will end up doing those very things you despise. You will subscribe to those very fears because you are avoiding what was and what is. Your mind, body, soul are brilliant. They will bring to life exactly what you don't want, if that is where you invest your energy.

Live in your fullest, with intention and purpose. Know what you stand for, and live as close to these guiding principles as possible. In the event that you fail to rise to these standards, surrender to asking for forgiveness. Make the shifts needed to live accordingly, and level up! Own the process of being both fallible and successful.

I Was Meeting Darkness in my Light

When I turned down the street to 68th Avenue in Arvada, Colorado, before I was even close to parking my truck, I spotted the camper. It was elevated up on my boyfriend's truck, with supplies, tools, and gear dispersed all around the vehicle. Music was blasting, and two guys, as happy as can be, were prepping their shelter on wheels for opening weekend.

The upcoming archery season would begin in a few days. These two men, my boyfriend Scott and one of his best friends had a palpable burning desire and 1,000% focus on their mission. They were unapologetic about making this camper experience exactly the way they had envisioned it. On every level, they were all in and clearly smitten with their plan.

This was about six weeks after I had relocated my whole life to Colorado in the late summer of 2011. They had planned this for a long time, and to be painfully honest, I was so excited for them. I thrilled for my boyfriend to venture out and fulfill his passion, which he had shared, openly and endearingly, while we had been dating. None of this was new or alarming for me, so it didn't scare me or intimidate me. I didn't feel anything but excited for them.

Then, when I got out of my truck and approached my boyfriend, he was cold, rude, and snarky. I was so disoriented by the behavior, it was a shot to my gut and my

ST(RIPPED)

heart, if I am being real. I've never considered myself easily ruffled or perturbed by any guy's action toward me, but this was different. I had just moved my whole life to his world and into a place where my only people, so far, were his. I was so st(ripped) of my certainty, this was an instant derail. I was taken aback by his behavior, and I immediately began to wonder what in the world I'd committed to. Who was this guy, really? I was spiraling quickly.

Please tell me you can relate to this through a moment in your life when your emotional state went from well to unwell in seconds. This was a clear sign to me I was not good. I thought I had everything cool and going well, but this interaction put me into a place of doubt so fast, and it shone a light into a side of him I had not seen. I was so disappointed. I realized this behavior was going to cost him, cost me, and cost us.

It was going to contribute to something bigger down the road. The cost was high because I hadn't fully identified all that was at stake for me. I hadn't paused while in my pursuit to truly check in with myself. I was in *Go* mode, and I had failed to check in with me. I was so caught up in being strong and driven, I forgot to acknowledge to myself, him, and my support circle that I was overwhelmed, fearful, and I little uncertain, despite all the certainty I had displayed.

In my eyes, I had two choices:

Brush it off and make an excuse for him.

Or call him on it and let him know I would not be treated that way or tolerate this as normal behavior.

Seems simple, right...?

I replied with my best snarky comments and looked at his friend with absolute annoyance. Then, my dorsal fin went up, and I headed inside.

I was devastated. It was so much more than immature behavior. I had silenced my internal voice. My strength was being tested in ways I didn't fully think through, before making this bold, all-in move. My exhaustion and fear were surfacing. In truth, I had fully leaned into this guy, his love, and his pursuit of me, but it was falling short of what I'd expected. I was falling short in my own expectations. I was experiencing disappointment and a level of disconnect that I couldn't fix, because I was way in over my head.

This brought me right back to the very lesson I had embraced and loved from my Papa: you can be deeply disappointed in someone while also loving them. This was disappointment on a deep soul level: disappointed both in this guy I had fallen in love with and in his actions. This experience was a call to action for me to dial in my needs and my asks and to be confident in doing so.

This experience was the start a years-long unraveling, a *big* misunderstanding between us. It evolved into a breakdown in communication that was detrimental to us for years. The disconnect was not the hunting. It wasn't the stupid behavior. It was the wall I threw up to counter the wall he was already building out of his own insecurities, to show me the love he deeply felt, to feel confident in his own actions, and to not care what his buddy thought. It was the wall of stubbornness and a need to be right versus doing right. It was holding firm to something and not calmly, clearly articulating what I was feeling and how it was unraveling for me.

I was so committed to "having it together," I was building a wall that would take years to dismantle. He was not only maintaining a wall that already existed, he was perpetuating a level of stubbornness and coldness out of

ST(RIPPED)

fear of his feelings for me and of not knowing how to articulate them. This would initiate a st(ripping) of what I thought was about myself and what actually was.

Scott and I started as a great idea, one that was certain to expose many ebbs and flows for every person in our lives, including us. There was a greater plan. When I sit back and reflect on the passion ignited fourteen years ago, it was a flame, a wildfire that had been kindling within me for years. It was a fire finally had the opportunity to spark and make an impact in so many ways. It was a fire that st(ripped) me of so much of my perfection and control. It reminded me that I'm a force to be reckoned with, while it also pushed me to seek deeper exploration of my capacity and purpose.

This fire wasn't new, but this form of the fire had met its perfect match in order to thrive, expose, and evolve. I knew it, and I had to pursue it!

I went *All In*.

There was no turning back. When this fire received the right "stoke," I was voluntarily st(ripping) myself of every comfort I had ever sought, in order to experience who I was in this next evolution of me. I wanted everything and anything that would come with this dynamic. I was terrifyingly bold, honest, and driven to evolve our match. It was honestly crazy to go from, "No, I do not want this" to accepting, "This is undeniable, and now I will take full ownership of it and never turn back. I will claim the victory of this discovered passion."

When I made my big move to Colorado in the late summer of 2011, I set up an adorable apartment and decorated it to a T. I had embraced my independence once again and was prepared to nourish this love thing I had moved for. When it was Scott and me, the fire could breathe and kindle at the same time. It was raw and vulnerable all at once. But it needed time and mentorship. We needed to embrace that. We needed to accept that love grows while we also evolve.

Instead, impatience often overcame us. This was a great example of when your very strengths are your worst weaknesses. Our drive, commitment, and relentlessness often interfered. We had cultivated this battle of strengths versus embracing friendship or the understanding that iron sharpens iron, and neither of us had to lose our edge in order to embrace the other. But we did need to loosen our grip on needing to be so strong and independent.

There is a bold, strong common thread between ignited passion and deep internal trust. During this chapter of my life, it revealed itself through love and soul connection. Earlier in my life, it was revealed in my commitment to my collegiate athletic aspirations. While the outcomes are the unique parts of my story, the common denominator for all of us is the power of your soul's knowing and desire to accomplish this mission at all costs.

We all have this deeper calling within us. We have to choose to harness it, to trust it, to get after it fiercely, and to go boldly in the direction of our ignited passions. On the other side is our soul's purpose. In this pursuit lies the beautiful st(ripping) of the necessary elements of our being that need an unraveling in order to boldly live out our soul's calling.

Do not fear the unravel. Fear the reluctance to discover it, the fear of not meeting who you are meant to become in the process of it.

ST(RIPPED)

The Impact of Your Formation As You Become

There is always room for two people to build and evolve off of each other's strengths; the danger is in the resistance to become the version of yourself that you deeply desire; to fully own the qualities and character you want for yourself and to share with others. This resistance can become the wedge that prevents you from the quality of relationship you envisioned for your life. This problem is not unique to marriage. It is a dynamic that plays a powerful role in all friendships and business partnerships, even parenthood.

I came into my love relationship hot, heavy, and sure. I came from a powerful home filled with love, deep connection, openness, respect, communication, and independence. I was young, a fresh twenty-three, but sure. What I lacked in age, I had locked down in my values and certainty about who I was and what I wanted in my life.

I had spent years studying the dynamics of many relationships I admired and also those I feared I might become. I had spent years knowing the love of incredible people, a family who wrapped me in support, connection, vulnerability, and trust. I gave with E-V-E-R-Y-T-H-I-N-G I had, despite the risk of losing it all.

I was no different from the version of Niccole who, as a junior transfer for volleyball, showed up and devastated with every ounce of my being. I was the girl who gave every bit of her integrity, grit, work ethic, honor, strength, and commitment, despite the conditions. I lived by the words "even if." I knew no other way to be other than by leading, loving, and fully giving by example. I was no different in these moments of being newly engaged and planning my life as a wife.

I had no plans to give up being me. I had no desire for my husband-to-be to give up himself for me. I did have every plan to demonstrate to the world, and especially to the man I was marrying, how it was possible to play all these roles.

It is hard to replace someone's uncertainty within themselves, something they have experienced for years, with your own confidence. I always learned you can lead by example, however, there is *no* guarantee you will be followed or embraced. People only know what they know until they choose to embrace something else. This rang true for many relationships in my own circle of life. Ultimately, you have to decide which hill you will die on or which hills you will choose to scale and evolve along with. Evolution ends when *you* choose to stop seeing life through an infinite lens.

Moments to Test Aligned Values, United in Surrender

We fell fast and hard. We started to build a foundation off of commonalities and aligned values, but we lacked depth around what our shared values were as well as deep appreciation for our individual strengths. There was an underlying insecurity and pride that pestered the process of fully surrendering to one another.

We both wanted the "more" with one another, but there was disconnect in achieving this "more." The surrender and growth required to unite in this particular way was not available. The lack of deep emotional connection would be the wedge that would eventually challenge our marriage in ways that we couldn't fathom.

Any ounce of doubt I had about my husband's understanding or appreciation of my grit and strength

ST(RIPPED)

evaporated as I labored and delivered our first child naturally. He was brimming with pride and love during this remarkable moment in our history, which was transformational for our relationship and would anchor for our evolving story.

I have always said the birth of our daughter was the best gift we could receive. It did something to my husband, to me, and to us that was undeniable and divine. It revealed the power of possibility and vulnerability. It united us in surrender. It also showed us our inadequacies and gave us each the power to choose to lean into each other and grow in this experience together.

I admit, I had been frustrated with him before her birth. We had spent nearly six years evolving our relationship and seeing one another through different challenges; I was desperately fighting for him to see me, value me in the ways I caught a glimmer of when we first started dating. It was as if time wore down the appreciation he once had for my independence, strength, and tenacity.

I had started to feel as if these qualities were now a threat to him versus a value. I did not think he was willing or able to go deeper with me at the time or to acknowledge my personal determination and will. But at her birth, he boldly advocated for my needs, my health, and our new baby girl. He saw my strength and determination in a way that humbled him. This built a connection that was truly a gift from God.

We were both in a place of surrender, and this breathed life into our ability to build a life together from a similar place. This experience reminded me of one of the most powerful stories I had listened to in my childhood from my Papa, when he was wounded in war, the humility and surrender he had to possess in order to move forward in the life he desired to share with my Grandma Ruby.

She met him with an elevated love and appreciation, despite his injuries. The challenge grew them. This was my desire for us, for this transformational moment to open my husband and in turn grow us. The "hard" proved easier to avoid in the everyday moments of our relationship, but the birth of our daughter left us no choice but to endure.

Chapter 9 Reflections

Part 1: My Rock-Bottom Realization

- Name a moment where you felt stripped, lost, or in the dark
- What belief, identity, or illusion was stripped away in that season?

Part 2: The Light That Found Me

Even in the dark, something began to take root.
- What did you gain or discover in the darkness?

Check any that apply—or write your own:

- ☐ Clarity
- ☐ Humility
- ☐ Resilience
- ☐ My true voice
- ☐ A deeper connection with God/faith
- ☐ A new boundary
- ☐ The real me
- ☐ A fire to start again
- ☐ The courage to let go

- One truth I found in the darkness was:

_____

Part 3: Becoming From the Bottom

Reflect on this:

"Freedom is found when we stop pretending that we're not broken."

"Becoming doesn't wait for perfection — it begins with surrender."

Complete these sentences:

"In the dark, I began becoming _____."

"The version of me rising now is _____."

PART III

UNITING PURPOSE X PASSION

"Think highly of yourself because the world takes you at your estimate."

Friendship and mentorship know no age gap. Freedom is in the ability to channel your gifts without limits, internally to externally. You can become who and what you deeply desire to be when you allow your mind, heart, and body to unite. When you move in alignment with your deepest calling, when your purpose meets your passion, you will not only find a way. You will become the way. I am convinced there is no limit you cannot surpass when you identify, own, and live out your true calling. I am proof.

NICCOLE HENDRICKSON

CHAPTER 10

The "Ripped" in St(ripped)

"I've come too far to quit."
—Sam Tinnesz

This st(ripping) of everything I thought I was and yearned to become changed everything, including how I showed up as a leader and as a friend.

I would never allow any physical pain to derail my tempo, because this pain was something I would embrace over any of the days when I lay, debilitated and unable to enjoy the simple pleasures, like just sitting at the dinner table, let alone being able to run, squat, serve, slide, and sprint. These were the things I yearned to do, when I couldn't even sleep or sit without disturbing nerve pain and mental interruption.

The constant, nagging pain and irritating nerve firing attempted to make me insane. I could not stay still, though, because stillness would aggravate or even heighten the nerve firing. At this point in my life, my tools for understanding of the nervous system were minimal. My understanding of my body and the way the body worked was far more advanced than most of my peers. However, I had *no* idea what was actually occurring within my nervous system.

The culprit in this debilitating debacle turned out to be the absolute dysregulation of my nervous system. Injuries have a unique way not only of making you appreciate what you had—the body, the mind, the presence, and the abilities—but also giving you the choice either to subscribe to a victim mentality or decide you'll be a force to redefine what is possible. You get a shot at showing what is possible when everyone else typically focuses on what is impossible.

This part of my life transformed my way of thinking, operating, becoming, and embodying. During this time, I also met some of my most impactful mindset mentors, people who helped me see through a new lens, who forced me to reach new depths of curiosity, and who presented to me ways of training and living that would transform my life on a cellular level. This was when I met my faith to a depth I'd never fathomed.

I would not let the darkness consume me. Rather, it would pave a path for light, a path I knew I could lean into. I would not fear the dark anymore. I became elements of this darkness to remind myself that we are not built in the comfort and ease of our lives, but rather in the trenches of our own personal challenges. This was me being st(ripped).

Choice. There is always a choice.

I met with countless medical professionals, most of whom told me to change directions in my life, to find something else to light me up and preserve my body for the long haul. After all I was only eighteen, but my back looked like a fifty-year-olds.

I scoffed at this idea, shook the spine specialist's hand, and said, "Thank you, but *no*! I will find another way."

ST(RIPPED)

His was an expensive and annoying recommendation. We had waited weeks to get into this appointment, and then an hour to see this specialist, paying him an exorbitant amount of money for ten minutes of his time and this useless suggestion.

As my mom and I exited the office, my wheels were turning. I was furious and empowered at the same time. These were the words I needed. This was the pushback I needed, Here was a living example of where Niccole would thrive... The naysayer, the person who would rather play it safe then find another way. The textbook says, "X," so must move forward with steps "Y and Z."

I said, *"Absolutely not!"* This was the moment in my life when I realized who I actually was, who'd been living in me this whole time, and the version of her who only came out when really, really demanded of, when pushed to no return. This would be the defining year of my life. This would be the moment I decided how I would be seen, experienced, and understood.

I looked my mom in the eye and told her, no, this would not be the path I walked. I would find a way, and I would not relent until the path was paved.

It was a defining moment for our relationship, too. She looked me back in the eye and replied, "Whatever it takes, sweetheart. Your dad and I are here for whatever it takes. We believe in you. We've got you."

Those three little words, "whatever it takes," became my guiding mantra. They rang in my mind alongside knowing their deep belief in me. This had zero to do with their understanding of my physical capacity. This went back to the little girl whose eyes they stared in during freshman year of high school and warned of the dangers of my mental drive. This was a full-circle moment, when they could reference my relentlessness at finding a way for the things in my life I was *passionate* about, the things that fueled my *purpose*.

This exchange between the spine specialist and me brought my mom to understanding firmly that her daughter was unstoppable, so she had to choose either to walk alongside me or join the naysayers. Mama D would walked alongside her people. That is what made her so special. This is where I came from: fifty percent of my wiring came from this gorgeous-souled woman, who gave her whole heart and belief when she was all in. This became a living lesson for me, as a strong woman, and this mindset and heart space became something I deeply desired to embody.

After this appointment, we were in agreement about moving forward, an agreement that embodied radical honesty and vulnerability. I knew I could do anything I set my mind to, but I also knew I needed a safe place to surrender to. I am so thankful it was in the arms of my mother. Her honesty mirrored the integrity I desired to live in. Her warm, cozy, compassionate arms were the arms I needed to collapse in. Her internal strength was the place I channeled my resilience from.

She would help hold the line for me until I got my footing again. She would help me see the long-game goals I was after and remind me who I was, when I succumbed to my fears and to my pain. She would remind me how good God is and to sit in my faith and rally my perseverance from what I know to be true: "I was built for this."

I would discover a new way to impact. I would learn what my voice really sounded like when st(ripped) of the power I had once harnessed to be my influence, my physical prowess. The energy I once took from my physical body would fuel my mind's ability to perceive what I thought was great. It was an "out of my mind and into my body" experience, which is powerful.

At this time, my body was broken down, and I needed to enter into my heart and mind, understanding these areas are not à la carte. I needed to unify them and their ability to lead and deliver. This was my introduction to my "parts." I was not done just because a part of me was hurting, injured, or debilitated. There was so much more to me than these "parts" that were temporarily out of order. I would unite with them and discover what all of me needed.

> *"There is no Life B. So, let your dreams come to reality. THIS is your life. Your ONLY one."*

I started to live boldly and fully, and I began to bear witness to my aspirations coming together in real time. I was a witness to my commitment to discomfort and to my passion to see what happens if I dared to live out what I wanted in a different way. I was writing my own story. it was truly a glimpse into my becoming as it transitioned into my embodiment.

Life was Fun, Adventurous, and Challenging

The holidays were fast approaching, and I couldn't wait to be home with my parents and older brother. I loaded my pup into my truck, and we headed out on our ten-hour road trip to sunny San Diego. The music blared, the roads were clear, and I had my pal riding shotgun.

NICCOLE HENDRICKSON

Once we made it home to my parents' house, we settled into the usual holiday hoopla. It was light and fun to be home with just the four of us. Each holiday was precious. It was clear we were entering the phase of life when these would soon be shared with our significant others, as well. It was fun to look forward to the possibilities ahead, but in this moment, it was still the four of us.

Despite the years we spent apart while I was in college and my brother was doing his life, he would always be my best friend. He would always be "Ant" to me and the person I called to help me, no matter the distance we were from each other, because he always proved he could fix, help, or navigate anything in my way; all it took was one call, one text, and he was there in whatever capacity he could be.

Christmas morning 2009 unspooled with ease. We sipped our coffee while sitting in the family room. My dad was in one recliner, my mom on the couch, I sat on the other recliner, and my brother, all 6'4" of him, sat sprawled on the floor, leaning up against my parents' ginormous coffee table. We were all laughing, no doubt at something silly our dad had said. Per usual, my brother laughed with his whole body. You could feel his light and enthusiasm.

Seconds later, his eyes got teary and full of panic. His huge hand went to his chest, and he immediately looked to our dad, letting slip the words, "Dad! My chest. I don't know what's wrong, but it really hurts. Dad, it's bad. It hurts!"

My dad immediately dropped to a knee to feel his pulse then told my mom to call 911. He asked me to move the furniture so there were zero obstructions for the paramedics to reach my brother.

ST(RIPPED)

Seconds later, my brother said he couldn't see, and he started vomiting. Everything was fast, but we were together, *thank God*. All I could think was, "*No, no*, this cannot be happening. Whatever this was, it cannot be our ending!"

My dad and mom remained calm, and, despite my brother's size, my dad kept him safe, anchored, and stable. Minutes later, the paramedics arrived. One blessing, a fire station was only four minutes from my parents' home.

The paramedics were efficient, poised, and compassionate. They loaded my brother into an ambulance and transported him to the hospital. My parents and I quickly dressed and followed close behind. Since it was Christmas morning, the roads were clear but the hospital was bustling.

We made it to my brother's room, where we found him in excruciating pain. He was disoriented, and there were no clear answers for what was happening to him. They were running every test, screening, and examination of his health history, hoping to quickly discover what was happening to and inside him.

I stood at the end of his hospital bed, my mind reeling. I watched my parents, the tension filling their eyes and the worry draped on their faces. The uncertainty was palatable, hanging over us like a black storm cloud ready to unleash at any moment. I didn't even know what to say, I was there, but I wasn't. I was lost in memories of me and my brother, pushing off the darkness of what could happen. A tug of war between belief and fear raged within me.

My dad spoke to my brother with love and some regret about things in the past. My mom told my brother he would survive this and we would get answers, to stay strong. As in every moment of my brother's life, no matter what, he stayed calm and strong. That is what made him *him*.

Nothing will ever erase that image of my big brother, age twenty-four, in a hospital bed, in absolute surrender. There was no denying it: this was all God's plan, and none of us could stop, control, or dictate what came next. We all had to surrender our fears and dig deep.

After many long minutes that felt like hours, the paramedics who had dropped my brother off came around to check on him. It turned out they'd played football for the same program as my brother, and they'd bonded in the ambulance. They also whispered to my parents that something was deeply wrong with him and not to settle for an easy diagnosis. *What the hell was that supposed to mean?*

Minutes later, a set of nurses came in to ask my brother about his pain level. It was still a 10, despite the morphine and other drugs they had given him. My mom pleaded for additional tests, any test, anything that could reveal something the other screenings had missed.

The nurses consulted with ER doctor and then wheeled my brother off. Minutes later, he was back in his room, and a man in a white coat arrived carrying a small whiteboard. He looked my brother over, asking him a few questions that confused him, greeted my parents and me, and then began to discuss what the latest test revealed.

Then, he drew an anatomical heart on the whiteboard, slammed the marker into it, and said, "Do you understand what this means, young man?"

We were all stunned, focused so intently on this doctor, we could have burned a hole through his white coat with our eyes alone. My brother had an aneurysm that was about to burst in his heart. Also, the doctor had a deep suspicion

ST(RIPPED)

there was something else graver hidden behind the aneurysm. He would need a team of six to operate, but if he couldn't get my brother stabilized and the team in house in time, he would do this open-heart surgery alone, because we only had hours to save him, if that.

> *"And she trusted God with the impossible.*
> *He would turn her fears to faith.*
> *He would turn her worries to wisdom.*
> *And He would turn her hurting to healing.*
> *And she never stopped praying."*
> —Lauren Fortenberry

December 26, 2024 became another day I would never forget. It is never our time. It is always God's time. If I had ever been uncertain about whether guardian angels existed, this day proved their existence to me. Their presence flooded the hospitals halls and hearts of each of us there. The feeling was palpable.

This was a surrender in real time. This was being st(ripped) to a level I'd never fathomed. We paced during surgery and waited for nearly ten hours. Though we were expecting a surgeon's debrief all day, the doctor's arrival caught us off guard when he came out of the operating room.

First and foremost, my brother was in the initial recovery stages, post-op. Thank God he had survived surgery. Second, the doctor explained the surgery had been tough and had presented the challenges he'd anticipated, but the team felt confident in the procedure they'd chosen to do. Behind the aneurysm was the main problem that was going to kill my brother first, a dissecting aorta. He'd noticed my brother had a few characteristics that aligned with this potential tragedy: he was tall and lanky with the roof of his mouth rising high in an arched shape, and maybe a connective tissue disorder, which can weaken the aortic wall and contribute to this kind of dissection or tear. But he was alive. That was all I could focus on. He was alive.

The days ahead would make or break his recovery. There were strict orders around visitation. The team working for the surgeon had very specific expectations, and so did we, as my brother's support system. I will never be able to unsee the fragility of life I witnessed when I saw my brother for the first time. I did not understand how surgery could take a person from vibrant to dull, robbing him of his internal liveliness. I knew, though, in a matter of days, he would start to get his color back, and weight would eventually return to his 6'4" frame.

The next few days were packed with precautions to prevent pneumonia and infection. My brother was an absolute warrior and made it out of the hospital in a week. Then, my parents and I solidified a game plan for his road to recovery. The heart surgeon had explained how the days ahead would be far different than how we had lived with him in the past. Patients who undergo open-heart surgery are never the same as before, so we would need to prepare ourselves for this revelation and evolution of my brother.

I had no idea what that meant, but I did know I was going to resign from my strength and conditioning job and role at the wellness publishing and production company, so I could move back home to support my brother's recovery. There was no doubt this was where I needed to be. This was the only thing that mattered.

Time froze.

ST(RIPPED)

My family was taken down to its foundation, which we knew was indestructible. This was a pivotal moment in all of our lives. This was an experience you don't wish on anybody, but you find yourself very thankful for everything it does for you and to you. Like any other moment of adversity, this was not the time to take on a victim mentality. Rather, there was opportunity awaiting each of us in this st(ripping).

As a family, we united in the unspoken truths that had flourished throughout years of love, trust, honor and commitment to one another. We would navigate the unknown with absolute confidence, because our home was built on deep love and friendship. This life-altering experience revealed everything I needed to know about how powerful faith was. It validated how resilience and strength are built in the darkness.

This was not my story. I couldn't claim a main role in it. I was not the lead character. I was simply *part* of the storyline. Yet somehow, during this experience, I bore witness to all the versions of myself that had evolved up until that point: all the hurt, all the obstacle, all the derailment, all the yeses when I should have said no, all the nos because I was scared. Every single moment when I had felt helpless and pathetic, only to discover my resilience and truth. All of this had led me into this exact point of time where *none* of it mattered. The st(ripping) I'd once believed defined my evolution and becoming meant nothing to me in the face of my brother's cardiac event and recovery.

As I studied my brother lying in the chair, weak, fragile, and sewn back together, I knew I had to reach far deeper in my own life. I had to vow not to play small or hold back. To show my love, my zest, and my passion, and to live it fully, because there were no guaranteed second chances. It didn't matter who received it or denied it. What mattered was that we each live out our lives fully. The land of playing it safe and predictable was for death, not for the time we have on Earth.

Throughout my whole life, my brother had demonstrated living in the moment and "going for it." I owed this to him, to my family, and to myself, to rip the safety bars off and *Go Hard or Go Home*. He recited these words over and over to me. There was no going back to tomorrow, only carving a different path to follow.

After all the visions I'd seen in my dreams, this was the life reminder that it was time. Time to step into these visions. I now had the opportunity to live them out without restraint. During this time, the best thing I could give my brother was my unwavering presence and strength, plus that pup I'd adopted before graduating college.

My little black-furred bundle of joy, Zoey, took a liking to my brother, and she became his healing sidekick. She was consistent, committed, and 100% cued into his new heart rhythm and needs. She found peace in the new tick you heard from his mechanical valve. She read him like a book before he gave us any sign that he had a need. She was determined to keep him soft, compassionate, and deeply seen throughout this healing journey.

I had a lot to learn from this pup and from this experience. This st(ripping) was life-altering for more than one reason. Reason #1: your foundation—it will make or break you.

I received this news flash: you think that you can't just get up and go and change course without thorough planning. *Wrong*! All it takes is a life-altering event for you to recognize how easy it is to simplify, to change directions, to relocate, to acknowledge what really matters in life, and boldly make the moves you need in order to facilitate the process. It becomes so much easier to carve out the path you need, in order to see through what is most important in life.

I have no idea why this happened to my brother. Truthfully, I haven't spent much time questioning God or the universe on what the bigger plan was. I simply surrendered and went in the direction that was so evident in its calling. I wanted to make this a key component of my life. The experience proved why it is imperative to know what we stand for, our guiding principles, and why it is important we know our non-negotiables in life. Through it all, we have to know elements of faith. It doesn't remove the pain, the anger, the fear, the hurt, the confusion, or the stress, but it allows you to stay dialed into your North Star.

Your faith, values, and guiding principles are what anchor you. They allow you to make decisions rooted in truth rather than be swayed by fleeting emotions or uncertainty. Without them, we drift unanchored and directionless; especially when life deals us a difficult hand. But when we are secure in what truly matters, we remain steady. No matter what comes, we know who we are and where we stand.

It was this st(ripping) that brought to life the most valuable lessons of my *becoming*: that my values and guiding principles are the foundation, no matter what.

There's Always Addition Through Subtraction

We live life hoarding our assets, our fears, our thoughts, and our dreams because we are terrified of letting something go in order to move on to the next level of our dreams. We are scared to let a relationship end out of fear we may not find something better. We are scared to scale back, fearful if we let the foot off the gas, we will lose headway toward our destination, our goal, or the "thing" we want to achieve.

While I am a firm believer in making progress one step at a time over an all-out sprint that covers an insane distance and requires a lengthy recovery before you are back on track again, it is important to note that methodical movement in life is the most valuable. Going in order to just go, while being fearful of letting up, when you have no idea where you are going anyway, you are just moving because you are terrified that, if you slow down, you will falter. This is mindless and detrimental to your wellbeing and your forward progress. In order to add, you have to subtract.

You have to subtract the mindless movement that is wearing you down. You have to subtract the outside chatter that is pure noise. You have to subtract the people who are not seeing your vision forward. You have to take a pay cut at times, when the work you are doing is costing you your sanity or your ability to thrive and live.

Our income is the easiest example of how powerful addition through subtraction can be. For example, there was a point in my career when I made a clean and consistent six figures. I'd established a dialed-in and consistent client base, a respected name for myself, and a repeatable method of success. However, I had minimal time for rest, self-care, personal growth, and freedom. My business was a monetary success, but my personal life was a slave to it.

While that might fulfill some people, I reached a point in my life where I needed to trim out certain elements of my business. This also meant trimming my income temporarily, in order to evolve my business model and make money without holding me hostage to hours I no longer desired to work. I had to put a temporary pause to some of my creation process to dial in another side of my business that would eventually make my day-to-day as a self-employed entrepreneur more efficient.

Obviously, the goal is never to lose money in order to grow. But the reality is: *something always has to give.* Whether it is your finances temporarily, your freedom, your sanity, or your quality of life. *You* ultimately have to decide what costs you more, temporarily.

With my business, I was able to go on and create something far more impactful and dynamic, when I temporarily cut one of my revenue streams because my brain and my soul were charged up. My mental capacity was able to innovate, and most important, I was able to detach. I was no longer in the business on the front lines at all times. The next significant example in my life, one of the most beautiful experiences of *addition through subtraction,* was my becoming a mother.

Nothing frees your time more than a life that depends on yours. Listen, ladies and gentlemen who are brave enough to read this book: as I mentioned earlier, I am a firm believer and advocate for women knowing and owning the wearing of as many hats as she desires. It is possible. However, it is only possible when there is a clear understanding that you will gain more than you can ever fathom during this stage of life, B-U-T it will require you to shed versions of yourself who no longer provide for this version of you. You will add to your life in ways that are unfathomable, but it will cost you the baggage you need to leave behind. It will cost you the negativity, the perfectionism, many people-pleasing tendencies, and, most important, any self-doubt.

Motherhood was the ultimate st(ripping) of identities, ones I'd had no idea I had breathed life into. It was the ultimate surrender to my greater purpose. It was the shedding of everything that no longer aligned with who I was becoming, and the building of the warrior woman whom it was my great pleasure to meet. I had glimpsed her throughout in my life, but was never fully acquainted with, until I became a mom.

The most dynamic version of me finally got the courage to ask the newly formed version of me (Hello, Mama!) to see my multifaceted drive in a new light. To embrace my new role and the possibilities that came with it. It didn't occur to me, beforehand, the detriment to the psyche and my self-worth, and the external pressures and encouragement to bounce back, to prove you can hold on to all that you did, prior to earning this new role as "mama." I never really thought much about it, because the women who came before me, who were essential in raising me and showing me what "being Mama" looked like, they didn't speak of the inability to hold the role. So, I didn't realize this wasn't the actual struggle.

I came to realize how the struggle, for me, was not in embracing the changes that happened within me, the new viewpoint I possessed. I was so busy once again proving things didn't have to change that I confused my mission to help women recognize the power and perspective that is born within them when becoming Mama is different than the thought patterning you have to surrender your power and impact, because you have become a mother. The power is in this ability to experience what is actually important. It is boundaries. It is protecting your energy, so you can show up as Mama. It is staying well and nourished because you are needed in big ways, when you return home to your babies. You do this by honoring yourself first, then your family, not through maintaining everyone's view of you and your capacity.

Motherhood built my internal matrix to a high standard and into an impenetrable landscape. It stretched my capacity to a degree I'd never believed was discoverable. It opened my heart to a place of sturdy. Motherhood made the resilience I thought I'd once fostered look like a speck of adaptability. Motherhood gave me credentials that no other degree or certification could ever award me. It was the ultimate example of addition through subtraction. It was to surrender in order to become!

"There's nothing more dangerous than the person who shows up every single day, even when the rewards are uncertain. The one who can tolerate the most uncertainty is the one who will eventually win."

—@RulesoftheWolf

The Grit Lives Within

When I arrived in Colorado, my first job was at a suburban 24-Hour Fitness; I took this simply to get me started in a place where didn't know anyone. While I had zero plans to dial in the protocols of the fitness bureaucracy, I did have every intention to meet as many people as possible and learn what was popping in Colorado.

I was on a mission: I would leverage my personal training certifications earned in college and my degree to grow a client base, to grow my impact, and to discover who

NICCOLE HENDRICKSON

I really was in this chapter. I was open, I was curious, and I was driven to create something of my own. Within the first week of work, one of my first clients asked if I would be interested in applying for the corporate wellness position at her work; she explained it was a superb benefit, provided to every employee. It paid decently well and in dire need of being revamped.

A project, a creation, a transformation: *"Yaassss, Please!"* This was right up my alley.

A few weeks later, I cruised to downtown Denver in my sunny-San Diego, white Toyota Tacoma, wearing big sunglasses, my hair in a top knot, and the music ridiculously loud. As I made my way to the heart of downtown, I was in a tizzy. I missed my turns multiple times and cursed the one-way streets, thinking how ill-prepared I was for downtown life. I felt like Little Miss Suburbia herself. It was slightly ridiculous!

Noted: get downtown savvy, Niccole. Do not drive in the wrong direction. *Oooof!*

I finally reached my destination and entered the building with a cheerful smile, my strong presence, and a carefully curated proposal in hand. Twenty-three-year-old Niccole was confident, sharp, enthusiastic, and ready to make moves. She was a little over the top for Miss Deb, though.

Miss Deb was moved by my energy but also couldn't believe my passion was real. This sort of energy was something found only in magazines, and here I was, alive and in living color, ready to own this assignment and determined to crack a smile on her face. I took note of her reservations and went out of my way to let her feel my gratitude for the opportunity and her time.

ST(RIPPED)

After she toured me through the onsite gym, she brought me around the building to give me a bit more intel on the social structure and relationships between each department. I truly appreciated the dynamic of this business. I was drawn to the gaps in the social hierarchy that had developed over time. This was an incredible opportunity, not only to foster better working relationships and camaraderie between the departments and teams, but a beautiful opportunity to strengthen individual performance and production.

I was confident in my ability to influence the esprit de corps among the people at this corporation. I kept thinking, if we could snag one to two people from each department, we could change the trajectory of the whole operation. I was bound to do this! I would do this.

We ended our tour in the HR office, where I had a chance to ask endless questions about the company, meet the head of HR, give my elevator speech, and then propose my vision. This was a turning point in my life. I was now living out the version of myself who pulled the chair up to any table she was interested in. This version of Niccole pitched what she wanted. This version of Niccole was embodied in strength, resilience, fortitude, and forward vision. This woman was ready to set the tone she had created. This version of Niccole was not threatened by a "no." In fact, she sought out pushback and the chance to counter.

A few days later, I received an email from the HR team proposing an offer that included a role as the corporate wellness coach and coordinator, as well as a variation of the schedule I had initially proposed. They confirmed my desired pay and start date; I smiled and thought to myself, in the words of Matthew McConaughey, "Green light!"

Pitching and accepting this role was my first big embodiment in my adult life. I was not only exhilarated at the opportunity to impact, but I was legitimately proud of myself. I knew in my soul, this role, this company, these people were going to grow me. They were going to stretch my maturity and bandwidth, and I yearned for it!

Curating and accepting this role were like putting the gas in a vehicle: it nourished a growth mindset for me, and it put me in a place where I could begin to see my life as a chess board, with each client and each role as a strategic move to my bigger vision. My role as a corporate wellness coach was a segue into building a name for myself in the training industry. It challenged my operating values, communication skills, and ability to hold the line. It proposed many obstacles for my life, but at the same time offered me a degree of stability and challenge I deeply craved.

This job let me work with a variety of beautiful humans who tested my ability to be malleable, to lead no matter the age gap, and, most important, to set the example. By month six of living in Colorado, I had secured my role at this corporation, left 24-Hour Fitness, and started my first official brand, Peak8Fitness. I led a weekly outdoor bootcamp, dabbled in a supplement company, rented space out of two personal training gyms, and locked down several in-home clients.

My life was nuts, and I *loved it*! It was the good kind of insanity at this stage of my life. I wasn't married, no kids, and my boyfriend worked out of town. I was bound and determined to create something of my own. Hard work,

ST(RIPPED)

tireless hours, grit, and commitment to something so much bigger than the present moment fueled my fire. I embodied relentlessness. I was the "ripping" to my st(ripping), building a foundation one day at a time.

Over and over again, the little things refined me and my process. Showing up for my standards when nobody was watching. Studying and connecting with anyone and everyone who shared a common interest. Endless coffee meetings to practice my voice and share my vision. Every single moment was a rehearsal for something so much bigger than the current moment. But also, it was recognizing how valuable the current moment was and celebrating it! I kept my eye on the prize, allowing each moment to evolve me. I was a sponge to the experiences and actively choosing to make my becoming tangible.

As I continued to grow and flourish this program, I was also growing my brand, evolving it at each new growth stage. I was ruthless in the hours I kept for myself. In the words of one of my beloved clients, "You need to tell that owner to give you a vacation!" The irony didn't fall on deaf. I really had kept brutal work hours, and I ended up learning some tough lessons, the longer I was growing my business.

I would not compromise my work ethic, but I was on a path to self-destruction, if I didn't start setting up some boundaries. I had returned to the kind of people-pleasing that would become merciless to my wellness. What became wildly clear was that I needed some business mentorship. I needed help with my structure. There was only one me, and I couldn't be in multiple places at one time, and I couldn't sustain ten-to-fourteen-hour training days every day, every week anymore.

Sure, the money had become intoxicating, but my ego was being nurtured in a way that was no longer healthy. I needed a time out. I needed a re-org of my business.

When you are willing to surrender, the universe blesses you with exactly what you need. My blessing come in the form of one the most tenacious women I had ever met. This woman, Kelly Forsyth, was of a combination of my Grandma Ruby, my father, and my auntie. I received the long-awaited gift of a brilliant, sassy, driven, loyal to the day of death, ride-or-die friend and mentor. Thank you, God!

She arrived in my life at the end of 2012 and greeted me with strength, audacity, and pure love. As I mentioned, I was nearing a level of burnout at the time, plus frustration at the direction of my growth. I was growing, but I wasn't necessarily in my niche. My passion was dwindling. I needed an audit.

Kelly had tenacity and engaged me in courageous conversations. She was bold but loving. She dared me to verbalize and then materialize the out-of-the-box ideas I needed. She helped me understand how to create a business plan, how to curate pitches, how to navigate clients, and, most important, how to *own* my power and purpose.

My breaking point was tangible. I was no longer having fun, and I was constantly navigating how I could fit in one more person. Something had to give. With perfect timing, like always, my parents came out for a visit. My dad and I went out to grab a coffee.

He looked at me and said, "Niccoley, you need to make a change. This pace is not sustainable or scalable. You have got to factor in down time and mental rejuvenation. You

ST(RIPPED)

cannot always operate with your hair on fire going 100 miles an hour!"

When I looked at him, tears immediately filled my eyes. After all, I was so damn proud of myself. I had created something beautiful, successful, and impactful. I was moving chess pieces in my life board, but damn, I was fried. I asked him the tried-and-true question: "Well, how do you do it then? You seem to be able to operate at a level that is not only admirable but successful and fresh. Plus, you always have an edge." This conversation was the igniter to my next "life move."

Between a Trace Deneke coaching session and Kelly Forsyth recalibration, I got back on track, ready to live out the next phase of my vision.

The relationships I have curated in my lifetime continued to be my backbone. They have lent support, insight, love, and courage in some of my most challenging moments. I truly believe the ability to surrender into the safety of our people, those who see us, love us, hold us, and believe in us to our core, are the reasons why I have continued to soar forward, even when taken down to ash. These support systems are my driving forces for paying it forward, cultivating community, and giving people permission to lean in. We need each other.

Grit is honed when you recognize that your *limits* are always you, not the hardships you face. Connection and impact know no age difference. Pour into those you love. Unshakable faith, grit, and gratitude are priceless. Listen.

Chapter 10 Reflections

Theme: Built in the Trenches

Choice, resilience, nervous system awareness, and becoming through pain.

Part 1: Nervous System Check-In

Before we go deeper—pause and take inventory.

➢ In this moment, my body feels:

➢ Right now, my nervous system needs:

- ☐ Stillness
- ☐ Movement
- ☐ Breath
- ☐ Release
- ☐ Nourishment
- ☐ Support

(Reminder: Awareness is power. There's no wrong answer.)

Part 2: My Own St(ripping) Moment

* What experience in your life stripped you of what you thought you were—only to lead you somewhere more powerful?
* What did you lose?
* What did you find or gain in return?

Part 3: Tool Rebuild

The author shared how her understanding of the nervous system was limited—and how that led to mentorship and transformation.

* What tool, support, or knowledge have you gained from your "dark season" that now helps you lead, live, or heal more fully?

* Who was a key mentor or guide during this time?

Part 4: My Choice, My Becoming

"I would not fear the dark anymore. I became elements of this darkness..."

* What is one belief, habit, or identity you are ready to leave behind in the darkness?

* What new identity or truth will rise from it?

CHAPTER 11

What No One Can Take Away...

"The lust for comfort murders the passions of the soul."
—Kahil Gibran

On Christmas morning one year later, we held our breath, wondering if the one-year mark of my brother's cardiac event would include some sort of second round of his and our unraveling.

It didn't.

My brother had been navigating his new life, his fresh start. My parents were in flow with their lives, and I was starting to lose my ever-loving mind!

I had lost touch with my own flow, my tempo, which I once found familiar. I had quickly realized how much of my worth was tied into what I was doing, not in who I had become and who I was evolving into next. I had lost touch with the unification of my passions and purpose. Truthfully, I felt behind, expired, passed over, and grasping for the rope to swing to the mountain I was scaling. But really, I was in free fall.

We crave freedom, but we panic the minute we have it, like *really* have it in our hands and in our lives. Then, I met a version of myself I needed to seek out and get curious with, this young woman living on the line between belief

ST(RIPPED)

and doubt on purpose. She was riding the edge of uncertainty as the fuel to drive her to the next chapter of her life. She was purposefully setting obstacles in order to see what would happen, to test out the resilience she'd built through all her prior derailments. I started to believe the only way I could actually step into the next portion of my becoming was by enduring something life-altering. So, I started to create life-altering situations to test myself, my grit, my bandwidth, and my intellect.

Whether I wanted to fully admit it or not, I was terrified about how easy it had been to slide right back into the ease of being at home, helping the family businesses, hanging with the circles of friends there, and saving money with ease because I was lucky to live in the comfort of my parents' home. I was in epic comfort, and I was going nuts, because that is not who I was to my core or a part of the woman I was building, brick by brick, in order to become. I would not allow myself to slide into this space. I would not allow a choice to be with my family during a challenging time morph into a blanket of indulgent comfort.

I was in a weird life spot and insanely anxious to navigate my next steps. I needed clarity. I craved a call to duty. I was fulfilled and empty at the same time. In my process of navigating what the hell I was going to do with my life, I was like an excavator on a job site. I literally cleared every path I was traveling: my relationship, my job, my circle of friends, my habits—all of it. A complete clearing. It was renovation time.

I saw one path and one path only: getting uncomfortable. Getting uncomfortable meant changing everything. In hindsight, I do not suggest you go about life this way. It was destructive, hurtful, and irrational, and the wreckage down the road cost me the freedom I'd once had inside me.

I was desperate to understand my role, to rekindle my connection to my purpose.

I had confused the shifting of my passions with a loss of my purpose. The truth was, I had a dream, a deep calling that nobody could kill, including myself. I needed to get out of my head and into my heart and body to navigate the steps ahead. I needed to give myself the permission to drop inward and listen to what Niccole needed and wanted now.

This version of myself was nowhere near the same girl as from before the life-altering event for my brother and our family. *I had to stop playing by the rules of engagement of my previous self.* I had to honor the power of "coming back home." In so many ways, I came back to the starting line that I'd deeply craved, but I was scared to admit I wanted a fresh start. I was scared to fully own that I could have a new beginning every damn day, if I wanted, but it would require taking ownership of those steps and surrendering to that calling. It would require me to tune out the chatter and tune into my inner knowing.

That was it. It was time to stop playing in the pathway of "this is next." It was time to create what was next, to own it and embrace the unknown.

> *"Feel the fear and do it anyway."*
> —Susan Jeffers

The root of my *why*, my *purpose* was in service and leadership. In the deep belief in a person's ability to achieve anything they united their mind and heart around. That was what fuelled me. It was this core element of my belief

ST(RIPPED)

system that got me out of bed every morning. It drove me to seeing nothing but possibility.

I wrestled around with what was next in my life, what the next steps looked like, felt like, and sounded like, with who would I *become* and what my impact would *embody*.

After all, I was st(ripped) back to my very foundation, to my core. This fresh start felt like a mix of "I am so behind" and "I am right on time." I decided to apply for physical therapy school, which was both intriguing and noble to me. I giggle as I type this: *noble*. Somewhere in my headspace, I didn't feel enough when I was personal training someone up to that point. It felt basic, simple, and lacked the depth and the impact I truly wanted to have on a person. The passion, energy, and love I felt as a strength and conditioning coach wasn't enough for me, long-term. Even that role had left me craving more depth and a lifestyle that could not be supported by that career path.

I was right back to the version of Niccole who was being forced to decide what her degree should be, her focus. It was haunting me all over again. The reality was I knew what I wanted to do, how I wanted to make people feel and the long-term impact on them, the collaborations I wanted to take place, and the freedom and fulfillment I wanted to embody, but I had no idea where to go next in order to step into this vision. The next best thing to my vision, which I couldn't seem to fully explain, was meeting my drive to create with more education and qualifications. So, I did.

I set out to return to school, to the very same junior college where I had started it all. It was déjà vu, as I wrote the next chapter to my story starting at the same beginning point. *AGHHHHH!* It was such a mess, yet I loved the comfort at the same time. Every step I took on my JC campus I had to remind myself I was already a college graduate and was simply back for more. This was not me going backward, but rather forward.

That summer and fall, I busted my ass to complete more chemistry and physics credits. I studied and added to my transcript in ways I never had before. It was painstaking and boring, but I was driven by the end destination: submitting my application to the Doctorate of Physical Therapy program. While I went to school, I started to work for a PT, while I also held on to my tried-and-true waitressing position at my grandparents' café. Eventually, I decided it was time to put my certifications to use and do personal training, as well. I was back as the full-force, high-functioning Niccole, juggling multiple roles with purpose, determined to discover which one truly aligned.

I was insanely busy and stretched mentally, but thriving at the same time. I was learning in ways that stretched my internal expansion. I was maturing into a young woman who was more aware of what energized her and what drained her. I was becoming while also observing who I was in the process. During this particular chapter of my life, I was all in, while getting a chance to edit the outcomes along the way.

My time working for the physical therapy office opened my eyes to an aspect of my wiring that brought forth the value of paying it forward. It exposed me to how important it was that, no matter what path I took forward, I always pay it forward. I never forgot the people along the way who had shaped me.

The PT office I worked for had a working contract with Project Walk. Project Walk is the world leader in treating individuals affected by paralysis and mobility-related disorders. Their mission is to provide an improved quality of life for people with paralysis through intense activity-based recovery programs, education, training, research, and development.

Frequently, we received patients from this recovery center. The PT I worked for gave me the rundown on each patient plus a small heads-up on what to expect. I was not prepared for what I felt when the first patient arrived one afternoon...

A sixteen-year-boy from Australia arrived with his mum and little brother. The door opened, and I had tears in my eyes immediately, I thought, *No! This is so damn unfair. How is this happening? Why?*

I composed myself and greeted them. We worked with the boy for over an hour. In that time, I got to know him, his mom, and little brother. I learned he'd had a dirt-bike accident. He was a skilled rider whose fall had ended his life of freedom instantly. This sucked my breath away. I was devastated and driven to help on a mindset level.

Pushing the parameters for regaining his mobility and strength were no-brainers to me. But in these PT sessions, I realized my passion for training the mind and heart to unite and, in turn, create the unstoppable force each patient could become, was second to none.

There, in that PT office, after all of the additional coursework, volunteering, physical training, and client and patient service, I arrived at my passion and purpose: through the demand of a dialed-in strength and conditioning regimen, I would facilitate men and women to harness their purpose, hone their mindset for growth and challenge, and live a life in their values.

NICCOLE HENDRICKSON

There wasn't a degree or certificate for recognizing this passion and bringing my purpose to life. This would require me to live it, and to be present. This would require I didn't settle into one program in order to bring this vision to life. It wouldn't be a single program, class, or occupation that would refine this skillset and my burning desire to expand my vision. It would require me to be a student in the everyday moments of my life. The growth and development would ask me to be the student and the teacher in all my exchanges. It would require me to stretch my comfort zones in all aspects of the life I was living.

I left the PT clinic that day both exhausted and invigorated at the same time. I didn't say a word to anyone. I just put my full application packet together for PT school, then I asked my mom to join me in submitting my application and seeing it off to the admissions office via U.S. mail.

When I returned to the car, I looked my mom in the eye and said, "It's not PT school that I want. I hope I don't get in."

Her eyes opened so wide, I thought they would come out of her head. She gasped and said, "Really? Why not? Niccole, I just watched you go back to school for additional coursework, volunteer tirelessly at a PT office, study for your GRE, take that test, and hold two additional jobs. Now, you do not want to go through with it? Why? What is going on?"

I looked at her and said, "That is correct. I don't want to be a PT. There are elements of it, just like being a strength coach, that light me up. They bring out the best in me, and in turn, I inspire the best versions of others. I help them harness their strength and grit. But there is more to me, and being stuck in that box is suffocating. Taking on tens of thousands of dollars in debt when I'm not all-in with the career path seems ridiculous. Why? For a title? For status? To say I did it? I simply cannot. I will not."

I finished all my classes at the JC, I wrapped up my volunteer hours at the PT clinic, and I continued to train at the gym while working at my grandparents' restaurant. I was free-floating and in a discovery phase. I was actively pursuing my options, dedicated to going back to school for something expansive, and most important, pursuing adventure. I was itching for adventure, craving the opportunity to live somewhere else and see who I could evolve during the experience. Who would I meet? Who could I join forces with?

This was perfect timing, because my childhood best friend was finishing up her degree, and she was game to explore all the possibilities, too.

Ride or Die in Action

If anything was true about my friendship with my childhood bestie, Kari, it was our relentless pursuit of fun and mastery of whatever we were doing and becoming.

I had been back in my hometown for just over a year. Most of that time I'd spent with my brother, helping him navigate his next steps, post-surgery. I went back to school and worked, too, but I also found time to connect with Kari.

We were in very different chapters of life, but yet were a lot the same. Plus, it never mattered with us. As long as we were together, it really didn't matter the external circumstances. We always seemed to meld back into each other's life, no matter the era we were living in.

NICCOLE HENDRICKSON

This particular chapter was a bit messy and unknown, but we each leaned into each other to pave a path ahead for our dreams. In so many ways, the dreaming part helped to clear the "clutter" of our current lives. The dreaming together recalibrated our internal compasses.

We started to dream about all the places we could move to and live. We started sharing the ideas of what we envisioned for our daily lives if we moved to New York, Florida, Arizona, Colorado, or somewhere else in California. Really, the sky was the limit. We just had to decide. Naturally, the only way to process all of these big dreams was through countless hours working out together, doing hot yoga, wine Wednesdays, concerts, bougie breakfast dates, and endless coffee from the Pannikan with our many beach walks.

We proceeded seriously with our dreams. I started to apply for grad school, while she started looking for jobs. We started to share this vision and materialize our plans. This was going to happen!

Personally, I was attracted to the idea of New York. I had long been in awe of its bustling tempo and the ability to walk anywhere and everywhere. I had fallen in love with the charm of Soho, plus I was ready to live a completely polar-opposite life than the one where I grew up. I craved a shift, something bold and new.

I was equally interested in Colorado. Every guy I had ever met from there was a catch. They were strong, masculine, steady, fun, and adventurous. There hadn't been one person I'd met from Colorado who didn't know how to work hard and play harder. I liked that. Plus, I had some friends there, so we would be decently set up for navigating a new life landscape. My bestie wanted Colorado over New

York, but she was ride-or-die and willing to explore wherever we decided.

We continued to pave our path for our move. We continued to dream about our futures and hold the vision of our move. And we continued to build memories along the way that only strengthened our bond, our sisterhood. This was a chapter of life when the memories together burned so deep in my soul, I still refer back to them and feel nothing but happiness, sisterhood, and the gift of our deep soul-sister friendship.

Our path was patient and evolving. It was on track. I was feeling good in my pursuit of continuing my education and experiences elsewhere. I was set on this being my next step to evolve my purpose and passions. After all I was only twenty-two years old. I had time.

And then my phone rang one winter evening. It was a friend from Colorado. I couldn't help but think this was a sign! She was calling to tell me she was engaged. (*Finally*, I thought to myself! She had only dated the guy for ten years, which was insane to me, but needless to say, I was thrilled for her!). They were planning their wedding, and she wanted to know if I was "in" for a cruise to the Caribbean.

"Well, of course!" I said. "Girl, I have nothing holding me back. Let's go! Let's get you married!"

This call reopened a dialogue and friendship that had always been there, but intermittently. She was a friend I'd made through another friend and caught up with a few times a year. We'd enjoyed some fun memories, but she was not a friend I spoke to often. Boy, was that about to change.

Weeks later, I was being pinged by her weekly then every few days. I didn't think much of it other than she was clearly excited to share her wedding plans, and this engagement had opened a door to evolve our friendship.

Then, a message rolled in. "Hey, I don't know why I never thought of this, but we have the perfect guy for you! Are you dating anyone by chance?"

My face flushed, my stomach went into knots, and my chest got tight. *Oh no*, I thought to myself. *Nooooooo!* I was frozen. This could not be happening. Just a few months ago, I had severed ties with a guy I'd been seeing, ending the relationship, which had shattered his heart plus broken my heart, too. And all because I needed freedom, clarity, space, and the opportunity to *live*! All I wanted to do was do me and hang with my best friend, somewhere else in the world, and now this. *What? No!*

I simply replied, "No, I am not interested."

She was aghast. She could not believe it was just a "no!" So, she didn't relent, despite my cold, dry answer. She added, "He thinks you're gorgeous. He is very interested. He already knows everything about you, and he wants to meet you! We are going on a winery trip, and I would love for you to join us and meet him!"

What was happening? *No*, I thought to myself again. This was not the time, this was not the chapter. I didn't want a boyfriend, I didn't want a distraction, I didn't want to care for someone else other than my bestie, and I certainly was not ready for my heart to open in the ways I had let it, before severing my previous relationship. I was in knots and tried like hell to stuff this text and phone conversation into a little box within me, the box where I stored all the inconvenient things until I could deal with them later. I told nobody about this conversation. I just kept it to myself, telling myself I would navigate it so it simply went away and became an afterthought.

Until it didn't! This friend's texts became more frequent. She was relentless about trying to introduce me to their friend, to this Colorado catch, and she was certain we were made for each other. In her opinion, too much time had already passed, we needed to be introduced already.

This was insane! I was starting to get distracted by just these texts. My life was in an ebb and flow. It was priming my path for the move my best friend and I would make later that year. But I found my curiosity growing into a distraction that was really getting in my way.

Finally, I shared what had been going on with my best friend and my mom. My bestie was, of course, intrigued and excited. I don't think any of us thought it would get in the way of our desired path ahead, so we indulged in the fun of it together, as gal pals. My bestie was there for me and my wandering, curious heart. My mom, on the other hand, had a sense about this. She seemed to empathize with my desire not to be distracted yet knew this distraction could be something long-term…

One afternoon, this friend's text messages transitioned into her taking a more proactive approach, which led me to ask for a photo of him. The photos came through as I arrived at the family grocery store, where my mom and aunt work. As I walked up to their office, my phone started going off. Picture after picture.

My face went pale! I said, "Oh, no. This is the guy you marry. I am not ready for this!"

Naturally, my mom and aunt were excited and wanted to see the photos. After looking they shook their heads and agreed. "Niccole, what are you going to do?"

I scoffed. With a coy smile, I replied, "Nothing. I am not ready for this. I am just getting my life going in the direction I have envisioned. I have just ended a serious relationship, and I need and want to do me, my life, my dreams!"

They said, "Okay…"

Then, I changed the subject and gathered some snacks for the fitness conference I was going to the next day. I kindly replied to my friend's twenty-something messages, saying, "He's very handsome, and I am sure he is wonderful. I am just not in the place to pursue something like this right now." I clicked send and threw my phone in my purse.

As I headed out of the store and off to my day, I couldn't think straight. I was so distracted by this whole life interference.

That night, she messaged me again. "We are with your guy, and he wants to know if he can have your number?"

I was furious and lit up at the same time! Come hell or high water, this guy was getting access to my life, and I couldn't for the life of me figure out *why now*!

I replied, "First off, he is *not* my guy. Second, you can, but let him know I am busy and not around much to chat!" After hitting send, I let out an exasperated sigh!

Four days later, I was cruising down I-5 with my windows down in my lifted white Toyota Tacoma, music blasting, sunnies on, and the perfect weather kissing my cheeks. Oddly for a Sunday, traffic was flowing, making the drive that much more energizing. I had just wrapped up a wonderful fitness conference and was on cloud nine, filled with creative direction, some new educational tips, and an ounce of freedom and fulfillment.

About ninety minutes away from home, I was set to cruise and reflect. But then, my phone rang. "Hi, this is Niccole," I answered without hesitation.

A male voice said, "Hi, Niccole, this is Scott, Matt and Abby's friend...!"

When Passion Ignites, Follow it, Trust it, and Go After it

That winter of 2011, an undeniable passion was ignited in me. A spark was lit when I was introduced to the man whom I am now blessed to call my husband. That March, though, I wasn't fully sure what was brewing within me, but I knew it was an undeniably kinetic, a palpably passionate connection that I couldn't deny.

First was seeing his photograph. Then, that first phone call, when I heard his voice. Good gawd! His voice did something to a part of my soul that woke me up, and I could not ignore it! The way he said my name, keeping a cool, calm tempo to his speech, it locked me in so I was ready to spill all the details. It hooked me in a way that I could no longer deny how he had piqued my soul's curiosity.

I was flustered, unraveling, touched by lust, desire, curiosity, and pursuit. I was dead set on exploring every aspect of this deep, passionate connection that had come out of nowhere. At least it felt that way at the time.

How could I, Miss Self-control—the extremely disciplined, knows what she wants, no barrier too high or too wide or too challenging to overcome—be so distracted and taken with a connection or a feeling that I stepped effortlessly and confidently into this relationship? How was it possible to be so overcome by a passionate connection that everything that had *nothing* to do with this connection started to feed into my passion and drive for this self-discovery that was unraveling. That's it! It was a revealing of myself, occurring while I was also discovering said person.

I do believe in the universe lining us up with a deep soul connection during our lifetime. I believe we are connected to certain people for a reason, and our lives will find said connection no matter the distance, no matter the challenge. Quite frankly, I believe God was doing His greatest work, leading me on this pathway, when He united me and Andi on the flight from San Diego to Monterey. This was no mistake. It led to what was to come in 2011, the uniting of my soul to my person, Scott.

This was a st(ripping) of me, my control, my level of expectation and ability to pivot, my desire to plan and know every detail. This one call that I chose to take changed my whole life.

There is such a thing as a positive derail; one that puts us in a mode to discover ourselves and our untapped magic. Throughout my life, I'd come to know the growth and reward that can come out of unplanned darkness, from the st(ripping) of what I had thought my identity was tied to. But this was a new kind of revelation, a new kind of growth and breakdown of what I wanted, what I thought I had dialed in, and what was actually revealed.

When I hung up that first call, my burning curiosity ran through me was like a moth to a flame. I couldn't stop my desire to know more. I couldn't deny what was happening within me, and I never wanted to forget what this felt like. There would be a reality check around the corner, at some point, but I didn't want to lose touch with this newly revealed passion and connection that was unspooling.

Sparks are Confronting in Real Life

Igniting a fire is hot. Stoking a fire can be the work you didn't know you wanted to involve yourself in. Keeping a fire lit despite the weather conditions is work with *no* shortcuts!

This "fire" and the process of nurturing it, managing it, and deciding if it was even smart to keep it lit became the best metaphor for this chapter of my life. In this chapter, I found my person, but more important, I began the revealing of who I was in the evolving moment and at the core of my existence.

The back and forth of our long-distance relationship was fun, intriguing, tiring, and confronting. It blasted levels of uncertainty within every facet of my being, while it also ignited a level of personal certainty that fueled me to go *all in*.

"Life is not a problem to be solved,
but a reality to be experienced."

Once I hung up with Scott and gathered my emotions, I grabbed my overnight bag and headed into my parents' house. It was a Sunday afternoon, so both of my parents were home and, better yet, in conversation at the island in the kitchen.

They looked at me, I looked at them, and they asked, "How was the conference? You look stunned. What is going on with you?"

I responded, "He called." Just two little words.

I quickly tried to change the subject back to the conference, back to anything other than what I had just experienced in the last ninety minutes. I was a floating, hormonally-entranced, emotionally-charged young woman, who was desperately trying to get a grip as I watched the look my parents exchanged. I knew they knew this meant something.

It meant something. It was going to be the conversation that shifted the trajectory of my life.

> *"Your visions will become clear only when you can look into your heart. Who looks outside, dreams. Who looks inside, awakes."*
> —C. G. Jung

I rode the escalator up to the arrivals area at Denver International Airport. I had my suitcase and a backpack full of reading material, because God knows I never went anywhere without ceasing the opportunity to learn something and stay on top of my studies. I was eager, a little anxious, but unrealistically calm at the same time. After all, I was "reuniting" with someone I had known several lifetimes ago. At least that is what I told myself.

I was quite literally stepping into a deeper calling, one that came straight from my heart. The entire unfolding of this connection felt like a dialogue between my heart and mind, led by intuition and inner truth. There was no interference *ever* from my logical brain. It was full steam ahead, honoring my heart's calling.

I made it to the top and there he was, waiting for me. All 6'2" of him, with a huge smile. He gave me a big hug and warm embrace as if we were longtime friends who had reunited after a year of traveling abroad. It was surreal!

I was alive and so goddamn sure of this, it quite literally terrified me. The girl who had denied this connection was now in the arms of the connection. She was living out the very thing she'd been avoiding, in order to see through her vision. Her vision, her impact, her purpose—which didn't seem to include the love story that was unwinding within her.

The irony of this revelation was pretty clear to me. I went from dreaming and observing to living out my vision. Taking ownership of my direction, my heart's calling, and my gifts had led me into a place of receiving. This led me to a place of wildly vivid pictures of what the future held for me on a cellular level. This started my embodiment.

> "Your heart tells you big things in little ways...
> listen."
> —Butterflies Rising

My best friend, Kari, recognized that what Scott and I shared was more than just a mutually liking. It was a deep connection I was fully dialed into it and intentionally pursuing it.

Six and a half months later, I was driving across four states to start a new chapter in Colorado. I left my Labrador in the loving care of my parents and said goodbye to my best friend, both holding pieces of my comfort and love as I stepped into the unknown. Once again, I as rolling on the highway of passion and vision with an open heart, ready to live my wildest dreams. If there had ever been a moment in my life when I was unreasonably certain, it was in the summer of 2011.

This man, this bond, this idea of starting from scratch and building myself from nothing in a place that knew nothing about me and my capabilities, my determination, my passion, and my unrelenting spirit to bring it to life absolutely fueled me. I was emboldened by the challenge, the unknown, the possibilities, and the probabilities. I was the certainty, the force, the drive, and the creator of the vision, and I would *not* look back.

I arrived with a vision to create a boutique mobile fitness business that would serve the professional on the go. I had a dream to create a movement through my dynamic collaborative business that would highlight the talents of other small business owners and serve the multifaceted individual. I knew no one but my boyfriend's friend group. They would not be the source for my business building or expansion. They would not be the people I leaned into

Little did I know they would be the very group who reminded me of how strong and dynamic I actually was by constantly putting my authenticity to the test. And let me be clear: the reminder was that the girl who saw herself in the mirror was strong, fierce, true, driven, independent, and assured of herself. They would not be able to bring me down. Their insecurities would not be my punishment to bear. Only send me to therapy. *Ha*!

My certainty and drive gave me the energy and tenacity to seek connections in order to expand and understand what I was working with in this new state, new town, and newly revealed side of me. It was invigorating, it was freeing, it was a field of endless open space, and I was there to claim my territory!

This part of my life was the initiation into my embodiment. I was living out what I had kept stored in my mind and heart for countless years. It was full throttle, stopping at nothing to try anything and everything to test out my vision. I would set my soul on fire!

ST(RIPPED)

This time, I was actively pursuing this chapter of st(ripping). I planned to tear my own walls down, ride through my fears, and subscribe to the derailment of everything I once knew. I went voluntarily into the fray. I craved it, and I would not be stopped or convinced otherwise.

It is fair to say, all the involuntary st(rippings) had primed my mental space to drive me forward with the degree of determination required to bring me into the light of my vision. Knowing I had nothing to actually fear because I had once, twice rebuilt myself from ash. This bold move would be no different.

"Whatever you do, do it with all your might. Work at it, early and late, in season and out of season, not leaving a stone unturned, and never deferring for a single hour that which can be done just as well now."

—P.T. Barnum

Reconnecting With My Passion and Pace

I live and will die by my work ethic, drive, and passion. Those are elements of my (ripping) that are not only important to my existence on this Earth, but also essential to the legacy I desire to leave. I believe this rings true for all of us: when our passion is united with our purpose, we are unstoppable.

But we require discipline to create boundaries around our pursuit of passion and purpose, so we do not sacrifice our wellbeing while pursuing our desired impact. There has to be a balance, a flow, a life to actually live, not just a grind. And this, my friends, was my chapter of life when I discovered that not only did I not know how to find a flow yet, I only knew how to build and grind at a level that would soon lead to my own demise.

My dad was an incredible strategist, leader, and time manager. I not only admired these qualities, I recognized how they yielded a high return, living a life full of enrichment and everlasting impact. I had to figure this out! I was determined to figure this out.

Like always, there was nothing that a good cup of coffee, a pen, paper, and time together couldn't problem solve. My dad and I sat down and got to work outlining all of my non-negotiables in my schedule, the things that couldn't move. We started grouping all the clients and commitments that yielded the highest return on my time spent. We made notes of where growth was possible and, most important, where I needed to make changes.

This encouraged me to get bold with my vision, to evolve it further. After we'd ironed out the day-to-day, next we time-blocked around the holidays and other historically slow times for business. Viewing my schedule through this lens gave me the foresight to plan ahead instead of operate in crisis mode, getting agitated about not having the time for the fun adventures that also fed my soul. I started to create a legit business strategy and a schedule that would soon afford me a life beyond just work.

One valuable point I'd like to share with you is that there are times when our passion fuels our drive to a level of burnout, because we fear losing our means to our end. We are afraid, if we say, "No," we will lose the demand or the respect of the client or the project. We tie up our worth in our doing instead of our being, our embodiment of.

It is imperative we shift our way of thinking into protecting our passion, so we can in turn see through our purpose. We need guardrails to support our doing, our pursuits. We have to possess a level of integrity with our boundaries, so we can preserve the essence of the gift we are striving to share with the world.

I needed guardrails, boundaries, and a reality check on sustaining tempo and impact.

Chapter 11 Reflections

Theme: "Subtract to Add: What's Worth Carrying Forward?"

1. Pause + Reflect

Name one thing you've been clinging to out of fear—fear of slowing down, letting go, or starting fresh.

2. The Pain That Changed Me

Write down one personal or physical pain that taught you more than comfort ever could.

- ➤ What did it teach you about your purpose, pace, or leadership?

3. Tempo Check

"Are you moving forward with clarity—or just moving to avoid slowing down?"

- ☐ I'm sprinting and burning out.
- ☐ I'm steady but intentional.
- ☐ I'm afraid to slow down.
- ☐ I need to recalibrate.
- ☐ I'm clear, aligned, and open to course-correcting.

- ➤ What's one way you can slow down this week without losing momentum?

4. My Next Becoming

- ➤ What's something you're ready to subtract... so that you can grow, lead, or create from a fuller version of you?
- ➤ What are you choosing to carry forward with intention?

CHAPTER 12

Passion Evolves, Purpose Stays

"Your dreams are non-negotiable—act like it."

Breathing New Life Into my Vision

In 2012, I met with one of the most impactful photographers and videographers in my area, we will call him, Dylan. He was tied into a side of the fitness industry I had never cared for, one I felt was missing the whole truth to living a life that was fully embodied and unified: mind-body-soul-purpose. I wanted nothing to do with it.

While I will never deny I was intrigued about possibly being part of such a tight community, like this one that sweated, tanned, trained, supplemented, and photographed together. But my deep inner knowing, what I had worked so diligently to meet, refine, and live out as a young girl, came full circle to meet me, and I knew that was a deal with the devil. So, I didn't go there!

I also bore witness to how detrimental this environment was to several women close to me. I knew there had to be a better way, and I was bound and determined to stay connected to what drove me. How could I share this message with the world so, in turn, my clients could fine tune what drove them?

When I met with the Dylan, I said very clearly, "Look I want to create a storytelling video. I am not into wearing skimpy clothing and showboating gear to articulate my message. I am an athlete, and I want to show up as her! I get it—sex sells. But I am here for a certain kind of client, and the client I am grabbing needs to see edge, grit, consistency, and perseverance. They need to see 'even if' in action. Are we clear?"

This photoshoot and video experience were nothing short of inspiring, incredible, uncomfortable, vulnerable, empowering, and raw. After I committed to shooting these photos and this video series, I knew I was onto something. I started to find my edge and messaging in the industry. I started to put my mark on the industry. Dylan met my goals while never forcing me into the fitness-competitor side of the industry.

As I sat in a recording studio for the voiceovers, I clearly remember thinking, "This is the missing piece to the industry that I love to hate."

I never intended to develop a personal training business and brand. That was always a stepping stone to my bigger aspiration. It was always a part of what I did on the day-to-day, to better understand people, including myself. Personal training was something I'd called, during my early years, "my hobby." What I finally began to realize was your hobbies can become your driving force to facilitate your passion's meeting your purpose. They can provide deep fulfillment into harnessing your purpose.

This introduction into who I wanted to be and who I didn't, in this industry, was a bold move on my part. In a space that had always been crowded by a certain way of thinking and doing, I stepped into it and said, "No! I will hold true to my values and belief that there is another way!"

From an early age, I had seen through my incredible parents and all they exposed me to, the power of discipline, grit, work ethic, and physical and mental perseverance. I had witnessed firsthand the tremendous benefits of training my body at a high level. I witnessed the power of community, connection, family time, and culture through my mother's Italian background. The blending of my parents' influence gave me an internal drive to help the world, specifically women. To help them understand the power of uniting discipline with joy and, in turn, living your best life.

Your best life doesn't come with deprivation at all times. In fact, it never should. It does require discipline, yes, but not a deprivation of good, balance, and enrichment, in order to look a certain way or be a part of a certain culture of people. This knowing and recognition began to separate me from my peers in my industry. It kicked me into a small subset of trainers focusing on my mindset and lifestyle.

I will be transparent: this is *not* exactly what the culture of training wanted at the time. While I am aware we now have many, many men and women leading and training others in this way, it may seem crazy to think that this was a tough buy-in back in 2012. But the truth of the matter is that the fitness and wellness industry has morphed and changed so much in the last ten-plus years. People have evolved to meet a more athletic, wellness, and longevity-based mindset and physical commitment. I can say with confidence, my drive to create what I wanted was well ahead of its time.

NICCOLE HENDRICKSON

It was lonely, though. "Going against the grain" came with the experience of also being st(ripped) of my confidence and certainty in my belief that what I felt was the way to evolve at the time. I had a deep inner understanding, but this was not the norm. I was tempted so many times to fall into the culture of what the fitness industry demanded, because—let me be clear—it drove revenue, it brought notoriety, it was "cool," it was well received, and it was the norm. The pressure to conform was high. The pressure to choose between the athletic world I'd been part of or the corrupt broken fitness industry was exhausting.

I had spent a lot of time in the athletic world. It was my passion and fulfilled a deep aspect of my purpose, but it was not my long game. I knew there was more to what I was destined to create and do in the world of wellness and fitness. I also knew the traditional fitness industry was so far out of alignment from my personal mission, vision, values, that I couldn't fully submerge into it, either. I walked a line that I'd created, and I teetered on my deep inner knowing. This was truly a test to my guiding principles. This was a powerful and pivotal lived-out st(ripping) of a world view versus my desired view. This was me standing in the power of what I didn't believe to serve me and my purpose and me building what I couldn't find.

It can be "lonely at the top," as Trace Deneke would remind me. But it isn't empty. When you authentically live your mission in integrity with your values, your soul is never lonely!

"When our hearts and our actions are true to our callings, God considers us successful."

—Tony Dungy

Taking Action in the Next Evolution of Me

2013, I was walking beside with my gorgeous mama at the mall. We were all smiles and nonstop chatter. We had finalized my last dress appointment at the Nordstrom Wedding Suite. We both knew I wasn't likely to find my dress there, but nevertheless, we knew it would be a "experience" for us to have together. It would add to our many memories of shopping side by side at this department store, with a beautiful interruption for coffee and a cookie in the Nordstrom Café.

As we strolled through level two, something caught my mom's eye. It was a tall, stylish chalkboard with a carefully-designed advertisement for fitness ambassadors for their signature athletic brand, Zella.

She paused and lightly tugged my arm. "Niccole, grab an associate and application. You need to apply. This is right up your alley!"

I grinned with a warm feeling of gratitude. I knew she was my mama, but her genuine approach to looking out for her people was admirable. She was always dialed in, no matter what she was doing or where she was. She always had an insane capacity for those she loved.

So, I did just what she'd suggested and leveraged my mom's company as I interacted with the sales associate. My mama listened, too, as I learned about the details of the program, and later briefed me on some of the little details I'd missed due to my exuberance.

NICCOLE HENDRICKSON

This was a special moment in my life. It kicked off an evolution of opportunity and audacious risk-taking, when it came to owning connections and experiences that were more in line with this bigger vision of dialing in community, connection, longevity, strength, embodied joy, and confidence. Thank you, Mama!

It had taken me nearly ten years to bring this mission to full fruition.

It had been a rollercoaster, at times. It was a road traveled and navigated with learning, triumph, failures, doubt, obstacles, frustration, and success. It was filled with drive, grit, discipline, overtraining, undereating, failed nourishment, imbalance, high stress, deep connection, deep fulfillment, incredible relationships, learning, studying, trial and error, and extreme attention to detail. It was a decade-plus of "keeping my eye on the prize." It was s(tripping) myself of a failed belief system that I was done staying in the lane of just focusing on women. Ha! That is funny!

When you deny yourself, you fail to deliver your mastery and overcome your own baggage. This was my shot to serve the very community I had once dreamed of igniting and bringing to life: the warrior-meets beautiful babe vibe. It was taking me back to my vision that had been born in high school. It was time to face down this denial and any resistance to my purpose.

Truthfully, I was burnt out from the disrupted culture and fabric of women after college and my team dynamics. I swore I would strike a balance by working with both men and women. In this process, what I came to realize is, if you don't like something, be a part of the change you desire to

ST(RIPPED)

see. That doesn't mean walking away from it. This was a humbling growth moment. This was me saying yes to this deep calling I had realized I was silencing, both because of fear and not fully knowing the "how to." I was tested throughout the process and pushed to face down the difference between validating myself and seeking external validation.

In summer 2014, shortly after I got married, I was chosen for a modeling gig with Nordstrom. They had launched a campaign to bring an authentic aesthetic to their activewear, a goal to help the consumer validate the fit, purpose, and visuals needed to bring an intentional connection to their clothing line. They deeply desired to bridge the gap between high-fashion activewear and the woman who was wearing it. This was a bold move in the retail industry.

At the time, models were models. No matter what they were wearing, it was still a chapter of life when every piece of clothing on display was carefully styled on a 5'10" or taller woman, with no curves, no muscle, and minimal shape. It didn't matter if she worked out or not. If she fit the mold of the fashion industry, the eye-catching vibe they defined as the demand, she secured the job.

This campaign was an effort to humanize the athletic clothing brand. It was an ask to actually bring reality into the clothing. Needless to say, I applied, and I was chosen. I headed to New York City, all expenses paid. I was on set the next day, and I was in way over my head. What I thought I'd signed up for, what I thought I'd been selected for, was not what I was on set for. It was insane. Think: *Devil Wears Prada* movie vibes meets a mass disconnect of vision.

The campaign Nordstrom had launched and the team executing the vision were not united. was the woman in the middle who would pay the price for that.

The very attributes I was selected for were my height and stature. But my long limbs, athletic build, and powerful legs were the very assets they had no idea how to work with. I started to get hot. My heart was racing, and my face felt expressionless. I was paralyzed by the glares of the on-set directors and by their borderline disgusted expressions, because I was not a professional model.

There were nine million people on set, but not one person who knew how to lead and explain what to do and how to do it. Listen, I had been photographed before. I had taken some gorgeous photos. But I had never modeled on a professional set. This was a nervous-system overload and a deep dive into a place of dark insecurity. I started to beat myself up, I was so defeated by not being seen the way I deserved, for not being embraced for what the casting call had said they wanted. I entered a dangerous mental loop.

Even more embarrassing, I started to think about what I'd eaten the night before. *Did that make me fat? Am I bloated? Should I have worked out this morning? Is my hair the right tone..."*

The list went on and on. Instant self-doubt and self-destruction. It was a red zone, and I had to get the hell out of here!

After hours on set, I finally said, "This is what was asked of me. How do you want this executed, because you are the expert in this area, not me! You direct me!"

This experience was nothing short of eye-opening and devastating. It was a true test of the power of owning your truth and worth, of not allowing others to dictate it to you.

ST(RIPPED)

The truth is this: you are not for everyone, as I've said before. This might hurt, but it is truth. The faster we all realize how our beauty and value are not dictated by anything external, the faster we live a life of power and unstoppable fulfilled purpose.

Although my mental state was strong, along with my perception of my impact and power, it was still painful to not be embraced. It was painful to be st(ripped) of the confidence and strength I had worked so diligently to build. In truth, I *wasn't* st(ripped) of my strength and confidence. I was freed. Freed of the thought pattern that someone else gets a say in my value and impact.

These lessons paralleled things I'd learned during my junior-year transfer. At the end of the day, all I could give was my all. If my coaches didn't have a way to utilize those tools, that was on them. In this photo shoot, I brought my best self. If that wasn't enough, that was on them.

I had to start embracing the idea that not every brick wall was designed for me to go over. Some were there to scale, and others to break through. These moments are bigger breakthroughs and contributors to our overall story, to our legacy, so stay in the fight of validating yourself not seeking it elsewhere.

Through my decade-plus of building and growth, I had learned this valuable lesson: "The best step or action to take is imperfect. It is progress over perfection."

Another lesson in st(ripping) the perfection element I had long struggled to overcome. It would continue to resurface and hinder my progress. What it really took was small, consistent action every single day to arrive at my desired destination that would unspool through the process of doing and boldly taking risks, being vulnerable, and embracing imperfect action. The desired end state doesn't occur if you stay in a never-ending planning and perfecting phase. It is action that provides insight.

> "The woman who follows the crowd will usually go no further than the crowd. The woman who walks alone is likely to find herself in places no one has been before."
> —Albert Einstein

The Band-Aid Ripped Off!

In June 2014, I was newly married. I teamed up this life event with evolving new elements of my business. It was time to centralize my operations and dial in my flow.

I knew what I wanted it to look like, so I started the process of curating the experience I envisioned. First, I would find a gym where I could rent space, establish roots, and grow! I'd use this step to propel me closer to my bigger vision, of serving the multifaceted and driven humans who deeply desired a dialed-in, realistic approach to their fitness and wellness regimen.

I'd resisted ever owning a brick-and-mortar business. I was keen on developing more of a collaborative operation that utilized established business venues and amplified small business owners. I wanted to foster the connections, curate the event, and take on minimal overhead. There was one way to find out what this would look like… Create it and test it out.

It is truly wild to think how far the boutique fitness industry in Denver has evolved over the last ten years. The spaces I sought were inspired by my New York City experience. I was in love with classic brick buildings, tucked up in swanky historic sides of town, the ones were you have to know someone in order to find them. Then, once you

ST(RIPPED)

discover them, you learn there is this a secret, power-packed community seemingly impossible to hide from the world, but they weren't hiding. You simply needed to know the right people in order to connect with this community.

Needless to say, I held this vision and experience I wanted not only to bring to life, but to foster. As I set out Googling personal training gyms in Denver, one or two options popped up. I started to feel annoyed and subconsciously even pushed toward, "Just create one, Niccole!" But I opposed this idea firmly, so that thought went into my little box within me, the place where I put all the inconvenient things.

The, I began to search by driving up and down the streets of downtown Denver, hoping I would stumble upon a hidden gem like the one I had discovered in New York City, years ago. I also leaned into my clients and contacts, asking them to keep their eyes open for me. I was in search of a very specific experience, and I just knew it had to exist.

One afternoon, in between my morning and evening clients, I sat down and turned to Mr. Google again. This time, I had new determination and will that I would essentially manifest exactly what I needed and hoped for, when I typed in all the key words. I typed in my search, took a deep breath, and pressed enter. The name of a gym popped up, and I thought to myself, surely this was recently added. How did I miss this?

The photos of the space grabbed my attention. It was simple, a little grungy, with roll-up garage doors, and exposed brick. It was in the heart of the area I was looking at. Now, I just needed it to line up with my needs: a space to rent, not a place of employment. I had worked diligently for two and half years to build what I had thus far, and I had zero interest in being someone's employee at this time, or anytime really.

I dialed the number and said a little prayer as the phone rang. A man answered. I introduced myself, asked a couple questions, and shared what I was looking for.

As if God was answering my prayers in real time, the man responded, "That is exactly what we are looking for—trainers with their own businesses who essentially just need gym space to run their operations. Why don't you come in and tour the space, and we can meet in person?"

I was beside myself with excitement and disbelief... *This is what it looks like, feels like, when you are clear and embodied. All the pieces fall into place exactly as it should. Another element of this vision (ripped), brick-by-brick. I was strengthening my process.*

The next day, I counted down the hours until my break so I could tour this space and hopefully take the next steps and settle my current, not-so-patient in-home clients into a new gym space. I was determined this would be my place.

That afternoon, I approached the gym on the side of a busy downtown street. The energy was bustling like most downtown days. The sun was beaming, and I was pumped for what I deeply hoped would be my next landing pad of operations. I took in the sunshine, the gym views, and the pulsing beat of music oozing out the rolled-up garage doors. I took in a deep breath and walked in.

There was a unique energy to the space, and I gave myself a moment to take it all in, every bit of it. There was a nostalgic aura in the space. I had a flashback to the first time I'd stepped foot into my high school gym with my brother: the clanking of the weights, the machines moving, the heat penetrating your skin, the focus, intensity, and diligent energy. I felt at home here.

As I made my way to the front desk, I quickly gathered myself and organized my thoughts. My "ask." I reminded myself how this was no different then the moment I toured the corporate wellness building. If anything, this was so much better than that had been. This time, I was my own established business, simply looking for a place to operate. It seemed easy enough to ask to pay someone for their space.

There wasn't anyone behind the front desk, but a man sitting in the office sensed my presence and glanced up. With a slight smile, he stepped out of the office and introduced himself. I shook his hand and introduced myself. Like most men who shake my hand, he immediately followed it up with, "Damn, that is a solid handshake."

I replied, "Thank you!" Pride and empowerment flooded my system.

I quickly thanked my father, too, acknowledging how powerful the mini but mighty lessons he'd taught me throughout my childhood and young adulthood. Respect, empowerment, and courage are rooted within. Stand in your power and presence with a solid handshake and eye contact. So, I did.

"Stop downplaying what you demand from your life to make someone else comfortable."
—Lori Harder

We sat across from each other, and I shared with clarity and absolute certainty what I was looking for in the current moment, including my expectations of the gym and my forward vision. He shared their expectations and vision. We shook hands, and I set out to inform my clientele where my new home base would be.

This gym would serve at my operating hub. I could start to put into action my creative direction and time-managing mentorship I'd gotten from both my dad and Kelly Forsyth, my business mentor and dear friend. I was embodying my mission and living out the vision.

New location, new area. It was time to get to know my surroundings and establish rapport with the small businesses. I always started with the coffee shops. My love language most definitely involved a good cup of coffee, so it was a no-brainer to start there.

I practiced a new approach to sharing what I was doing. I remained diligent and open to what this new environment offered to me, while also keeping my bigger vision in clear view. By this time in my career, I'd noticed how easy it was to fall victim to the grind and lose sight to what I was actually intending to create. I had to stay focused and dialed in to the plan. Thank God I had Kelly to keep my ass in line with going for it and not settling for comfort.

As my days rolled into months, I started to find my groove at this training space. I invited my contacts in to train and to experience a new perspective on their training. I began seeing myself as the professional I sought to be, and I was ready to elevate my offerings. I started to implement a lifestyle component, bridging the gap between the training and the rest of the hours in each client's day.

My heart sang for depth and the mindset. I loved programming and kicking someone's ass in the gym, building confidence and courage, and upleveling someone's skill set and physical prowess, but my heart

ST(RIPPED)

roared to bring out the edge in someone's mental grit, specifically in women. At this stage of my life, I not only embodied my vision, but I saw clearly it was time to make my way back, not only to training, but to focusing on the female population.

I held onto the highs and lows of the mental, emotional, and physical components of getting married. I'd been married one year, so I was freshly out of the spectacular chapter of planning and living out that vision. As I sat in reflection of what I wanted to accomplish with my career vision, the first place to test out this idea was brides.

Training them to feel their best physically wasn't the main goal. I wanted to put a spin on it. This was my moment to bring all of the elements of sisterhood, joy, celebration, and being in the moment, to help them tap into recognizing the ebbs and flows, and not succumbing to the script of stress and burnout, rather to stay in presence and prioritizing the WHY of the event. I was determined to shift the narrative around wedding prep and bring to life glimmers of love, family, celebration, community, and joy that had been modeled to me in my family.

I wanted to curate an experience for women to look back and smile when they thought of all the fun they'd had with their girlfriends, leading up to a life-changing commitment. I wanted women to feel so good in their bodies, not because they were skinny and starving, but because they were strong and well nourished. I wanted women to show up in their power on that day, because they were honoring their true north in the process. I would rewrite the script for wedding prep. I set out to cultivate community and connection along the way, highlighting other incredible professionals who served the bridal industry.

NICCOLE HENDRICKSON

This was my era of shining unapologetically, of embodying hope, connection, exuberance, and impact. I laugh when I think of how many coffee dates I went on with other small business owners. This chapter of life definitely beat my college years' coffee drinking. This chapter of life was one I liked to call small business courtship.

I made it my mission to meet and experience the services provided by each of these badass business owners. My cardinal rule for collaboration was that I had to not only align with the values of the business, but I also needed to fully buy into their services, in order to authentically promote them. This was not only about creating authentic contracts. It was a known expectation. The same went for me. They needed to believe in my mission, vision, and values, or it wasn't worth the time investment.

This process was eye-opening. It is one thing to have expectations and a vision. It's a whole other thing to hold the line and be courageous enough to implement them. I learned a lot in this process. It was humbling to learn the truths behind the scenes.

I spent a couple years going hard, evolving these collaborations, running the corporate wellness program, and starting the initial steps of building an online platform. The online space was in its infancy, and I started to deeply desire some time freedom. I deeply yearned for a change of pace from the mundane hours I was keeping, and I wanted to develop residual income.

Life has a beautiful way of opening up your perspective and facilitating a new lens. Like every big realization of my past, I was in sunny San Diego for a summer visit, and I felt exhausted and sick. So sick, like sick to the point of over-the-counter meds to assuage my poor, burnt out nervous system and fatigued body. I found myself in bed and down for the count. I felt the haze of slowdown and the peace of not being able to do anything, because I was not only sick, I was so dysregulated that I was going nowhere. This was a st(ripping) I surrendered to.

I rested and leaned into the love and care of my mom. No matter my age, the comfort of her presence has always brought me instant internal peace. She has the gift of sharing the purity of compassion. She's an angel in action, always, unconditionally.

Later that trip, I learned I was also pregnant with my first child. This would ignite a shift in my life for the greater good. Once again, God always knows how to wake me up! The universe responded to the shifts I'd started to cultivate, and then the dominos began to fall into place. They weren't always an easy fall, but they were a necessary one.

I worked myself to the point of exhaustion during this pregnancy. I was determined to shift the perspectives on what is possible when crossing motherhood with entrepreneurship, and I did not relent. Once again, my struggle was evident. I experienced my inability to have a healthy balance of flow and production. *Gahh*, this was getting annoying.

I began to lose steam in my approach. I was at a crossroads, building out something sustainable and beneficial for the long term, but a slave to the knowing and intoxicating gratification that came with the money I made putting in long hours serving clients.

That fall 2016, I lost four clients because of the election results. This was a painful lesson to learn: *Not all money is good money*. It was painful and brutal. Let me be crystal clear: I never mixed business and politics, but I also never hid my values and guiding principles. These clients sought out disagreements with me. They picked apart my upbringing and my husband's career, and they began to despise me because I wouldn't agree to battle them. Instead, I'd suggested it was okay that we had differing viewpoints; it cultivates a healthy world, with varying perspectives. They did not feel the same way.

This was a *huge*, eye-opening call to action around how I was operating. At the same time, the leadership shifted at the corporate wellness program I was running. These shifts involved power-hungry, disgruntled employees on a mission to blow up the fluidity of anything that didn't serve them or that had served the previous leader. I reflect back now and see I was simply a structure in the path of this leadership's storm. While this new leader didn't truly know me or have a personal issue with me, he had issues with the prior leadership members who had thought the world of me. This role was bringing more stress than benefit to my life, so I knew it was time to resign and end my nearly six-year role there.

The necessary st(ripping) was happening. Every time it was less difficult than the times before. I began to notice a beautiful pattern in this embodiment. I noticed a yearning for the derailment. This was my subconscious, my higher self, speaking and demanding a change. I started to surrender more easily and to embrace what was to come.

I spent the months leading up to the birth of my first child making shifts and leaning into what felt the most nourishing. This time period will forever be sacred. My dad retired from his teaching career and came out to spend a month with my husband and me. This was the gift of a lifetime. He greeted me early, at 4:00 a.m., with avocado toast, and he packed lunch for my work day. He was there for me in ways for which I will forever be grateful. His presence in my life during one of the most pivotal chapters of my life, my entry into motherhood, gave me the mental, emotional, and physical nourishment to fully step into my next chapter.

His presence and care reminded me how strong I was and how impactful I was just being me. Our endless conversations and his strong presence were gifts to my soul. Without even knowing it, he healed parts of me that truly broke when I made the move to Colorado. I was brave, determined, and drowning in my work ethic. I'd forgotten how truly spectacular I was without any of those accolades. He reminded me of how worthy I was, no matter what, and said this next step in my life would be the greatest accomplishment of my lifetime. Own that, he told me. Embrace it, and allow myself a new embodiment.

His presence in our lives was selfless and truly a gift. Another lesson I would learn as a parent, myself: the power of presence.

Ain't No *Hood* like the Mother*hood*...

When it was time, I was ready. I fully embraced the role— the hat, the title, this new aspect of me. It was full throttle into the becoming.

I wasn't always sure that motherhood would be part of my story, but once I became a mother, I knew exactly how I wanted to show up. An undeniable shift happens within us when we begin to grow a human. It's not something you can take lightly. That internal transformation required that I surrender immediately any illusion of control I'd thought I had over the direction of my life.

NICCOLE HENDRICKSON

Despite my several prior experiences of being st(ripped) of what I'd believed was my power, identity, and impact was, motherhood forced on me a level of surrender that grew me, freed me. I believe women can define this role. They can construct and embrace their desire. But more times than I care to admit, I have fallen into the confines of what society tells us our st(ripping) should look like, embody, and reveal. *No! No!* Ladies, that is not how it works. *You* get to decide how you want your role in the *"hood"* of mother*hood* to look. It's up to you to decide and to bring to life your values and impact in this chapter of your life. It's in how you choose to care for yourself and advocate for your wellbeing. It's in the boundaries you set and the level of vulnerability you provide for yourself. It is in how you choose to parent and navigate your marriage. Babe, you get to decide.

How?

It all begins with choosing to discover you first, your needs, and then taking ownership of them. Advocating for yourself, and knowing the value of your wisdom within. Trusting your inner voice, which deserves listening to and acknowledgment. We are quick to outsource everything. Stop, pause, and check in first with your heart, mind, and gut. Then go from there. When you start with your inner knowing, there is a clearer pathway to understanding what you need from the external.

There has to be an undeniable degree of faith and surrender. You have to relinquish this idea that you can control it all. If motherhood shows you anything, it's how little you actually have control over. But you do have control over your faith and mindset. Nourish this and own it!

ST(RIPPED)

"Becoming a mother leaves no woman as it found her. It unravels her and rebuilds her. It cracks her open, takes her to her edges. It's both beautiful and brutal; often at the same time."
—Nikki McCahon

In March 2017, I welcomed my little gem into the world. I waited patiently for her to come. She had no plans to make a move on her own and was over a week due. As I waited, though, I started to succumb to fear, and my stress increased. I had episodes when I could not feeling her move. I started overthinking. I was ready to surrender into this chapter, but I needed to meet her.

I opposed the potential path ahead if I waited too long, but I also opposed what could unravel if I moved forward with induction. I was terrified of a C-section; it was a longtime fear of mine. I took peace in my faith and focused on what I could control, which was my mindset.

I had spent years dreaming about delivering my babies naturally, with minimal interference. I was never someone who enjoyed substances or really anything that would interrupt or alter my internal wiring. I didn't like the feeling of being out of control because of something. I could take myself to a place of euphoria on my own. Hell, yes!

I headed into the doctor's office after an evening of uncertainty. I wanted to hash out my options and create a plan. I asked my husband to join this appointment. I needed to lean into the very qualities that made me insane with him at times, the quality of being overly logical, fact-driven, and with impeccable discernment.

I left that day with a plan for induction. I would report to the hospital well fed and ready to go! I felt a mixed bag of emotions. I still yearned to be the woman whose water broke and was rushed to hospital to deliver her baby shortly after. But, no, that would not be my story. I would drive in, check in, be connected to all those machines, and monitored.

Once the magnitude of my reality set in, I started to walk a line of freak out. We met with the delivery team, and I explicitly outlined my desire to have a minimally invasive delivery, while I was also agreeing to a cervix softener, hoping it would cue my body to start making moves. I still deeply wanted to remain drug-free and in my body. The team was on board... initially.

Soon, my patience was waning and the scenery was suffocating. I thought to myself, *What have I done?"* I soon realized the power athlete in me was now in an endurance race. I needed to shift my headspace and put my focus on the end result, fully owning that the process was unpredictable and out of my control. I could own my mindset around it. I could stay dialed into my heart.

As the hours passed, my body was initially slow to respond, which put me in a head-spin. Let me note how unaligned the hospital setting is. They won't feed you while you are in this marathon, so my body was starting to fatigue at the same time the intensity of my labor occurred. The very moment I needed fuel for this endurance event, I couldn't have it. *Annoyed*! I snuck in an orange, threw it up instantly, and begged my husband to excuse us so we could walk the halls.

The nurse was annoyed with me, but I had no apologies to give. I needed out of that room and to move my body. I made it maybe ten steps before I thought I would collapse. This s(tripping) would be different. I would have to honor

ST(RIPPED)

the desire of my body to collapse, and then I would remind it, "the body may get weak, but the mind is strong and determined!" I took three more steps and returned to my room.

I took a bath, bounced on the ball, and surrendered again to the bed. Eventually, it was game time. My little gal decided she was ready to make her debut. I was able to hold my vision of a drug-free delivery and live out this portion of my story. I was able to surrender to the help of the cervix softener and let go.

The process of delivering her was invigorating, terrifying, and empowering, a front-row seat to how wildly human doctors are. My delivery doctor started to fold under pressure and fear. To this day, I thank my husband for keeping this woman in check and reminding her to have a semblance of faith and patience. She was quick to shift gears and go for interventions when my daughter wasn't coming out at the tempo she wanted. Soon, though, my little gem made her way into the world, and I would never be the same woman. I was now Mama.

My first days of motherhood were a blend of beautiful, dark, eye-opening and soul-filling. I was caught off guard by how difficult it was to be so far from my family, my community. I had been in a chapter of life when I "had me." I was able to take care of myself and navigate the challenges alone, despite being in a very close family that rallied to do life. My whole life, I'd witnessed the beauty of the "village." If anyone knew how to take care of one another, it was the Italians, and this had been my example. This is all I'd ever known, yet I'd been willing to live in a different way to follow love and build a life in Colorado.

NICCOLE HENDRICKSON

My choice came with the strength and fortitude I had channeled from my grandmothers, the ones who had boldly stepped into their purpose with absolute courage. I knew I was wired for this. I just needed to navigate the tools I required and then grant myself permission to receive them. I would often think, "I can do this. If they did motherhood alone halfway across the world without the ability to text and call their mothers, friends and family, I can do this!"

I had entered my Colorado chapter thinking I was immune to the darkness that would come with this challenge. I overestimated my strength and underestimated what my heart sang for. I was a mix of being ashamed at my sadness and loneliness plus so happy to be with my baby and evolving my life. My driven, strong, independent mind and heart tried to lead me out of sadness and loneliness. I battled, and I allowed myself into the darkness. It was there, in this chapter, that I would identify how challenging it was to discover how to thrive. But, I did, in turn, pass on the lessons learned to other mamas. This, too, became an experience I would recycle and create from.

Another version of me was flourishing before my eyes. Through the darkness, I discovered a small ember and let it ignite.

> *"The ocean does not apologize for its depth and the mountains do not seek forgiveness for the space they take. So, neither shall I."*
> —Becca Lee

Ten weeks postpartum, I was itching to renovate the brand I had created. After all I was not the same woman, so the brand I had developed couldn't be the same anymore, either. I connected with a branding company and got to

ST(RIPPED)

work with the next steps of Peak8Fitness. This time, I dared to step further into my bigger vision, to stretch myself into zones of growth in which I had zero background. This was a bold move and a promise to the new version of myself who emerged, postpartum.

Motherhood st(ripped) me to my core. It exposed me in ways I am grateful for. The absolute shedding of the mentality, "I've got it all, and I don't need to lean in," quickly left. Those were defense mechanisms for the loneliness I was able to fill with production and growth in my company. The truth is, I was married to someone in law enforcement, which is a relentless career that can be brutal on family life. While I knew what I had signed up for, when I got married, I will not deny the strain on me as a new mom with no family around. A woman needs a community. She needs her people. At this, I needed my husband, and I needed people. But they were hard to find and challenging to lock down.

This made me stronger but also harder. My internal wiring became harder and cold. I started to lose touch with the woman I once knew, the fun, open, light, exuberant woman. I had to fight to find her, and that fight involved me creating a community. I moved from the desire to serve the mutifaceted, driven individual who lived life on the go to the multifaceted, driven female who worked diligently in her career and life and needed a facilitated team of wellness professionals to amplify her life.

I deeply desired to navigate the driven-motherhood niche, but to be very honest, I was way too raw to jump into that world. I often felt I needed to iron out my motherhood credentials before placing myself in that niche. However, what I did know was this: women need one another, and they need circles of women to evolve and grow their values and their strengths, to bounce ideas off of, and to celebrate with. Down the road in their evolutions, whether into motherhood or not, it would be a hell of a lot easier to write their stories and live them out.

Mission number one, postpartum, was dialing in my ideal client by putting myself into the circles of women I wanted to serve. Before I knew it, I was in my crowd, and my passion had been sparked by the driven female entrepreneur. This evolved version of me was ready to see women show up for other women and to build their networks through collaborative events. I firmly understood how "iron sharpens iron" and the only way we evolve and grow is with a healthy dose of people.

Once I started curating these events, I started to feel like Colorado was more of my home. It took me years to start to find my people and to experience an ebb and flow that was truly in line with my values and forward vision. This new endeavor breathed life into my purpose. It showed me the way out of training and into leading in new ways. It validated how impactful we are as business owners, when we lean in and allow ourselves to be st(ripped) of our egos and embrace when others in our circles do well.

After I came back from maternity leave, there was a palpable shift in all of my work environments. I know a large part of that had to do with me. I was no longer the same young woman. I was Mama. I was the woman who had delivered her baby without pain meds, the one who walked through the darkness of the early months of motherhood alone and then navigated what was needed in order for my heart to sing again. I would not apologize for the depths I was ready to hit and would go after. I started gaining the attention of some of the coaches at the gym where I rented space. Suddenly, it went from okay to build your brand to jealousy and disdain for not building theirs.

The golden lesson I discovered in this chapter of my life was the power in knowing your strengths, staying in alignment with your values, and never selling your soul for validation.

Chapter 12 Reflections

Theme: "Flourishing Through the Ember"

1. Rooted in Her Strength

Think of someone in your lineage (or life) whose resilience shaped you.

* Who comes to mind and what strength did they pass on to you?
* How do you honor that strength in your life today?

2. The Power of Permission

"I just needed to... grant myself permission to receive."

* What support, resource, or kindness are you resisting?
* What permission do you need to give yourself right now to move forward?
  - ☐ Permission to rest
  - ☐ Permission to ask for help
  - ☐ Permission to slow down
  - ☐ Permission to rise
  - ☐ Other: _____

CHAPTER 13

Fearless in your *WHY*

"When your intentions are pure, you don't lose anyone. They lose you."

For me, I will go to the end of my time on Earth leading women to the realization that it isn't one way or the other. You can and should wear many hats in the iterations of your life. It will not be easy, but suppression awaits the woman who believes she is limited to one hat or two.

I believe every woman has the capacity to be multifaceted and own all her roles, but it begins and ends with her standing confidently in her truth, power, and *Why*. When you are clear on these elements of you, you can and will withstand the uncertainty of those around you, including your mate, your person.

I was ten-plus years into the business I had built, in a training industry that, truthfully, I'd never seen myself building in. And I was desperate to shift the flow in my life. I had felt hints of this longing after having my first child. But once I was pregnant with my second child, I yearned deeply for more quality time with my family and better health for myself.

NICCOLE HENDRICKSON

I wanted to share my purpose in another way, to push myself out of my comfort zones. I started to dream of my life without doing personal training. I started dreaming of writing again, of speaking and coordinating events on a larger level. I was drawn to giving back and navigating a life where I could make money and have freedom.

I was desperate to put the training life to rest. This was an identity I barely related to anymore, and I was tired of battling the profession's culture. While I was dreaming and evolving my vision, I started to work out with a trainer I will call Jess. She also rented space at the gym where I rented space. This was a strategic decision not only to get to know her, but to see through a new lens. Mine was foggy and strained. She had a heightened sense of energy in her sessions, and the inner athlete in me desired a program facilitated by someone else.

I needed some people on my life team, so I chose her. Training together gave us the opportunity to get to know each other, to push each other with courageous questions about our bigger goal, and to open a door of curiosity. It was the connection and camaraderie I'd missed from when I was a collegiate athlete, the fierce female relationship where we elevated each other in ways by holding the bar high.

I had been running my business out of the downtown gym for almost six years. Expectations had shifted, and the atmosphere was evolving into a vibe I was not interested in. That, in turn, pissed off the owners' egos. Then, my evolving friendship with the newer female trainer, Jess, threatened the staff. My commitment to my brand and life flow was only agitating the owners even more. This was a great example of what happens when your vision shifts and you fail to honor that other people may not be united in

ST(RIPPED)

your shift. The tension grew thick at this facility, and my disdain for the culture grew thicker. I had to get out!

It was time to get bold and honest with myself and what I wanted in this next phase of my life. While this was my job, it was so much more than that. As an entrepreneur and creator, your life is intertwined, because you are living out your passion and purpose in all that you do. Owning this mindset forged the path to unveiling the realization that I was wasting my energy and time, showing up to a space that did not value me for who I was and what I brought to the table.

However, it is important to note that I had a choice. I could complain all I wanted, I could keep seeking external validation and stay suffocated in the mediocrity box, or I could acknowledge that it was me who possessed a level of uncertainty and fear in the next level of my aspirations, so I was staying. I was choosing this, and it was up to me to change it.

This was a me problem, and it was time to address it.

Navigating the hard and the unexpected will demand you know who you are at the core. How you respond to the st(ripping) of your comforts will be determined by your guiding principles and core values.

"Your body is the vessel through which your soul speaks. To be embodied is to listen and respond with grace to its wisdom."
—@orderyourwish

The days blurred together, the weeks ran in a sprint, and the months turned over faster than I could keep up with. After building a flourishing fitness business in Colorado and starting a family, I began to explore how to fulfill my WHY in new ways.

There is something to having children: it's like the clock runs faster and you lose minutes and precious moments so quickly. I was bearing witness to how fast time was going as my daughter shifted from baby to toddler to fierce big-sister-to-be. I was expecting baby number two, and I was also on a mission to create the next iteration of my bigger vision. Injuries and pregnancy had that effect on me. Ha!

One late morning, I spotted my training friend, Jess. She was on the StairMaster, her happy place, wearing large headphones, a "don't interrupt me" attitude, and working out at a pace that meant business.

I hopped on the StairMaster next to Jess, grabbed her attention, and laid it out. I went for it. Maybe I did this for her. Maybe it was my need to vocalize my bigger aspirations and put them into the universe. Maybe it was an invitation to dream bigger together. Regardless, I showed up big and let myself be heard.

I asked Jess what her plan was with her career, because there was no way it was just the gym where we were renting space. I refused to allow her to settle on that as her end goal. I peppered her with ideas and asked she considered looking at the bigger view and long game.

She looked at me and answered with a "You have some serious audacity!" look, and said, "Wow, thank you for bringing your energy to life!" However, she stated the obvious: I was pregnant and thus had to be unsure about what life would look like, postpartum.

I let out a laugh and looked at her in the eye, telling here, "This is not my first rodeo, and motherhood is the event that feeds my rebirth of beautiful ideas. Don't fear. I will show you what it can look like."

We agreed to stay in touch and courageously push each other in our goals.

I spent my next eight weeks dialing in my business to support a more fluid maternity leave. This time around, I would test drive a whole new model for maternity leave. I started to create a blueprint for what I dreamed life could look like with a team, with systems far beyond me. I used my maternity leave preparation as practice.

During this time, I had a chance to look at a space to rent and to build out this vision I was starting to share with clients and friends. The same one I'd bombarded my friend with on the StairMaster. I invited her to look at the space, as well. I was still walking that line of fear and doubt around anything brick-and-mortar, but my subconscious was speaking. My heart was demanding that I get more audacious in my aspirations. The space was not the right fit or timing, but it was a step in the direction of my embodiment.

Three days into maternity leave, while still awaiting the arrival of my second baby, the world started getting weird. The time I had invested in building out programming for clients so my team of training friends could work with them became null and void. Little did we know it, but the world was shutting down because of Covid. It was absolute chaos!

The timing, though... was so perfect in so many ways.

"Your future self is begging you to leave behind the people who only want the old you."

—Lori Harder

NICCOLE HENDRICKSON

Five days before Colorado was shut down, my son was born. My little warrior made his way into the world with strength and gusto.

I was in active labor with this guy for days. I did everything during this pregnancy with the deep hope of avoiding induction. I was bound and determined to not travel the same pathway as I had with my daughter. However, it turns out, my babies loved their womb and did not want to exit, so induction it was. Second delivery, similar experience. Gone was the unexpected water breaking and rush to the hospital; hello to the check in, get changed, and let's get this process started.

I arrived, I changed, and I was greeted by a familiar face. Somehow, this gave me instant peace. This gave me the knowing and ease I so deeply desired. I was a mix of emotions this round, I knew the power I'd felt when bringing my daughter into this world. It had been a rite of passage, an experience of strength and inner warrior that no one could rob me of. It was me, my body, my mind, and my will.

I tried like hell through every contraction to be in it, to absolutely allow myself to surrender into the pain and presence of my body. This was an element of my experience that I loved and craved. It was when I felt the most alive in my body, knowing I had the power and capacity to endure. The female body is spectacular. This would be my final experience in this kind of power, and I didn't want to lose touch with one second of surrender. Labor and delivery were two of my most desired s(tripping)s.

From when I entered the hospital to when I exited, the world became its polar opposite. The transformation was quite honestly unbelievable. Luckily for me, this changed

ST(RIPPED)

very little for me initially. I was focused on bringing my new baby home to meet his beautiful big sister and two furry Labrador friends. I yearned for the peace and surrender that was going to come with being home, while I knew I was in for a whole new world: a toddler and new baby. Still, this was the pause I deeply desired and craved. I wanted to be home, to slow down, to only care for my kids and my health. I wanted to permission do nothing.

I badly needed the change of pace and ability to feel like Mama was good enough. I didn't need to be all things to everyone. I didn't need to make events and collaborations happen, to produce a certain income. For a hot second, I wanted the simplicity of spit up and toys everywhere. I wanted cold coffee and lullabies. I am not sure why I didn't think I could have these moments and also work, but something was pulling at me to just be.

By three and a half weeks into my mamahood of two, the Internet was exploding with online programs and platforms. The fitness industry was transforming overnight. Every industry was, actually. The online space went from a nuance to the mainstream of delivery.

I was overtaken by this pressure to produce, to make something happen because I could, and now, it was expected. The platforms were there, and the people wanted the content! I wrestled with this. In many ways, I felt robbed of the maternity leave I dreamt of taking, the one I had redesigned, the one that would set me up for a rewire. The one that would grant me surrender. Short-lived!

Another two weeks passed, and my pal, Jess, whom I'd bombarded on the StairMaster, called me to check in and let me know she had an opportunity for me to consider. She had a spot where we could possibly bring our visions to life.

She gave me the rundown on the location and potential. Suddenly, my desire to surrender transformed into an ignited fire.

Two days later, I met her at the location in Wash Park. We walked the space, did a quick rundown on how we would set it up, as if we had planned this all along. From there, we agreed to a conference call with a third gal who was interested in this endeavor. After we said our goodbyes, I loaded up my little guy and sat in my car for a minute. I had to ground myself and breathe. I was in absolute disbelief... This was happening.

The next day, with exuberance, we hopped on a call with the third gal to share the details about the space and to share our visions. It became crystal clear we were forging a brand experience, not a personal training gym. The third gal kindly declined, so it was us, the two of us, diving into further exploration and making a choice. I was A-L-L I-N without a second thought.

The brick by brick was forming a path, and this was the reality of my unshakable strength, my truth... A brick-and-mortar, a business partnership, and a brand.

All of the steps, risks, connections, roles held, clients worked with, and collaborations led me down the path of meeting my new business partner. I'd had no intention of ever forming a partnership or hell ever having a brick-and-mortar. In fact, my husband had often encouraged me to do this, pinging the idea of opening my own space, and I'd always told him, *"No! Absolutely not!"*

Ha...! Look at me now. I had said no so often to the very thing I actually now held as a deep desire. I had been uncertain of what it looked like, but instead of exploring it, I had rejected the idea and closed myself off to it.

ST(RIPPED)

As I am living proof, though, God had other plans for me. Finally, I entertained them, relinquishing my control. I'd surrendered to faith and guidance and marched forward into cocreating another level of my dream. It was raw, messy, and another level of unraveling. It was a s(tripping) of one thought process to embrace a new level of another. It has paved a path to emerge and bring light to other facets of my being. I am st(ripped) of what was in order to reveal what is.

Chapter 13 Reflections

Theme: "I Am Many: A Hat Ceremony"

A reclaiming practice for the multifaceted woman.

1. The Hats I Wear

"Suppression awaits the woman who believes she is limited to one hat or two."

Prompt

List every hat you wear in this season of your life — roles, titles, or identities, both seen and unseen.
I wear the hat of a...

- ➢ Circle the ones you're **proud of**.
- ➢ Underline the ones you've been **hiding**.
- ➢ Put a star next to the ones you're **ready to embrace more fully**.

2. Your Truth. Your Power. Your Why.

"When you are clear on these elements of you, you can and will withstand the uncertainty..."

Prompt

- ➢ **My Truth Is:**

What is undeniably true about you, no matter what life looks like?

- ➢ **My Power Is:**

What inner strength shows up no matter the role you're in?

➢ **My Why Is:**

Why do you keep going? What is the fire that fuels all your iterations?

In your journal, complete these sentences:

- ✳ My truth is...
- ✳ My power is...
- ✳ My why is...

NICCOLE HENDRICKSON

CLOSING LOVE NOTE

Truth and strength are found in the resilience that is discovered in darkness and the unexpected.

St(ripped) is the revealing of the character and grit harnessed when we are without our believed comforts.

It is the discovery of strength that is built and earned.

You are not meant to live life safely tucked inside one label, one title, or one identity.

You are *many things*—and that is your superpower.

As you close this book, ask yourself:

What are you ready to st(rip) away?

What parts of you are ready to be reclaimed?

What fire is asking to be reignited?

ST(RIPPED)

The world doesn't need a perfect version of you.
It needs a present, powerful, grounded one.

So, rise.
Lead.
And never forget:

You are the mission.

With love,

Niccole

NICCOLE HENDRICKSON

If you're interested in learning more about Niccole's consulting services and coaching, reading her work, or if you're looking for a keynote speaker for your next event, please visit:

www.niccolehendrickson.com

Follow @niccolehendrickson on Instagram
Subscribe to her Substack:
https://niccoleh.substack.com/subscribe

ACKNOWLEDGEMENTS

First and foremost, I want to express my deepest gratitude to my family—especially my children and my husband—for their boundless love, unwavering patience, and constant encouragement. You are the foundation of my life, and this book would not have come to fruition without your steadfast support.

To my parents, whose teachings of resilience and self-belief have been the pillars of my journey, I am forever indebted. Your unconditional love, faith in me, and guidance have ignited my passion and purpose, shaping me into the person I am today.

To my closest friends—Kari, Andi, Allison, Jorgi, Kelly, and Kayla—thank you for being my anchors in the storm. Your unwavering presence and strength during my darkest moments have been a constant source of comfort and inspiration.

To my mentors, both in business and life, thank you for your invaluable wisdom, the challenges you've set before me, and your belief in me, even when I couldn't see it myself. Your guidance has helped me uncover truths within my own story that I never knew existed.

A heartfelt thank you to my publisher, editor, and team, whose expertise, dedication, and professionalism transformed my raw words into something I am proud to share with the world.

Finally, I want to acknowledge everyone who has crossed my path and contributed, in both big and small ways, to the evolution of this story. Each of you has played a role in shaping the person I've become and the journey I've taken. For that, I am truly grateful.

ABOUT THE AUTHOR

Niccole Hendrickson draws from her rich upbringing and experiences as a mother of two to share the foundation of her passion, drive, and deep sense of connection. A former collegiate athlete, fitness professional, and entrepreneur, she empowers multifaceted, driven women to channel their grit and ambition—aligning passion with purpose to create unstoppable momentum in their lives.

Through relentless pursuit and unwavering resilience, Niccole has discovered that true power is never lost—it lives within. Her mission is to empower women to stand firm in their values, own their purpose, and rise unshaken. Setbacks aren't the end; they are the proving ground. Legacy is built not by settling in the struggle, but by evolving through the darkness and turning every challenge into unstoppable growth.

Today, you'll find Niccole chasing her two kids and British Labradors around their seventeen-acre ranch in the foothills of Colorado, savoring a hot cup of coffee as she journals at sunrise, crafting charcuterie boards at sunset, lifting heavy weights, drumming up the next move for business growth and leadership at KALO Fitness, and indulging in every travel adventure with her family. She remains loyal to the sea—and to the infinite opportunity to

NICCOLE HENDRICKSON

grow something deeply rooted in the unification of passion and purpose.

Niccole is a serial entrepreneur, deeply committed to growth and impact through public speaking, paying it forward, and fostering meaningful community. She believes true leadership is measured by the ripple effect of how we serve, empower, and elevate others along the way.

www.ingramcontent.com/pod-product-compliance
Lightning Source LLC
LaVergne TN
LVHW011415080426
835512LV00005B/59